SHOW
us the way

The *New* Christian Way Series 2

Maura Hyland
with the assistance of
Máire Daly

VERITAS

Published 1992
by Veritas Publications
7 & 8 Lower Abbey Street
Dublin 1

with the co-operation of
Maryvale Institute of Religious Education,
Archdiocese of Birmingham

Imprimatur
✠ Desmond Connell
Archbishop of Dublin

This text is a re-presentation of
The Christian Way 2
by Raymond Brady, first published in 1980.

ISBN 1 85390 159 8

The Author and Publishers gratefully
acknowledge the contribution of all the
teachers who took part in the piloting of
the material in this book.

Design by Bill Bolger
Cover illustration by Jeanette Dunne
Illustrations by Jeanette Dunne,
Bill Bolger, Brenda Duggan
Cartoons by John Byrne
In-house editor, Eithne Doherty
Origination by the Type Bureau, Dublin
Printed in the Republic of Ireland by
Smurfit Web Press

Contents

another year

In Your Religion Journal

Make out an advertisement encouraging parents to send their children to your school.

St Paul's
Post-Primary School

Help your child prepare for the future
APPLY NOW
to St Paul's for

✓

Excellent Examination Results

✓

Professional Career Guidance

Come and see our up-to-date facilities.
Meet our highly qualified staff.

Phone: John Hurley (Secretary) (01) 367984

Find Your Group
Discuss

What have you been looking forward to about returning to school?

What have you been dreading?

What are your hopes for yourself for the year ahead?

What do you think you can do to ensure that these hopes are fulfilled?

Once again a new school year begins.

What preparations have you been making?

In Your Religion Journal

Write a letter to your cousin in Australia telling about the beginning of the school year.

Another year!

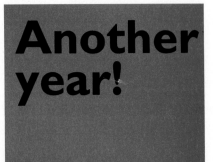

It was the night before the first of September. In the Hughes' household it was all action. Preparations were well under way for the return to school which would take place in the morning.

It would be young Brian's first day at school. He was really excited about his shiny new school-bag, the uniform hanging in his bedroom, the lunch box and his flask.

Looking on, his older sister Anne wondered if, indeed, her mother was just as excited as Brian was about his first day at school. He was the youngest and had always been regarded as the baby.

Anne, on the other hand, was beginning a crucial year in her school life.

Next summer would be exam time for her. In the

meantime she knew there would be lots of hard work, extra study and less time to see her friends and do many of the things she most enjoyed, nevertheless, she was excited. It would be a challenge. This was the year she had looked forward to and worked towards for ages and she hoped that it would be worth it in the end.

Then there was Paul. Paul was starting his second year in post-primary school. He looked on at the others and remembered how he had felt this time last year. He was starting secondary school. He had been excited then and maybe a bit anxious. Now, things were different. He had made many friends. He knew the teachers and he was familiar with the subjects. He was just a bit sorry that the holidays were over. He would miss the long days with nothing to do except enjoy himself. There would be no more free evenings of football, friends and, later on, his favourite television programmes to watch. However, he was also looking forward to getting back to school and meeting his school friends again. There would be stories to swap about the holidays and plans to make for the year ahead.

'A penny for them, Paul', said Anne. 'You're looking very thoughtful.' 'Well, as a matter of fact I'm just trying to decide whether I'm glad or sorry that it's back to school time again,' said Paul. 'And now, I must go and see if I can find my school-bag and books for the morning.'

Discuss

Why do you think Paul felt as he did ?

If you were Paul's mother and heard his thoughts what do you think you would say to him ?

3

In Your Religion Journal

Write out six words which describe how you felt as you got ready to return to school.

4

Discuss

Why did the little fish want to leave his old life behind and begin a new life on the shore ?

Why do you think he did not realise the consequences of his action ?

When in your life did you feel like the 'Little Fish', wanting things to be different ? Tell your story!

What can we learn from this story ?

The Little Fish

A happy little fish was swimming and frolicking near the bottom of the ocean. There he enjoyed the company of many friends. He could eat as much food as he wished and never seemed to lack for anything.

Then he began to swim upwards, higher and higher. He had never swum so high before.

'I wonder what it's like up there,' he said to himself. 'It seems to be growing much lighter and I can see things far more clearly than I could down there.'

Before very long, the little fish reached the surface of the ocean. He was amazed to see how beautiful the sky looked and wondered what it must be like to go through the top of the water. He even managed, for a second, to push his head through the surface.

'How beautiful it looks ! How exciting!' he gasped, seeing the edge of the sandy beach.

When he found himself once again beneath the waves, he felt despondent. Why should he have to go back down to that dark, gloomy life at the bottom of the ocean ? It was so bright and warm outside. Why couldn't he go and live outside, where it was much brighter and warmer ?

The little fish decided to jump out of the water as high as he could. He then felt the warmth of the sun even more. He could also see much further, beyond the beach, and as far as some rows of trees, beautiful flowers and a street full of picturesque little bungalows.

He soon made up his mind to reach that shore and begin a new life. Nothing would now deter him, as he began swimming eagerly forwards until he eventually found himself washed up on the sand.

'Free at last,' he cried. 'I'm now ready to enjoy a wonderful new life, far away from that dull, cold life at the bottom of the water....'

Suddenly he felt a choking sensation. 'Oh dear,' he murmured, 'I must have taken too much out of myself. I've tried to swim...too fast...too...quickly....'

He again tried to catch his breath but the choking feeling remained. A few minutes later, the little fish lay dead on the beach.

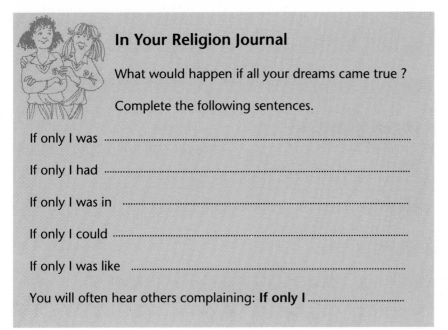

In Your Religion Journal

What would happen if all your dreams came true ?

Complete the following sentences.

If only I was ....

If only I had ....

If only I was in ....

If only I could ....

If only I was like ....

You will often hear others complaining: **If only I** ....

A Time to Pray

Let us thank God for all the opportunities we are being offered in our lives right now.

For the opportunity to get to know ourselves.

For the opportunity to learn more about our world and how to care for it.

For the opportunity to prepare for the life that lies ahead.

God our Creator, we give you praise and thanks.

For the opportunity to get to know others.

For the opportunity to develop our gifts and talents.

For the opportunity to take on new responsibility.

God our Creator, we give you praise and thanks.

For the opportunity to get to know you better.

For the opportunity to learn how to show thanks to you for all the gifts we have been given.

For the opportunity to help others get to know you.

God our Creator, we give you praise and thanks.

Let us also thank God for the summer holidays which we have enjoyed.

For the people we met.

For the fun we had.

For the freedom to enjoy all the gifts which you have given us.

God our Creator, we give you praise and thanks .

God gives each of us a place in life; depending on our situation, our abilities and opportunities, we can get the best out of life. We can accept ourselves and the circumstances in which we find ourselves. We can become aware of all the good things we have been given. On the other hand we can put all our energy into wishing that we were elsewhere and concentrate on what we do not have, rather than on what we have.

We should remember that happiness is to be found in what we are and wherever we are.

Every stage in life brings with it some pleasures and some pain. It is important to be aware of the opportunities which are offered to us in all the different situations in which we find ourselves in life. If we wish to move to the next stage as better, more mature people we must be willing to face up to reality and to make the most of all the opportunities that are available to us.

There are probably some things about school which you enjoy very much and some which you find quite difficult.

Find Your Group

Discuss

What do you like most about school ?
What do you like least about school ?
In what way do you think you can make life at school more pleasant for yourself and those around you ?

In Your Religion Journal

List all the opportunities which are being offered to you in life just now!
List some things which you could do in order to make the most of these opportunities.

**Unit One
Creation**

in the

Poem from a Three Year Old Brendan Kennelly

And will the flowers die ?

And will the people die ?

> And every day do you grow old, do I
> grow old, no I'm not old, do
> flowers grow old ?

> Old things – do you throw them out ?

> Do you throw old people out ?

And how you know a flower that's old?
The petals fall, the petals fall from flowers,
and do the petals fall from people too,
every day more petals fall until the
floor where I would like to play I
want to play is covered with old
flowers and people all the same
together lying there with petals fallen
on the dirty floor I want to play
the floor you come and sweep
with the huge broom.

The dirt you sweep, what happens that,
what happens all the dirt you sweep
from flowers and people, what
happens all the dirt? Is all the
dirt what's left of flowers and
people, all the dirt there in a
heap under the huge broom that
sweeps everything away?

beginning

Why you work so hard, why brush
and sweep to make a heap of dirt?
And who will bring new flowers?
And who will bring new people? Who will
bring new flowers to put in water
where no petals fall on to the
floor where I would like to
play? Who will bring new flowers
that will not hang their heads
like tired old people wanting sleep?
Who will bring new flowers that
do not split and shrivel every
day? And if we have new flowers,
will we have new people too to
keep the flowers alive and give
them water?

And will the new young flowers die?

And will the new young people die?

And why?

In Your Religion Journal

Write out all the questions you can find in this poem.

Do you remember asking questions similar to these?

These questions are examples of the kind of question that children have asked since time began:
Where did I come from? Where do flowers come from? Where do dead people go etc? And why ... always why ?

The questions are often concerned with how things began, how they will end, where they came from and where they will go.

As children grow to adulthood they continue to be concerned with questions about beginnings and endings.

Where did life come from ?
How did the world begin ?
Where did the first human beings come from ?
Where do we go after death ?

In Your Religion Journal
Write your own poem containing the questions of a fourteen-year-old.

Activity
Listen to some of the poems written by your class.
Compare the questions with those in 'Poem from a Three Year Old'.

Where did the Earth come from?

For centuries scientists have been trying to find answers to their questions. Over the years different theories have been put forward by them, but still the search for answers goes on. The universe is four thousand million years old at least, that is 4,000,000,000 years. Further research may yet prove that this figure is too small.

Scientists look at the universe as it is at present and from the evidence that is available, they try to work out what it was like at the beginning.

One theory about the origin of the planet earth is as follows: the universe contained huge clouds made up of very large amounts of dust and gas. One of the clouds began to condense. As it condensed, it began to spin. It spun faster and faster and flattened as it spun. It became shaped like a pancake, thick at the centre and thin at the edges.

The slowly spinning centre condensed to make the sun. The outer parts, however, were spinning too fast to condense in one piece. They broke up and condensed separately to form the planets. One of these is the earth. This is known as the dust-cloud hypothesis.

Discuss

What do you think of the dust-cloud hypothesis?

How do you feel when you think about the universe: excited; confused; uncertain; afraid; amazed; full of wonder; scared; thrilled? Can you think of other words to describe how you feel?

In Your Religion Journal

Draw a picture entitled, 'The beginnings of the planet earth'.

Research

Research other theories from science about where the earth came from. Present them to the class.

The Story of Life

As far as we are aware, the earth is the only planet on which there is life. There are millions of different forms of life on the earth, varying from tiny organisms like the protozoa to huge creatures like the whale.

The smallest unit of living matter is called a cell and most living organisms are made up of millions of these.

During its early stages the earth was too hot for life to exist. Later, when it had cooled and when water had begun to fill the low places, it was able to support the first life.

The theory of evolution states that forms of life on earth have changed from original, simple, fragile creatures to larger and more complex forms of life.

The earliest creatures lived in the oceans, more than two thousand million years ago. As they developed and became more complex they became capable of living on the land and in the air.

Millions of kinds of beings have lived on the earth in the past. Many of them no longer exist. As conditions on the earth changed, life became impossible for them and so they became extinct.

They have been replaced by the kinds of life that are successful on the earth today. More and more information is continually being discovered about the earlier forms of life.

9

Find Your Group
How many different forms of life can you name?

Research
Can you find out about some of the species which have become extinct ? Share this information with the class.

Evolution and Human Life

Evolutionists say that human life is the highest point of evolution. Human beings possess an intelligence that is far superior to that of any other organism. In structure the human body is closely related to that of chimpanzees, gorillas, orang-utans and gibbons.

From their study of fossils, scientists think that ancient human beings and apes had common ancestors, millions of years ago. They think that humans and apes evolved in different directions and became adapted to different ways of life.

More fossils of the earliest people on earth are being discovered each year and more accurate ways of dating them are being developed.

The theory of evolution is, however, far from explaining the complete story of the evolution of human life and might well have to be revised as new information comes to

10

light. It seems that the earliest people on earth were skilful hunters. Gradually they perfected the ability to talk with one another. They discovered fire and learned how to make it.

For thousands of years they lived in caves, on the open plains and in the jungles. Then they began to train animals and grow plants for their own use. As time passed they learned more and more about the earth's resources, about how best to develop these resources and about how to use their own abilities.

Today we are still trying to discover more and more about ourselves and the possibilities which we possess for growth and development.

We must remember that human life is a late-comer on the scene, existing for only about two million years, which is one-thousandth of the time that life has existed.

None the less, human beings have already had more influence on the face of the earth than any other form of life.

Find Your Group

Discuss

List as many ways as you can in which human life is superior to animal life.

There is still much to be uncovered about how the universe began and how life developed.

For Christians however, one thing is clear. We believe that all things are created by God; in particular, we believe that the human soul is created by God in his image. God is the Creator of the universe and the Creator of life. We believe that God created all things out of nothing. We do not know how God created everything.

These are the truths which we find in the first chapters of the Book of Genesis. The biblical writers set out to answer the questions of the Hebrew people – questions about beginnings.

Where did life come from?

How did the world begin?

Where did the first human beings come from?

The Hebrew people believed in God as someone who loved them, who saved them from their enemies and who wanted their well-being. God had delivered them from slavery in Egypt. God had led them through the wilderness and had given them the richness of the Promised Land.

The following piece from the Book of Deuteronomy describes how they felt about themselves:

My ancestor was a wandering Aramean, who took his family to Egypt to live. They were few in number when they went there, but they became a large and powerful nation. The Egyptians treated us harshly and forced us to work as slaves. Then we cried out for help to the Lord, the God of our ancestors. He heard us and saw our suffering, hardship and misery. By his great power and strength he heard us and rescued us from Egypt. He worked miracles and wonders and caused terrifying things to happen. He brought us here and gave us this rich and fertile land (Deut 26:5-9).

The biblical writers wanted to assure the people that the one God, in whom they believed, created the universe and everything in it. Everything God created is good. Human life is the high point of God's creation.

Discuss

Which of the following words do you think the Hebrew people would use in their description of God: loving; terrifying; saving; punishing; cruel; kind; thoughtful ?

Which of the following images do you think they might apply to God: loving parent; builder; shepherd; taskmaster; creator ?

The beginning of the Book of Genesis

This is the story of the making of earth and sky: in the very beginning, God made them both.

Earth was formless chaos
lost in darkness
with stormy winds
sweeping over the vast waters.
'Let there be light!' said God –
and everywhere there was light,
splendid in his eyes.
He marked off light from darkness
calling light 'day'
and darkness 'night':
so came the evening and the morning
of the **first day.**

'Let there be a vault,' said God,
'separating the waters above the vault
from the waters on the earth below !'
The great vault was made;
he called it 'sky':
so came the evening and the morning
of the **second day.**

'Let all the earth's waters
be gathered together!' said God.
'Let dry land appear!'
He called the dry land 'earth'
and the gathered waters 'sea' –
splendid in his eyes.
'Let the earth grow plants and trees!' said God,
'seed-bearing plants and fruit trees!'
Plants and trees appeared –
splendid in his eyes:
so came the evening and the morning
of the **third day.**

'Let there be lights in the sky,' said God,
'marking off day from night,
signs for festivals
for seasons and years!
Let the lights of the sky
shine down on the earth!'
He made the sun,
dominating the day,
the moon and the stars
dominating the night –
he set them in the sky
to shine on the earth,
day and night,
light and darkness –
splendid in his eyes:
so came the evening and the morning
of the **fourth day.**

'Let there be fish in the waters!' said God,
'and birds flying in the sky!'
And there they were –
great sea monsters,
shoals of fish,
flocks of birds –
splendid in his eyes.
God blessed them all –
'Be fertile,' he said,
'swarms of fish in the sea,
flocks and flocks of birds in the sky ':
so came the evening and the morning
of the **fifth day.**

12

'Now for the animals!' said God.
'Let there be living creatures on the earth,
domestic animals,
reptiles and wild animals!'
He made all the animals –
splendid in his eyes!

'Let us now make man in our image,' said God,
'like ourselves,
to be master
of fish and wild birds,
of domestic animals,
of reptiles and wild animals!'
He created man in his own image –
in his image both sexes were created.
He blessed them too –
'Be fertile' he said, 'and increase!
Fill the earth and conquer it,
be master of all living creatures.

Plants and trees
shall be your food;
green plants
food for all living creatures –
animals, birds, reptiles,
everything alive.'

It was all splendid in God's eyes:
so came the evening and the morning
of the sixth day.

Earth and sky were made,
crowded with life.
On the sixth day
God finished his work;
on the seventh day
he stopped working.

He blessed the seventh day –
the day he stopped work.
He had brought into being
everything he had set himself to make.
(Genesis 1:1-24)

Some things to note

The Book of Genesis does not claim to be an eyewitness account of creation. The biblical writer is not interested in the historical, factual accuracy of the way in which these happenings took place. The author simply wants to affirm the truth that everything that is, comes from God and that it is good. The account clearly identifies human life as the high point of God's creation.
The account of creation in the Book of Genesis is not a scientific account. The author does not try to tell us how the work of creation was accomplished. The author tells us that creation is the work of God.
It is not meant to support or deny any particular scientific theory.

There are certain patterns in the account of Genesis.
The work of creation takes place in seven days. The description of what happened in each of the days falls into the following five-part pattern:

1. **Introduction;**
2. **Command from God;**
3. **The command is carried out;**
4. **God sees that what has been created is good, 'splendid in his eyes';**
5. **The day is named.**

The seven days fit into a pattern of three days; three days; and one day.

The first three days are days of **separation** – the light from the darkness, the dry lands from the water and so on.

The second three days are days of **repopulation** – creatures of the land, the sea and the air are created.

The last day is a day of **rest**.

At the time when the earliest scripture passages were written the printing press had not been invented and so written materials were not easily available.

Most things were passed on by word of mouth. The type of writing used in this passage, almost like poetry, would probably have helped people to remember it when they heard it.

The way in which the biblical writer wrote about the creation of the earth, the sky and so on was influenced by the way in which people who lived at that time understood the earth, the sky and the ocean.

For instance, it had not as yet come to light that the earth was round. People believed that the earth was flat. This is a picture of what they thought the earth looked like.

WATER OVER SKY

THE DOME OF THE SKY

THE EARTH

WATER UNDER THE EARTH

The fact that we understand these things more accurately now does not alter the truth of the message which the Book of Genesis wants to bring us, that the whole universe, however we picture it or understand it, is the work of God's creative power.

Find Your Group

Can you discover in the creation story from Genesis, how that particular view of the earth is borne out in the words of the writer ?

In Your Religion Journal or as a Class Project

Illustrate the seven days of creation.

OR

Draw your favourite image of the moment of creation.

The Earlier Account

In chapter 2 of the Book of Genesis we find another account of creation. Biblical scholars now know that this was in fact written earlier than the account which we find in chapter 1.

I n the very beginning no prairie bush was yet to be found anywhere; no wild grain had started to sprout. No rain had fallen on the ground; there was nobody to till the ground if it had – there was only the water rising up from beneath the ground and covering the land.

Then GOD moulded Man from the ground itself and breathed into him the breath that made him a living creature.

He then planted a park away in the east, in Eden, and gave it to Man as his home, planting all sorts of lovely and useful trees. In the heart of the park he planted two special trees – the Tree of Life (the fruit of this tree made those who ate it immortal) and the Tree of Knowledge.

GOD put Man in the park to work in it and guard it.

'You can eat the fruit of any tree you like,' GOD told him. 'But the fruit of one tree you must never eat – if you do, it will mean certain death. That tree is the Tree of Knowledge.

'It is bad for Man to live here all alone,' GOD went on. 'I must make a mate for him !'

So GOD moulded all the wild animals and the wild birds – again, out of the ground itself. He led Man to them to see what names he would give them – these would be the names they would always be called by.

Man gave names to all the domestic animals, the wild birds, and the wild animals. But none of the animals could be a mate for him.

So GOD put him into a deep sleep. While he slept, he took one of his ribs, healing his body afterwards. He then built the rib into the Woman and led her to Man. As soon as he saw her, Man exclaimed –
This one at last
is from my very bone,
from my very flesh.
She shall be called 'Woman' –
from Man was she taken .
(Genesis 2:4-23)

Find Your Group

Discuss

What differences can you find between this account of creation and the earlier account ? What similarities can you find ?

Can you list the principal truths which you think the biblical writer wanted to communicate to us in the first chapter of the Book of Genesis; about God, about the universe, about ourselves?

What do you think is the most amazing thing about the universe ?

The glory and power and love of God which we can see in the story of creation inspired the writers of the following psalms. Read the extracts slowly and reflectively.

In Praise of the Creator

When I look at your heavens, the work of your hands, the moon and stars which you created –
Who are we that you should be mindful of us, that you should care for us ?
You have made us little less than gods and crowned us with glory and honour *(Ps 8:3-8).*

You created the moon to mark the months;
the sun knows the time to set.
You made the night, and in the
    darkness
all the wild animals come out.
The young lions roar while they hunt,
looking for the food that God
    provides.
When the sun rises, they go back
and lie down in their dens.
Then people go out to do their work
and keep working until evening.

Lord, you have made so many things !
How wisely you made them all !
The earth is filled with your creatures.
There is the ocean, large and wide,
where countless creatures live,
large and small alike.

All of them depend on you
to give them food when they need it.

You give it to them, and they eat it;
you provide food, and they are
satisfied.
When you turn away, they are afraid;
when you take away your breath, they
die and go back to the dust from
which they came.
But when you give them breath,
they are created;
you give new life to the earth
(Extracts from Psalm 104).

In Your Religion Journal

Write your own psalm in praise of creation.
OR
Write into your journal your favourite lines from the above extracts of the Psalms.

Activity
Make a collage illustrating your favourite lines from the above.

Activity

Look at the
following two
pictures, one of
a city scene and
the other a
picture from
the countryside.

In each picture
point out five
places where
more care and
respect should
be given to the
environment.

Lesson Three

The

Earth

Discuss

You have identified ten places in these pictures where disrespect has been shown towards the environment. Have you ever been responsible for showing disrespect towards your environment ?

Our world is not just for us. It is also home for all kinds of living creatures from roses to reindeer, pine trees to pears. But because we are careless in the way we treat the environment, nature is having a very tough time.

TheGreenNewsletter

ISSUE NO. 1

IN THE RACE TO SAVE THE ENVIRONMENT FROM FURTHER DAMAGE... THERE IS NO TIME TO LOSE. ON THE TIME-CLOCK OF ENVIRONMENTAL DISASTER WE ARE FAST APPROACHING MIDNIGHT !

Our roving reporter has uncovered some interesting facts which we should all be aware of. You'll be amazed, read on...!

Pollution

Air and water are two of the most important elements on earth. Without them we couldn't live. But we are making them so dirty with fumes, chemicals and rubbish that in some places the air is too dirty to breathe and the water can be too polluted to drink.

In some areas where there is a lot of traffic passing through, or where a large industrial estate is located, there are problems with lead pollution.

This is caused mainly from the use of leaded petrol. Research has found that lead pollution can seriously damage the health of children.

Smog

Smog usually occurs in cities where warm smoke, mainly from the burning of coal in homes, as well as fumes from car exhausts, is prevented from rising by a still layer of cold air. This usually happens in winter during cold, calm conditions.

Smog can cause severe breathing problems for people with asthma or for elderly people. During the winter of 1952 in London, 4,000 people died from breathing difficulties within just a few days.

Smog can also do damage to buildings.

In recent years laws have been passed in many countries banning the burning of all but smokeless fuels in built-up areas. This has greatly reduced the amount of smog in the atmosphere. However, another similar problem has now arisen – smog caused by the action of prolonged sunlight on high concentrations of car exhaust fumes. Los Angeles is one place where this causes major problems.

Acid Rain

Acid rain is the term used to describe polluted rainfall.

The air is made up of lots of gases. Fumes from cars and factories combine with these gases and make our rain acidic. This means that raindrops actually damage plants, trees and in some cases even whole forests, like the tropical rain forests of South America.

Greenhouse Effect

Humans have produced so much of the gas carbon dioxide that it has formed a thick layer between us and the sun and this stops the heat getting out. The increase in the earth's temperature, or global warming, as it is sometimes referred to, can be compared to living in a greenhouse.

While we all enjoy being warm, too much heat doesn't do us any good at all. The greenhouse effect means that in time we won't be able to grow crops and our rivers will run dry. Eventually the polar ice caps may start to melt, making the sea swell so much that coastal towns may disappear.

The Ozone Hole

In the sky there's another layer of gas called ozone which helps us by blocking out some of the sun's harmful ultraviolet rays. But certain gases called CFCs and halons, found in fridges, aerosols and plastic foam, have floated up to the ozone layer and made a hole in it. This means that the dangerous rays of the sun can reach us on earth, and in some cases cause skin cancer as well as damaging plants, crops and marine life.

Activity

Complete this crossword.

Across

2. Name given to planet which is 92,000,000 miles from the sun. (5)
6. World-wide warming of the earth. (6)
7. Product which contains CFCs. (7)
9. The surroundings in which a person lives. (11)
11. Place of captivity for animals, some of which will soon be extinct. (3)
12. Container holding drink, which can be recycled. (3)
14. Type of pollution caused by petrol. (4)
16. Any substance used to produce heat. (4)
17. Polluted rainfall. (8)

Down

1. Used for heating, can also cause pollution to the sea. (3)
3. Name given to the causes of damage and destruction to the environment. (9)
4. Place where tomatoes grow. It also gives its name to the increasing rise of the earth's temperature. (10)
5. Name of forests which can be found in the southern hemisphere. (8)
8. London had a great problem with this earlier this century. (4)
10. A layer of gas which protects the inhabitants of the earth from the sun's harmful rays. (5)
13. Often abbreviated, chlorofluorocarbons. (3)
15. The environment is in urgent need of help. Another word for help. (3)

In Your Religion Journal

Choose five words from the crossword and explain how each one contributes to the pollution of the environment.

STOP PRESS

Late Edition No. 232

There was an uproar in court today, as the trial of the century began. The human race has been charged with reckless behaviour, damage to property and neglect of the earth's environment. The counsel for the prosecution will require the defendant to answer the following charges:

(a) The six basic elements necessary for life (Carbon dioxide, Hydrogen, Oxygen, Nitrogen, Sulphur and Phosphorus) have been carelessly squandered;

(b) The tropical rain forests are in the process of being destroyed;

(c) There has been a mindless slaughter of certain mammals, birds and reptiles;

(d) The air necessary for sustaining human life has been polluted and poisoned, through neglect;

(e) Food and water has, to a large extent, been contaminated;

(f) The ozone layer is being destroyed through the use of CFCs in aerosols;

(g) And finally the most serious charge has been that the environmental damage which has been caused is as a direct result of the defendant's own materialistic attitude and greed. Added to this charge is one of ignorance and inaction which maintain the problem.

The courtroom buzzed as the defendant pleaded **Not Guilty** to all seven charges. The trial began, with the prosecution opening the case.

Activity

Continue this courtroom drama by acting out the case for the prosecution and the defence.

Discuss

What is meant by the assertion that the health of the environment depends on the daily choices made by millions of individuals?

List five ways you can improve the environment by choices you make in your own life.

List five ways in which you are already caring for the environment.

QUESTIONNAIRE

How well do you care for the environment?

In Your Religion Journal

In what ways do you need to change your attitude to the environment?

Complete the following questionnaire to see how well YOU care for the earth.

Answer **Yes** or **No** to the following statements.

	Yes	No
1. I have discussed environmental issues at home with my parents or at school with my friends.	▪	▪
2. I never throw litter.	▪	▪
3. I never dump rubbish in the countryside.	▪	▪
4. Before buying/using an aerosol I always make sure that it is ozone-friendly.	▪	▪
5. I collect old newspapers so that they can be recycled.	▪	▪
6. I buy/use recycled paper for my school-work.	▪	▪
7. I bring glass bottles to the bottle bank so that they can be recycled.	▪	▪
8. I would like to help to organise a bottle bank for recycling bottles /cans in my neighbourhood.	▪	▪
9. Any cans/tins I drink from, I make sure to put them in a bin so that they can be recycled.	▪	▪
10. If I have a choice, I prefer to walk or cycle to school rather than use a bus or get a lift in a car.	▪	▪
11. I am worried about the future of the planet.	▪	▪
12. I belong to an environmental organisation.	▪	▪

Activity

As a class you could make up your own questionnaire on the environment and how to care for it, and circulate it throughout the other classes and the teachers in your school.

Some of the environmental damage we do is caused by the fact that we want an easy lifestyle. Try to find out, within your own neighbourhood, in what ways people are damaging the environment for the sake of convenience.

Report back to the class !

The Green Newsletter

ISSUE NO. 2

ATTRACTIVE DETACHED RESIDENCE

Believed to be unique, this magnificent dwelling has been sadly neglected in recent years. Some outstanding features have been lost. However, it still offers an exceptional home to those prepared to maintain it with care !

In Your Religion Journal

This is the opening headline of the second issue of the *Green Newsletter*. As a reporter, you are to write an article for the newspaper, which will encourage students in schools throughout the country to think of ways in which they can improve and care for their environment. Remember, you are trying to remind them that the future of the earth is in their hands.

Find Your Group
Discuss

What do you think the earth we live on has to say to us at this time ? Describe a beautiful natural scene you have witnessed and say how it made you feel.

Activity

Design a poster to be included in this issue of the *Green Newsletter* for an advertising campaign entitled, **Caring for the Environment.** Your poster will need to have an original advertising slogan!

What has the environmental crisis got to do with religion anyway ?

The environmental crisis has become a world-wide issue. However, we often think that caring for the environment is the responsibility of others. Most of us are in the business of hoping someone else will take care of it. After all, what can we do as individuals ?

Those who do get involved in work to protect and preserve our environment can find support from within the Bible. We only have to look as far as the first chapter of Genesis, where, each time God creates an element of the universe, the author tells us: 'God saw that it was good' or in other words, 'it was splendid in his eyes'.

The sea, the land with its vegetation, the sun, the moon, the stars, all the creatures of the land and sea are created out of God's own goodness. They all speak to us of God – a sunset, a waterfall, a snowfall, even a water lily. In them we see the power, the beauty of God reflected in our world and so it is our responsibility to listen and respond carefully to the world in which we live.

Activity
Read and act out the following short play.

Characters: Three readers; the other students in the class are the audience.

The Bright People

Trio:	Oh, we are a bright people !
Reader One:	We know so much !
Reader Two:	For example, we know all about lightning.
Reader Three:	We also know what causes floods, earthquakes and plagues of locusts.
One:	Since taking dominion over all things, we know that a lightning bolt is not a spear thrown by the Almighty.
Two:	We RESPECT lightning, mind you, but we are not TERRIFIED by it.
One:	And so it is with many of the so-called dark things of nature....
Three:	We have conquered the fear.
One:	We have eliminated the terror of the unknown darkness of nature ... By devastating nature herself.
Trio:	Oh, we are a bright people !

Pause for two counts; with new energy....

One:	Yes, we are a bright people !
Two:	We have changed the very chemistry of the planet;
Three:	We have altered the biosystems;
Two:	We have changed the topography...
Three:	...even the geological structures of the planet.
One:	Such structures and such functions, I might add, have taken hundreds of millions, even billions of years to bring into existence. We changed them all !
Two:	That certainly shows great intelligence.
One:	Within a historical snap of the fingers we changed it all.
Trio:	We could not have done that if we were not a bright people.

Pause with a fresh start....

Trio:	Oh, we are a bright people !
Three:	We know ENOUGH, you can be sure of that.
One:	We know enough to know that we are playing for high stakes.
Three:	The beauty...
Two:	...the grandeur...
One:	...even the survival of the earth is in our power. But we are also an honest people...
Two & Three:	...a bright and honest people...
One:	...and we'd be the first to admit that a few minor compromises have been made along the way.

In quick succession, overlapping slightly.

	Yes, it is true that we have contaminated the air, water, soil...
Two:	...we have dammed the rivers, cut down rain forests...
One:	...destroyed animal habitat on an extensive scale.
Three:	We have driven the great blue whale and a multitude of animals almost to extinction.
Two:	We have caused the land to be eroded, the rain to be acid.
Three:	We have killed ten thousand lakes as habitat for fish.
One:	But that's what we call 'playing for high stakes'.
Trio:	

Suddenly very bright and exuberant.

	We are moving into a new technological wonderland !

Pause for one count; very loud.

	CAN YOU HELP US FIND IT?
One:	

Reassuringly calm.

	We ARE a bright people. We MUST be moving towards something magnificent that is worth the necessary destruction of the natural world.
Three:	We must survive --- you know that !
Two:	We must provide food and shelter for our children...
Three:	...and of course, consider the energy we will need to work all our machinery...
Trio:	WE THINK IT IS WORTH IT.

Towards audience.

	DO YOU THINK IT IS?
Audience 1:	I may not be very bright, but I ask you: what benefit is worth giving up the purity of the air we breathe ?
Audience 2:	I may not be very bright either, but I challenge you: what benefit is worth giving up the purity of the water we drink?
Audience 3:	Come, come, bright people. Ask yourselves again. Is it worth it? Is it worth it?
Audience 4:	Dear bright people: did we hear you correctly? Did you say future 'wonderland'? Is any future 'wonderland' worth giving up the air we breathe, the water we drink, the life-giving soil in which our food is grown?
Trio:	

Facing each other.

	Will we find the answers ?

Facing the audience.

	Will we find the answers?

Jesus and the Environment

Jesus was a man who knew how to listen with respect and attention to his environment. He used nature and the environment as the basis for many of his parables. In one of his parables, when he was explaining the meaning of the kingdom of God, he used the image of a mustard seed to encourage his followers to think about what God's kingdom is like.

Read Luke 13:18 -19.

Jesus showed his followers how God was always at work in the world, forever renewing and sustaining life. He appreciated that the earth was a gift from God and given to the human race in trust to nurture and conserve for the next generation. Jesus knew how God cared for even the smallest creature on earth. He said 'Aren't five sparrows sold for two pennies ? Yet not one sparrow is forgotten by God' *(Lk 12:6)*. 'Even the lilies of the field' *(Lk 12:27)* 'and the birds of the air', *(Mt 6:26)* are protected and cared for by God.

Through his example, Jesus taught his disciples not to exploit nature but to live lightly on the earth. He warned them against hoarding possessions and allowing their hearts to be enticed by the lure of materialism. He was careful not to waste anything – especially where food was concerned. For instance, after feeding the five thousand, he instructed the disciples to gather up the pieces left over, so that nothing would be lost.

St Francis of Assisi Patron of Ecologists

In 1979 Pope John Paul II named St Francis of Assisi (1182-1226) the patron saint of ecology, and when one looks at the life of this man it becomes obvious that this title is well deserved.

During his lifetime Francis displayed a deep reverence for nature. He saw nature as the work of God; he saw in all things God's creative touch, by which everything in nature becomes a stepping-stone to God. Francis embraced the world because he saw in it a reflection of God.

For Francis, all created things were his brothers and sisters. He saw himself as a living creature, one member of an immense family of creatures of God. Because he felt at one with all created things he respected them. He didn't approach nature with a superior attitude nor was it a mere plaything for him. He didn't want to transform or dominate nature – he lived in perfect harmony with it.

Francis offers to Christians an example of genuine and deep respect for the integrity of creation. He reminds us all of our serious obligation to respect and watch over all created things with care.

In today's world many consider something valuable only if it can be used. We are often interested only in the 'purpose' of things, and not so concerned with the meaning a thing has in itself, namely that it glorifies God by its very existence. This is the message of Francis – a steward of creation.

The challenge for us as Christians is to respond in a positive way to the environmental crisis which is taking place in our time. We are called to pay attention to our world, to attend to our environment with reverence and respect and to listen to it attentively.

Research

Find out more about St Francis of Assisi. Make a picture display in your classroom illustrating some incidents from the life of St Francis which show his respect for nature.

Class Activity

Set up a display board in your classroom displaying information from newspapers, magazines etc, about caring for the environment. Divide the board into two sections showing both the positive and negative aspects.

A Time to Pray

Leader

Let us pray to God the Creator. We offer prayers of thanks and praise to God for bestowing on us the privilege of caring for the earth. Help us to appreciate our environment and accept the responsibilities we must face each day in caring for it. Help us to make the right choices in our daily lives which will save the environment from further damage.

Reader 1

I the Lord am the God that made you; and as I made you, so have I made all living things and a fit place for each living thing and a world for all living things to share in interdependence. And so that my creation may be cherished I command:
>   You shall not act carelessly
>   towards the world of nature.

Reader 2

You shall not act in any way which makes the world less able to sustain life:
not by destroying the soil;
not by destroying the living seas;
not by laying waste the wild places;
not by releasing poisons;
nor by causing great changes in the climate.
You shall not encroach on a species' habitat, or destroy its natural defences, or reduce its numbers to the point where its survival is endangered.

Reader 3

I am the Creator of the world; treasure it as your Creator's treasure. Honour the life of all living beings and the order of nature and the wildness of the wilderness, and the richness of the created world, and the beauty of lands undefiled by your works; and seek the holiness I have placed in these things, the measure of light I have lent them; and preserve these things well; for these are my gifts to you from the dawn of time and their life will not be offered to you again.

Reader 4

And in the fulfilment of these commandments, be not half-hearted and do not err on the side of your greed and your convenience; but act with all your ability to love. If you will not attend to me and instead live contrary to my way, your own acts and choices will become the means of your undoing.

Leader

'As a friend of the poor who was loved by God's creatures, St Francis of Assisi invited all of creation – animals, plants, natural forces, even Brother Sun and Sister Moon – to give honour and praise to the Lord. The poor man of Assisi gives us striking witness that when we are at peace with God we are better able to devote ourselves to building up that peace with all creation, which is inseparable from peace among all peoples... And may he remind us of our serious obligation to respect and watch over them with care.'
(Pope John Paul II, New Year's Message 1990)

Song: **Canticle of the Sun**

Petition Prayers

Reader 5

We pray for the indigenous people who see their land invaded, their forests destroyed, their animals exterminated and their hearts torn by the greed and irresponsibility of the so-called civilisation of consumerism.

All:

Lord, help us to treat your world with kindness.

Reader 6

Like St Francis of Assisi may we too have a genuine and deep respect for the integrity of creation.

All:

Lord, help us to treat your world with kindness.

Reader 7

You have given us the resources of the world to care for and share; help us not to waste these precious resources.

All:

Lord, help us to treat your world with kindness.

You may now wish to add your own petition prayers.

All:

Creator God, we see you in our earth; we see and feel your love and care for us; your earth feeds us and clothes us.

Forgive our greed and our selfish use of this gift.

May we learn to share the earth, to work it and care for it, so that all who live now and in the future may enjoy its care for us.

Lesson Four Human Life
the high point of Creation

image image

We use the word IMAGE to speak about the way a person looks.

Usually there are images that are in fashion at a particular time and other images that are not in fashion.
Often people are expected to present one particular image in order to be acceptable to others.

PRESENTING AN IMAGE

Activity Find material from magazines to illustrate the images you have discussed. Did you find any other images that are popular in the world of fashion today ?

Sometimes people try to present an image which is false in order to make an impression. For example, someone who lacks confidence might try to appear full of confidence. Someone who is shy might try to appear very outgoing. Someone who is gentle might try to appear tough.

Find Your Group Can you think of times when you tried to give the impression that you were different from what you actually are ? Say how you did this!

Advertising

People who advertise various items on television try to find ways to make the things which they are promoting attractive to the viewers.

Find Your Group

Discuss

What kind of images are used to advertise the following:
cars; coffee; alcohol; jeans ?

Activity

In your group decide on a product which you would like to advertise. Now think up a television advertisement for the product.

DO YOU KNOW YOUR OWN IMAGE ?

Complete the following questionnaire and find out what image you present to the other students in your class.

Find Your Group

1. You go into your local music store, what record would you buy ?
   - (a) Country & Western
   - (b) Soul
   - (c) Reggae
   - (d) Heavy Metal
   - (e) Pop
   - (f) Other

2. Which of the following would you choose from a menu ?
   - (a) Burger & Chips
   - (b) Pizza
   - (c) Vegetarian food
   - (d) Salad
   - (e) Fish
   - (f) Other

3. You go on a shopping spree; where are you likely to buy your clothes ?
   - (a) Local market
   - (b) Second-hand shop
   - (c) High Street chain store
   - (d) Boutique
   - (e) Make your own
   - (f) Other

4. What would you choose to wear ?
   - (a) Jeans & T-shirt
   - (b) Hippy gear
   - (c) Latest trendy gear
   - (d) Punk
   - (e) Sports gear/track suit
   - (f) Other

5. Your favourite colour is ?
   - (a) Red
   - (b) Black
   - (c) Green
   - (d) Blue
   - (e) White
   - (f) Other

6. You have a choice of programmes on TV, which do you choose ?
   - (a) Film
   - (b) News & current affairs
   - (c) Documentary
   - (d) Wildlife/nature
   - (e) Comedy/soaps
   - (f) Other

7. What's your favourite hobby/ interest ?
   - (a) Sport
   - (b) Reading
   - (c) Music/dancing
   - (d) Computer games
   - (e) Clothes
   - (f) Other

8. What type of film would you choose to go to ?
   - (a) Romantic
   - (b) Comedy
   - (c) Thriller
   - (d) Horror
   - (e) Science fiction
   - (f) Other

9. Which hair-style would you choose ?
   - (a) Perm
   - (b) Short/straight
   - (c) Bob
   - (d) Punk
   - (e) Longhair boy
   - (f) Gelled back

10. If you had a choice what would you like to do ?
   - (a) Teach
   - (b) Act
   - (c) Scientific research
   - (d) Model
   - (e) Own your own company
   - (f) Other

Using the following categories try and analyse the answers given and decide what image is being presented by others in your group. An individual may fit into more than just one of the categories suggested. You may use other categories where you think it is suitable: trendy; conservative; shy; outgoing; intelligent; easy-going; adventurous.

Describe the image which you would most like to present to others.

He's the image of his father!

He's the image of his father!

Discuss
What do they mean ?

If someone who didn't know you saw your photograph, they would then have an image of you. We have images of various people we don't know, people we've seen on the television or in films.

An image of someone is not the person but it shows what the person looks like.

He's the image of his father!

Read again the accounts of the creation of human life from the Book of Genesis which you can find in Lesson Two.

Congratulations, he's the image of his father!

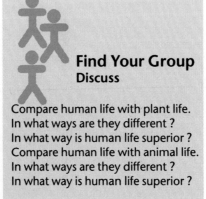

Find Your Group
Discuss

Compare human life with plant life. In what ways are they different ? In what way is human life superior ? Compare human life with animal life. In what ways are they different ? In what way is human life superior ?

One of the things which the creation accounts in the Book of Genesis have in common is that they tell us that the creation of human life is the crowning glory of God's creation.

Human beings are created in God's image.

More than anything in the universe, we reflect God. We can show others what God is like. People can get some idea of the love of God through experiencing the love of other people.

In Your Religion Journal
Put the caption, *God's love through people,* at the top of a page. Illustrate the caption with pictures, photographs or drawings.

We can guess at the goodness of God through seeing the goodness of people. There are many people in the world who reflect the goodness of God. Who do you think of ?

Discuss
Think of someone you know who, for you, reflects the love and care of God.

Find Your Group
Make a collage for the classroom wall to illustrate the caption, *God's goodness through people.*

We can be helped to understand the creative power of God through the creativity of people.

Artists, writers, poets, scientists, and builders are all people who use their creative powers in the world in various ways. We can all be creative in some way. In what way can you be creative ?

In Your Religion Journal
Write about the different ways in which you can be creative.

Most important of all, we are like God because we, above all creatures, are personal beings. We can form personal relationships with each other and with God.

In the book of Genesis we read: 'Then God said, "And now we will make human beings; they will be like us and resemble us. They will have power over the fish, the birds, and all animals, domestic and wild, large and small"' *(Genesis 1:26)*.

Human beings are free, intelligent persons. They not only reflect the freedom and intelligence of a personal God. They are able to use their freedom and intelligence. They can grow in their understanding of the world of nature. They can shape and organise the world around them in ways beyond what is possible for any other creature. They can use their intelligence and power to stand back from nature, analyse it and, using their initiative, find new ways of harnessing its powers. In this, they reflect in a small way the complete power which God has over creation.

If human beings are to be true images of God they need to have the kind of attitude God has to all he created and they have to use their superiority and independence responsibly. God puts his world into our hands. He wants us to use his gifts wisely and to care for them.

Discuss

If we are created in God's image, what obligations does that place upon us?

How can we reflect God?

Activity

Using pictures and captions from magazines and newspapers make some class posters to illustrate the title, 'In God's Image'.

In Your Religion Journal

You are a citizen of a distant planet. You have been sent by your people on a fact-finding mission to earth. They have heard about a Creator called God, who, they have been told, created the entire universe. They have become very curious about this God and have sent you to have a look at what God created in order to see if there are any clues available as to what God is like. Write a letter telling them about what you have found on earth.

A Time to Pray

The psalmist who wrote Psalm 8 was convinced that human life was, in fact, the crowning glory of creation.

The Majesty of God and the Dignity of Humanity

O God, our God
how glorious is your name over all the earth !
Your glory is praised in the heavens.
Out of the mouths of children and babes
you have fashioned praise because of your foes,
to silence the enemy and the rebellious.
When I look at your heavens, the work of your hands,
the moon and the stars which you created –
who are we that you should be mindful of us,
that you should care for us ?
You have made us little less than the gods
and crowned us with glory and honour.
You have given us rule over the works of your hands,
putting all things under our feet:
all sheep and oxen,
yes, and the beasts of the field;
the birds of the air, the fishes of the sea
and whatever swims the paths of the seas.
God, our God,
how glorious is your name over all the earth !

In Your Religion Journal

Write your own psalm in praise of the glory of God and the dignity of human life.

Test Yourself.

Do the Looking Back exercises on page 224.

Lesson Five
The Gift of Life

When God created living things, he also created the plan whereby each species reproduces itself so that life continues. God is still re-creating life in the world through the people, the animals, the plants and all living species which continue to co-operate with God's plan for creating new life.

There are many different varieties of living things but the most important which we can see with the naked eye are plants and animals.

In the animal kingdom there are several different classes such as fish, birds, reptiles, amphibia and mammals. The mammal class is particularly interesting for us, because as human beings we belong to this group.

Mammals are somewhat different from the other species of the animal kingdom. They do not lay eggs. Instead their eggs are fertilised internally within the female and grow there for several weeks or months, depending on their species. This period of time is called pregnancy. In the case of a human baby it lasts for forty weeks, in the case of mice for three weeks and in the case of elephants for two years.

Human Life Begins

Your life as a human being started when your father's seed, which is called sperm, joined with your mother's egg, which is called the ovum.

This is called conception. At the moment of conception aspects of your identity as a person were decided; sex, hair colour, height, and so on.

Your father's seed carried his characteristics and your mother's egg carried her characteristics. You inherited a combination of these.

We all resemble our parents in varying ways and to varying degrees. We resemble them not only in the way we look but also in the temperament and various talents which we have. When we grow we develop other characteristics and talents which we did not inherit from our parents. As we get older we are more in control of the way in which we are growing and developing. For instance we can decide to become more of an outdoor-type person and we can do things to make this come about.

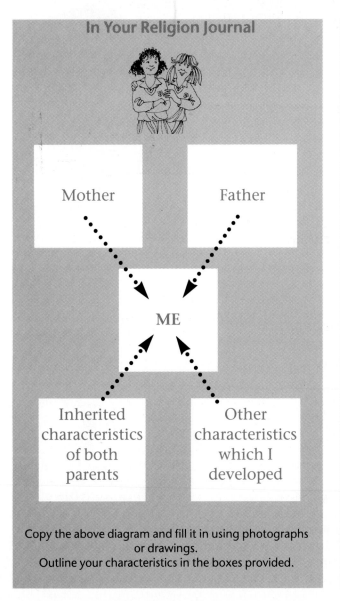

In Your Religion Journal

Copy the above diagram and fill it in using photographs or drawings.
Outline your characteristics in the boxes provided.

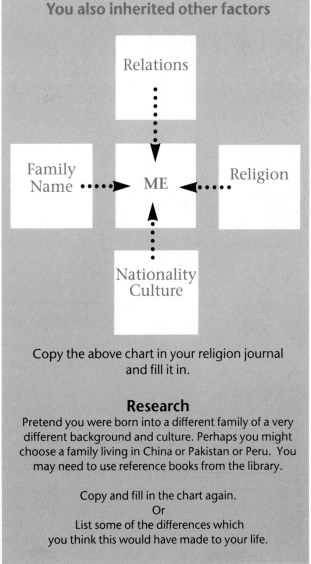

You also inherited other factors

Copy the above chart in your religion journal and fill it in.

Research

Pretend you were born into a different family of a very different background and culture. Perhaps you might choose a family living in China or Pakistan or Peru. You may need to use reference books from the library.

Copy and fill in the chart again.
Or
List some of the differences which
you think this would have made to your life.

Pregnancy

About seven days after conception the new human being or foetus moves into the mother's womb or uterus. There it is enclosed in a bag of warm fluid which regulates its temperature and protects it from germs and other injuries. The foetus nestles into the soft lining of the womb and around it the placenta is formed. This is connected on the one side to the mother's blood supply and on the other to the foetus, by means of the umbilical cord, which contains arteries and blood vessels.

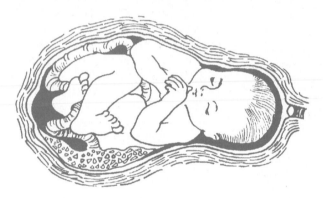

Through the umbilical cord the baby gets its nourishment and also gets rid of its body waste during the period of pregnancy.

If the mother drinks alcohol, takes drugs or smokes cigarettes, the harmful materials which go through the umbilical cord will affect the growth of the foetus.

At birth the umbilical cord is cut and the baby now breathes in its own oxygen, takes in the nourishment which it needs to live and to grow and disposes of the waste products from its body.

However, it is still totally dependent on the adults around.

You are a unique and special individual. There is nobody else in the whole world quite like you. You may resemble your parents or your brothers and sisters in many, even remarkable, ways. But you are not quite the same as any of them.

The ability that parents have to create new life is a gift from God. The way in which life is created is part of God's plan for the world. In creating new life, men and women become co-creators with God and God continues to create life through them.

In Your Religion Journal

Use paint or ink to make your fingerprint on a page of your journal. Nobody in the whole world has a fingerprint that is the same as yours. List the characteristics which make you unique.

Discuss

When are you most like your mother or your father ? In what ways ?
If you have brothers or sisters, in what ways are you like them or different from them ?

Find Your Group

List all the ways in which a new-born baby is dependent on the adults around him or her.

In Your Religion Journal

Illustrate these using photographs or pictures from magazines.

Development and Growth

Birth to Four Years

The first four years of a child's life are years of tremendous learning and growth. At first, babies spend most of their life eating and sleeping. Then they gradually begin to spend more time awake. They come to be able to see more clearly and to take notice of all that is going on around them.

They are extremely interested in their surroundings and love to explore spaces and shapes. They love to touch and taste things.

They learn to smile and parents wait anxiously for their baby's first step. They make the first sounds that will eventually be shaped into words. They learn to respond to love, care and warmth. They learn to trust people. From these early experiences of love, care and trust they will eventually come to know and understand the love and care of God.

By three years of age, babies can eat soft foods, use a spoon, say quite a few words, are toilet-trained and they can walk and run around.

Four to Twelve Years

Around about four years of age a child starts going to school. This is a big step in the child's growth and development. They learn to interact with a much wider group of people. They learn to feel secure and happy when not surrounded by their immediate family and the people they know best. They love learning. At this stage they are excited about learning new things, such as reading, writing and mathematics. They learn to co-operate with others, to work as a team both in school projects and in play. Their bodies grow and get stronger and sturdier. They learn to run and jump and enjoy all kinds of physical exercise.

Adolescence

Adolescence is an in-between time, the time when you are in between being a child and an adult. You are no longer a child, however, neither are you quite an adult as yet. Sometimes you will find yourself acting more like a child, at other times you

will act more like an adult. For instance, one day you may long for independence and wish to have the freedom to make your own decisions, while the next day you may find yourself wishing that your parents or some other adult would decide so that you would not have the responsibility of making your own decisions.

In Your Religion Journal   Illustrate each stage of a child's life with pictures or drawings.

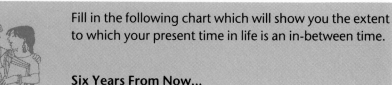
Twelve to Twenty years

With adolescence, comes an important milestone in a person's growth and development. The human body grows and matures very rapidly at this time due to the fact that it begins to produce special chemicals, called hormones. These are released into the body from the glands and this leads to the stage of growth which we call puberty.

This starts at different ages for different people. Most of you are probably at this stage of development at the moment, or if not you soon will be. It is a time of rapid growth and change. We will look in detail at the various kinds of change and growth.

Physical Changes

Changes in a Boy's Body

His voice deepens and breaks.
His penis and scrotum enlarge.
His testicles begin to produce sperm.
Hair grows under his arms, on his face, chest and pubic area.

Changes in a Girl's Body

Her hips widen.
Her breasts develop.
Her ovaries begin to produce eggs or ova and each month she begins to have menstrual periods.
Hair grows under her arms and on her pubic area.

This time of enormous physical change which happens in early adolescence is called puberty. Both boys and girls can feel quite awkward until they get used to the changes that are taking place in their bodies.

Both boys and girls are physically capable of becoming parents after puberty but in many ways they are too young to take on the huge responsibility of parenthood.

Emotional changes

During puberty, because of the new hormones which are active in a young person's body they can experience mood swings. They feel quite happy at one time and then for no apparent reason can become quite miserable.

Because of this they often feel misunderstood at home and with their friends. They tend to fly off the handle or burst into tears. They feel frustrated and ashamed of themselves. They sometimes find it difficult to ask for advice or help. It is also a time when they can discover more clearly than ever before their own strengths and weaknesses.

Above all it is a time when they can relate with sensitivity and understanding to other adolescents who are experiencing similar difficulties.

Intellectual Change

At this stage the young person is capable of a more in-depth type of learning and understanding. Often it is at this stage that a particular interest emerges – a young person can become particularly interested in science, in reading, in outdoor activities and so on. Young people love discussion and the exchange of ideas.

Social Changes

Until now a young person's life centred almost completely around parents and family. When they looked for advice, support and understanding it was almost always to their parents and family that they turned. Now they begin to look outside the family for some of these. Friends of the same age, the peer group, become extremely important in a young person's life. They like to take part in group activities. They need to feel accepted by their peers and that they belong to the group.

Twenty Years to Forty Years

Adults have become physically fully developed. As people mature they become more able to control their emotions. They gradually learn what their strengths and weaknesses are and try to be happy to live with these.

They become aware of the limitations of human nature and many adults deepen their trust and confidence in God. They learn to look carefully at all that is taking place in the world around them, to discover what is good and what is bad and to make mature thoughtful decisions. They learn to develop meaningful personal relationships with a small group of close friends. They come to understand in a deeper way what it means to love and to be loved.

Forty Years to Old Age

For many people, reaching forty means that they have come to the stage when they can really relax and enjoy life. Many feel that they have already achieved a great deal in their lives. They have become aware of all that they have to contribute and they now have a greater confidence in themselves.

As people grow older changes occur which indicate that their bodies are slowing down. They are unable to be as active as they had been; their skin becomes wrinkled and their hair turns grey. They can, however, be quite healthy for many years if they treat their bodies sensibly, by eating proper food and taking exercise.

In Your Religion Journal

Illustrate each stage of a person's growth with drawings or pictures.

Activity

In groups, make posters using cut-outs from magazines or newspapers illustrating the main characteristics of a young person who is going through the adolescent stage of life.

In Your Religion Journal

Which stage of a person's life do you think is:

(a) easiest?
(b) most exciting?
(c) most difficult?
(d) most confusing?
(e) most enjoyable?
(f) most interesting?

If you had a personal problem and you needed to talk to someone would you:

(a) talk to your father?
(b) talk to your mother?
(c) talk to your best friend?
(d) talk to someone else?

Give a reason for your choice.

Find Your Group

Discuss what you have written. Compare your responses with those of the others in the group.

Each stage in life is a stepping-stone to the next stage. When we leave behind any one of the stages and step into the next stage it usually involves some difficult adjustments.

The most traumatic of these is probably the moment of birth when the baby leaves behind the comfortable, secure warmth of the mother's womb and emerges into the cold open space of the world.

In turn the young child has to leave behind the familiarity and security of the family and step into the life of the school.

Adolescents have to become more and more independent of their parents as they grow to adulthood. At the end of each stage of life, we long for the happiness and fulfilment which, we believe, we will arrive at eventually.

Primary school children long to be in post-primary school. Teenagers long to have left school. Young adults long to have greater independence.

The final stage in life is death.

Our Christian faith tells us that Jesus has won for us eternal life and that he offers it to us. If we accept his offer in faith and if we show our love for God by working for justice, freedom, peace, love and happiness for all people during our lives on earth, then, after death, all our desires and hopes will be fulfilled beyond our wildest expectations.

St Paul tells us about: 'Things that no eye has seen, and no ear has heard, things beyond the mind of man, all that God has prepared for those who love him' (*1 Cor 2:9*) when he speaks about life after death.

Jesus, when he speaks about life with God in heaven, compares it to a great wedding feast to which we are all invited.

Every step of our lives from the moment of conception to the moment of death is part of God's plan for us and for all of creation.

If we truly believe this we will be able to face each step with courage and confidence and there will never be any need for us to be afraid.

A Time to Pray

Read, slowly and reflectively, the following version of Psalm 46.

If we know anything at all about God
we will know he is someone who
takes good care of us.
God our Father is someone we can
trust.

Blessed be God !
He listens to me.
He hears me,
when I pray for help.

Blessed be God !

I trust the Lord,
for he is strong.
I thank the Lord,
for he takes care of me.

Blessed be God !

Something else about God our
Father –
he is a person who will be gentle
and kind with us.

We don't mind
even if the earth shakes –
even if the sea is raging.
Even if the hills fall down
we don't mind !

God is like the gentle river
that flows beside the House of Prayer
bringing water to our city
to make us strong
and make us glad.

God lives with us
in our own city.
Whatever happens
we are safe.

Come and see the great things God
can do.
Everywhere he stops the people
fighting
he breaks their bows
he snaps their spears
he burns their shields.

Stop all your fighting now – he says –
and come to me.
I am the Lord of the whole wide
world.
Listen to what I have to say:
Be still
and come to me.

I am your God.

Lesson Six

Family Life

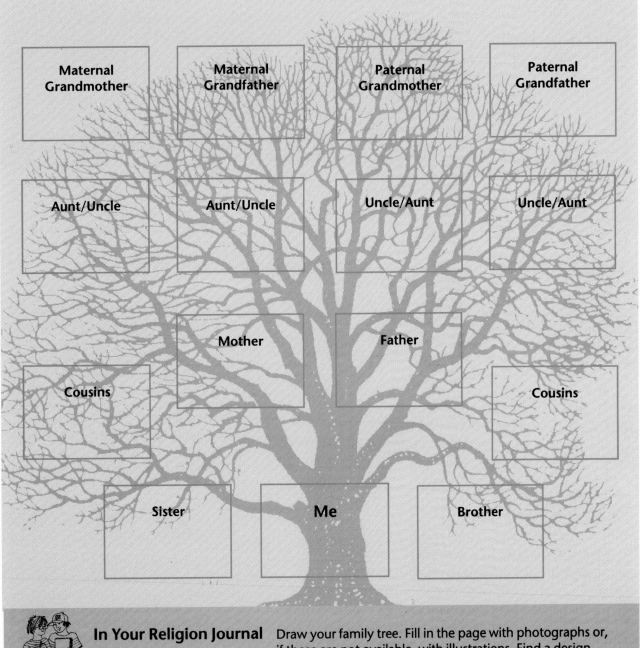

Maternal Grandmother

Maternal Grandfather

Paternal Grandmother

Paternal Grandfather

Aunt/Uncle

Aunt/Uncle

Uncle/Aunt

Uncle/Aunt

Mother

Father

Cousins

Cousins

Sister

Me

Brother

In Your Religion Journal Draw your family tree. Fill in the page with photographs or, if these are not available, with illustrations. Find a design which best suits your family.

The family is the first group of people that we belong to. It is also the most important group. It is where we first learn the meaning of love, care, friendship and companionship. It is where we can be safe and secure in the knowledge that here are people who really know us as we are and who love us as we are.

Families come in all shapes and sizes. There are different numbers of adults and children in different families. Some children live with adults who are not their natural parents, but who love them and take care of them.

Each family has its own special identity, its family history and the stories that are handed on from one generation to the next.

The family is the place where we first learn about relationships. The relationships between parents and children and between brothers and sisters are very special. As years pass the members of a family grow and change. Their needs are different and they develop new gifts and talents. The relationships in the family change also.

In Your Religion Journal

Write and illustrate one of the stories which you have heard and enjoyed about your own family's past.

Find Your Group

In what way is the relationship with your parents different now from what it was when you were about three years old?

Carmel Smith

Carmel Smith is ninety-two. Her husband has been dead now for twenty years. She had just got used to living alone again when her health began to fail.
She began to suffer from bad arthritis which makes it very difficult for her to get up, get dressed, move around the house, prepare meals for herself or do any of the hundred-and-one things which need to be done each day. The last straw came when she suffered a mild stroke last year and the doctor pronounced that it was unsafe for her to live alone any more.
Carmel was very distressed by this news. Difficult as it was, she valued her independence and had grown accustomed to her restricted lifestyle. The neighbours had been good to her and, by and large, she had been quite content with her lot. However, her son insisted that it was out of the question for Carmel to continue living alone. He was married and his wife shared his wish that Carmel would now come and live with them. Carmel knew that what they said was true. She knew that it would be foolish, even if it were possible, for her to continue her present lifestyle. However, she did not look forward to the move.

Find Your Group
Discuss

What kind of relationship does Carmel now have with her family?
How do you think it is different from the relationship she had with her children when they were young?
How does it compare with the present relationship you have with your parents?

In the beginning the small child experiences the care and love of parents and responds to them by relying on them with total dependence. As the child grows he or she discovers the ability to become more and more independent. The adolescent sometimes longs for total independence. The more mature person knows that it is never possible to become totally independent and the ideal situation is one where people learn to relate to one another in a way that recognises interdependence. There will be times when, even as an adult, you will need to depend on your parents. On the other hand there will be times when they will need to depend on you.

Adolescence

Adolescence can be a very difficult time for parents as well as for young people. Parents realise that their sons and daughters are no longer children. They know that they cannot continue to treat them in exactly the same way as they used to. They know that they need some extra independence and freedom. This is essential if they are to grow into mature adults. They also expect more from them than in the past. They expect them to take extra responsibility. They expect that they will be more able to respond to the needs of others.

However, they also know that an adolescent is not quite an adult. They know that given too much freedom too soon, young people can make serious mistakes which can do real damage to themselves and to others.

This is further complicated when a young person acts in a very mature and adult way one day and in a highly immature and childish way the next day.

It is important to realise that adolescence, while it is a time of frustration and questioning for young people, is also a difficult time for parents. It is important to be open and honest, to discuss difficult situations when they arise and to respect the other people in your family even if you disagree with them.

Parents generally want nothing but the best for their children. They want them to grow up healthy and happy. They want them to develop into mature well-balanced adults. They want them to enjoy friendship. They want them to develop their skills and talents so that they will be able to gain satisfaction and enjoyment from doing the things they are good at.

42

Martin's Night Out

In Your Religion Journal

Write about a recent situation where you showed adult characteristics. Write about a recent situation where you showed childish characteristics.

Which of the following words and phrases describe someone who is able to behave in an adult manner, and which fit someone who is still behaving in a childish manner:

selfish;

responsible;

respectful;

thinks of other's needs;

makes hasty decisions;

flies into temper tantrums;

sulks;

puts others down;

thinks carefully about how to spend time;

tries to understand another's point of view ?

Martin has been pleading with his parents for some time to allow him to stay out later on the nights when he doesn't go to school on the following morning. He said that all the others in his class were allowed to stay out later than him; that obviously his parents didn't trust him; and that he was tired of being treated like a baby. His parents thought long and hard about the situation. They really didn't want to treat Martin as if he were a child. They wanted, however, to be sure that he would not get into any difficult situations which he might be too young to handle. They knew he was a good lad and they trusted him, but they also knew that there were some others in the neighbourhood whose behaviour left a lot to be desired.

Eventually though, they agreed that on Friday nights Martin could stay out until eleven o'clock. Martin was delighted and told the good news to his pals. 'It's Susan's place tonight,' said Harry, 'Her parents are away. Be there at nine.' Martin felt really grown up that night as he set off. He set out to Susan's a little late. When the door was opened he heard the shouts and shrieks of excitement from within. He wondered what was happening.

On the kitchen table there were half-empty bottles of cider and vodka. 'Get some of this into you,' said Jean, 'you can pay your share the next night.' Martin was annoyed, he never thought that this was what his friends got up to. He didn't really want to drink but he didn't want to be laughed at either. 'I'll have the cider,' he said.

Friday Night at Paul's

Mark's parents had decided that when he would be fourteen, Mark could stay out until eleven on Friday nights. Last week Mark celebrated his fourteenth birthday and the last thing he said to his friends as they left was, 'Don't forget, I'll be there on Friday night'. 'We'll be in Paul's,' one of them replied, 'See you then around seven.'

On Friday Mark set out. Immediately he rang the bell the door was opened. 'Come on, hurry,' said Elizabeth. 'We've the video all set up. We're ready to start. But first we're going to have a game on the green.' They divided themselves into two teams, and played a lively game of football. Afterwards they went back to Paul's to see the video.

The film was one that had recently done the rounds of the cinemas. Only one or two of the gang had seen it and they liked it so much that they said they didn't at all mind watching it a second time.

It was an anti-war film. Paul's parents had left crisps and cans of soft drink. As they munched and watched the screen they wondered how anyone managed to live through such terror.

Discuss

What was the difference between the situations in which the two fourteen-year-olds found themselves ?

How do you think the parents in each case would react to what happened ?

How do you think you would act if you had been in Martin's situation?

Martin had some cider because he didn't want to be laughed at. Talk about a time when you have felt like this.

Find a Group
Discuss

What do you think are the ten things which parents most want for their adolescents ?

What kinds of things do parents do to ensure that these actually happen ?

In Your Religion Journal

Think of a time when you really felt that you were part of a group. What were you and the others in the group doing ?
Describe what it was like or draw a picture to illustrate what it was like.
Now think of a time when you felt ignored or left out.
How did this happen ?
Describe what it was like or draw a picture to illustrate what it was like.

44 | Peer Pressure

A group of people who are about the same age are often referred to as a peer group. Young people, in particular, are very anxious to belong to their peer group. They want to feel that they are liked and accepted by others of their own age.

I like Simon. He wears really trendy clothes. His hair is dishy and he goes to all the best discos.

Why can't I have my hair dyed yellow?

Because it would look absolutely ridiculous.

I can't stand Sandra. Just look at the clothes she wears. And she never goes anywhere with the rest of the group. She's a bore!

But all my friends have their hair dyed!

I don't care. You'll do as you're told!

It's just not fair!

Joanne is a really nice girl. She's very thoughtful. She helped me out with my awful maths homework last week. And she always seems to know when someone needs a helping hand.

Discuss

Has anything like this ever happened to you ? Describe it.

Have you ever sneered at someone or ignored them because they did not wear the same clothes or take part in the same activities as others in the group ?

Discuss

In your opinion, which of these judgements was the most valid? Why ?

Sometimes we judge people just by looking at them on the outside. For example, we can write someone off as being boring, but if we take time to get to know the person we might find that he or she has many qualities which make a really good friend.

Discuss

Have you ever felt rejected by your friend or by a group because of the kind of clothes you wear or because you refused to join in?
How did you feel?

Young people often feel pressurised to join in whatever activity the group is interested in, to wear the same clothes as everybody else, to listen to the same music, to have the same hair-style, etc. We call this peer pressure.

Consider the following:

All John's friends smoke. John knows that this is silly. He knows how damaging cigarettes can be to a person's health. And he also knows how difficult his parents found it to give up smoking. However, he finds it really difficult to say 'no' and he knows that sometimes the others laugh at him behind his back.

Discuss

Have you ever been in a situation such as this?

Activity

Organise a class display of posters warning of the dangers to health which can be caused by smoking.

Roles in the Family

There are many tasks to be done in the family if the life of the family is to run smoothly. These are divided out among the various family members.

In Your Religion Journal

Write out a list of the tasks which need to be done in your family.

How are these allocated to the various family members?

What happens when one or more of the family members fail to carry out the tasks allocated to them?

In Your Religion Journal

The family functions by providing various things for its members. Copy the following diagram and illustrate it to show how the various functions of the family which are outlined in the diagram are fulfilled in your own family.

What the Family provides

MORAL STANDARDS · RELATIONSHIPS · INTERESTS · EDUCATION · RELIGIOUS BACKGROUND · CUSTOMS/CULTURE · LOVE AND SECURITY

ME

A Time to Pray

Spend some time quietly thinking about your family.
Perhaps you could do this before you go to bed at night.
Think of all the good things that come to you through your family: love; companionship; care; a sense of belonging.

What else can you think of ?
Think of each member of your family by name.
Silently in your own heart ask God to bless each one of them in whatever ways you think the person most needs God's blessing.

Pray Together

God, our Creator, we thank you for our families:
for the love we feel for our parents, brothers and sisters;
for the companionship;
for the support and advice;
for the fun we have together;
for the celebrations which mark special occasions.
Help us not to take our families for granted.
Show us how we can play our part in the life of our families.
Through Christ, Our Lord. Amen.

Find Your Group

Discuss

Are there boys and girls in your family? If so, are they treated differently in any way?

For instance you could think in terms of the following headings:

colours of clothes;

kinds of clothes;

things adults say to them e.g. 'Big boys don't cry'; 'That's not ladylike';

jobs they are expected to do;

games they are taught to play;

subjects they are encouraged to learn at school.

When people presume that all boys like to wear the same clothes, play the same games etc. or that all girls read the same magazines and watch the same television programmes we call it stereotyping.

What do you think is the result of stereotyping ?

Class Project

Families have very different experiences and customs in various parts of the world.

Compare your family life with that of families in places which are different from your own country because of climate, economic position, culture, religion and so on.

For example, you could choose a family in the Sudan, South Africa, India, Chile or New York.

OR

Explore ways in which you could find pen-pals in other countries. Then through your correspondence you can find out more about how people in these countries live.

Friendship

The members of the youth club had been looking forward for months to their weekend camping in the country. As the date drew near, the preparations were completed and the excitement grew. There were a number of meetings and the leaders discussed with the young people the rules which would be necessary for everybody's safety during the trip. They would go mountain climbing on one of the days and there would also be an opportunity to visit some interesting ruins.

At last the weekend arrived. On Saturday morning they set off to climb the mountains. They travelled by bus to the place where the climb would commence and they started the long slow trek to the top of the mountain. There was a lot of laughter and fun and it was obvious that everyone was having a good time, that is all except Martin.

Martin found it difficult to make friends. He was shy and was inclined to spend a lot of time by himself. He had gradually dropped back behind the others and was soon walking by himself. No one noticed, until Mike looked back. Everyone enjoyed Mike's company, he was always cracking jokes and helping to create a good team spirit. The others in the group looked up to him.

'I'll wait for Martin,' he said. No one was more surprised than Martin. He had become used to being left on his own and though he often longed for company he was too shy to take the first step. In fact he'd had doubts as to whether he should come on the camping weekend at all.

He was always afraid of being the odd one out. Now he found that he and Mike had lots to talk about. They were both interested in football and both supported the same team. They made plans to exchange tapes of some pop music which they both enjoyed listening to. They had become so absorbed in the conversation that they hadn't noticed that they had gradually lost sight of the rest of the group.

They decided to stop and have something to eat from their packed lunch. But as they sat and chatted and enjoyed their lunch, a mist fell over the mountain. They soon realised it would be impossible to continue on. They thought that the best thing for them to do, would be to make their way back to the foot of the mountain and to wait for the others.

They began to move slowly and carefully back in the direction from which they had come. The going was difficult but they were doing OK until Martin slipped on some loose stones and fell. His ankle was badly twisted and when he tried to stand up it was so painful that he almost fainted.

'Lean on me,' said Mike, 'that way you won't put pressure on your bad foot.'

However much he tried, Martin still found it impossible to move without screaming out in pain.

Mike shivered. It was getting colder all the time. He began to get worried. How would Martin ever manage to get down to the foot of the mountain? He decided that he would have to get help. He took off his jacket. 'You take this,' he said to Martin. 'Find the most comfortable place and sit down. Wrap this around you, it'll keep you warm. I'll go down and get help.'

Martin was quite glad to sit down. But he knew that Mike was really putting himself out on his behalf and he felt that he had ruined his day. Mike set off. It was difficult. He could only see a few feet in front and there were loose stones and gravel which caused him to slip and slide dangerously. At last he reached the foot of the mountain. As he had hoped the two bus drivers had just arrived back to wait for the group to return. They went back with Mike to where Martin was and without a lot of bother they were able to carry him down the mountain.

From then on Mike and Martin became close friends. In the beginning, Martin was amazed that anyone would want to be friendly with him, but slowly he began to get more confidence in himself and to mix more easily with others.

When he looks back on the camping weekend, he remembers that it was one of the best weekends he's ever had !

The Camping Weekend

Discuss

What do you think it would have been like to be in Martin's shoes at the beginning of the story ?
What kind of person do you think Mike was ?
Martin really needed a friend. Have you ever needed a friend ?

In Your Religion Journal

Write about an experience which has taught you to value friendship.

Friends are important at all stages of our life. As young children we make friends very easily and there is no great depth to our friendship. Friends are simply the people we sit beside in school, the children we play with, those who live next door. For young children, friendship is very much a one-way process and friends are the people who make us feel good, who are nice to us and who are fun to be with.

As we grow we certainly choose our friends more carefully. We also come to be capable of seeing friendship as a two-way process, in other words, we don't think only of what we can get from our friends but also of what we can give to our friends.

As small children we find it easy to be friends with other children of either sex. Boys and girls play together easily. Then there comes a time when girls want to play exclusively with other girls and boys with other boys. About your age boys and girls once again tend to want to mix freely with members of the opposite sex.

The Importance of Friendship

Unlike our family, we can choose our friends and we are linked to them by shared interests, attitudes and activities. We can have friends of both sexes. Our choice of friends can sometimes depend on our parents, e.g. through their approval, the district they choose to live in, their choice of school for the children etc. We are pleased when we find that those we have chosen as friends are liked by people who are important to us – our parents, our brothers and sisters, our other friends.

In Your Religion Journal

Answer the following.

How many close friends have you ? Write down their names and the things you have in common.

Do you make friends:

(a) very quickly ?
(b) only after a long time ?
(c) depending on the person, sometimes quickly, sometimes a lot longer ?

Are your friends at the moment:

(a) mostly the same sex as yourself ?
(b) mixed boys and girls ?
(c) mostly the opposite sex ?

Do you think it is easy to make friends with the opposite sex ?

Why/Why not ?

Which of the qualities listed below do you most value in a friend ? Why ?

(a) trustworthiness;
(b) similar interests;
(c) the fact that he/she is like you;
(d) the fact that he/she is not like you;
(e) intelligence;
(f) generosity;
(g) being funny;
(h) beauty;
(i) something else.

Find a Group
Discuss

A. What kind of people do your parents like for you as friends ? Why do you think this is so ?
B. In what situations can you make new friends (school, disco, youth club) ?
C. What sort of friend are you ?

Try the following quiz

1. If you and a friend were waiting for a bus and the driver only had room for one more passenger, would you:

(a) suggest that your friend gets on and meets you later ?
(b) suggest that you get on and meet him/her later ?
(c) both refuse to get on and wait for the next bus ?

2. Your friend has a habit of interrupting you in every conversation. You are talking to a group of people and he/she again interrupts. Would you:

(a) tell him/her to shut up ?
(b) say something like, 'Do you mind ? Can't you see I'm talking ?'
(c) let him/her know privately afterwards that he/she has this habit?

3. Your friend is doing badly at maths, whilst you are quite good. He/she suggests that you help him/her in the forth-coming maths exam. Would you:

(a) agree willingly ?
(b) say something like 'It's not worth it. We could get caught '?
(c) arrange to give him/her some help with maths after school before the exam ?

4. Your friend is telling a joke you have heard before. Would you:

(a) interrupt and finish the joke for him/her ?
(b) listen while he/she tells the joke without interrupting ?
(c) say something like, 'What a terrible joke' ?

5. Your friend buys a new shirt, jumper etc. which doesn't suit him/her and asks you whether you like it. Would you say:

(a) 'It's awful. Whatever made you buy it ?'
(b) 'It looks great,' and hope he/she believes you ?
(c) 'I don't think it's quite right', and then offer to go with him/her to the shop to exchange it ?

6. Your parents disapprove of a friend without even knowing him/her properly. Would you:

(a) bring the friend home, so that they can see what he/she is really like ?

(b) tell them it's got nothing to do with them who your friends are?

(c) sulk and refuse to discuss the matter ?

7. Your friend tells you that he/she cannot go to the disco until some household chores are finished, which may take some time. Do you:

(a) say, 'What a pity,' and go ahead on your own ?

(b) arrange to go later when she/he has finished the chores ?

(c) offer to help with the chores and then both go together ?

8. Your friend wants to join a school club that you are not interested in. Would you:

(a) tell him/her it's a stupid, boring club and that you don't know why anyone would be interested in it ?

(b) join another club at the school that you are interested in and which is held on the same night ?

(c) lose interest in him/her and try to find another friend with similar interests ?

9. You and your friend audition for a part in the school play. Your friend gets the part that you really wanted, while you get a smaller role. Would you say:

(a) 'Oh great, I'm pleased you got it,' and mean it ?

(b) 'I'm pleased for you, but wish I'd got it' ?

(c) 'You always get your own way. It isn't fair' ?

10.You find out your friend was cheating in his/her exams. Would you:

(a) tell him/her that they were just right to cheat ?

(b) advise your friend to go the teacher and own up ?

(c) do nothing, but change your friend ?

Quiz Scores	1. (a) 1	(b) 0	(c) 2	6. (a) 2	(b) 0	(c) 0
	2. (a) 0	(b) 0	(c) 2	7. (a) 0	(b) 1	(c) 2
	3. (a) 0	(b) 1	(c) 2	8. (a) 0	(b) 2	(c) 0
	4. (a) 0	(b) 2	(c) 0	9. (a) 2	(b) 1	(c) 0
	5. (a) 0	(b) 1	(c) 2	10. (a) 0	(b) 2	(c) 0

Scale		
	18-20	Excellent
	14-17	Very good
	10-13	Good
	6-9	Fair
	5 or under	Poor

One of the true characteristics of real friendship is love.

Real love leads people to treat one another in particular ways.

People who love others are prepared to:

put the other person's needs before their own;

respect the other person at all times;

have a sense of responsibility towards the other person;

be understanding of the other.

In Your Religion Journal

What rules should exist in friendship ?
Write out five qualities which you think are important in a friend.
OR
Make up five sentences that begin with: A friend is ...
OR
Try to compose a poem about the kind of friend you would like to be.
OR
Select and write out the words of a song that you like which describe the qualities that you would look for in a friend.

Find Your Group

How could you show each of the characteristics of real love in the way you treat any one of your friends ?

Give practical examples.

Jesus and Friendship

All through his life Jesus showed us, in the way that he related to others, what true friendship is like. Read the following extracts from the gospels: Luke 7:1-10; 7:11-15; 7:36-50; 10:25-37;10:38-42; Mark 10:13-16; 10:46-56.

Discuss

What qualities did Jesus show in the above stories ?

Activity

Pick one of the following situations and write a story showing how someone might show the same qualities today.

Margaret's baby gets very ill and is rushed to hospital. There are other children in the family.

There's a fire in David's house. The house is not damaged beyond repair though all of the furniture is destroyed and it will take quite a while to rebuild the house.

Jonathan is preparing for his exam. He has been working hard all year and was depending on having three good weeks of really concentrated study before the exams. Then with eighteen days to go he ends up in bed suffering from a very bad flu and a high temperature. The doctor says he won't be able to go back to school for ten days.

Jesus said that we must be prepared to put other people's needs before our own. This is what he did in his own life. In the world today many people do this. Parents almost always are prepared to put their children's needs before their own.

In Your Religion Journal

Write about a time when you put someone else's needs before your own.

Read the following newspaper report.

A young mother's heroic effort to save her baby ended in her own death early today. The woman, Mrs Teresa McCormack, saw a car go out of control and swerve towards the pram where her sleeping baby waited for her to return from the supermarket. Teresa lunged towards the pram and pushed the baby to safety. The driver, however, was unable to avoid hitting the woman, who died later from her injuries.

Discuss

What do you think of what the woman did ?
Can you think of other situations where a person might give his or her life for someone else ?

Jesus said that if we really loved someone we would be prepared to give up our lives for them. Jesus told us what real love and real friendship demand of us when he said:

The greatest love a person can have for his friends is to give his life for them. And you are my friends if you do what I command you. I do not call you servant any longer, because a servant does not know what his master is doing. Instead I call you friends because I have told you everything I have heard from my Father (John 15:13-15).

Jesus himself was prepared to lay down his life for his friends. That is exactly what he did. He expected his followers to be prepared to give all for their friends, their time, their love, their care. We are his followers today. We will hardly find ourselves in a situation where we are being called upon to give up our lives for our friends. However there are many situations in our experience where we are called upon to make sacrifices of one kind or another for our friends.

Captain Oates

The famous British explorer, Captain Scott, led an expedition which attempted to be the first to reach the South Pole. Unfortunately he suffered many delays on the way and this not only meant that his rival, Amundsen, got to the Pole first but also that by the time Scott did arrive there the worst of the Antarctic weather was beginning.

On the way back Scott's party was short of provisions and suffering from frost-bite. One of the party, Captain Oates, was particularly badly affected. He knew that there were not enough provisions for all of them and he also knew that he was slowing up the rest of the expedition. On one occasion they were all sheltering in their tent from a raging blizzard. Oates knew, and everyone else knew, that nobody could last for long outside in those terrible conditions. He got up from his sleeping-bag and said to the others, 'I am going outside and I may be gone some time'. He then went out into the blizzard and that was the last they saw of him.

Find Your Group

Discuss

What do you think of what Captain Oates did ?

How do you think the others in the group would have felt about what he did?

Talk about the practical real life situations where you might be called upon to make a sacrifice for a friend.

Your Friendship Motto

Read quietly the following sayings from the Bible about friends and friendship.

A friend means well, even when he hurts you (*Proverbs 27:6*).

If you are polite and courteous, you will enjoy the friendship of many people (*Sirach 6:5*).

Some people will be your friends only when it is convenient for them, but they won't stand by you in trouble (*Sirach 6:8*).

A loyal friend is like a safe shelter; find one and you have found a treasure (*Sirach 6:14*).

A person who listens to the Lord will find real friends, because he will treat his friends as he does himself (*Sirach 6:17*).

Friendship is like wine. It gets better as it grows older (*Sirach 9:10*).

I will never be afraid to protect a friend and I will never turn a friend away if he needs me (*Sirach 22:25*).

When things are going well it's hard to tell who your real friends are, but in hard times you can recognise your enemies (*Sirach 12:8*).

The greatest love a person can have for his friends is to give his life for them (*John 15:13*).

Now decide which of them you would like to use as your friendship motto.

A friend means well, even when he hurts you.

A loyal friend is like a safe shelter; find one and you have found a treasure.

In Your Religion Journal

Write the motto you have chosen into your religion journal and decorate the page.

Project

Find some greeting cards about friendship. What are your favourite sayings about friendship from these cards ? Make a collage of these sayings for the classroom and make your own friendship cards.

Test Yourself.
Do the Looking Back exercises on page 224

Lesson Eight

Free to Grow

In what ways do you think the following people are free?

In what ways are they unfree?

1. Paul has to go to school today. He'd really like to stay at home and watch the big match on TV.

4. Mark would love to go to the pictures tonight but he has spent all this week's pocket money and his parents refuse to give him more.

2. Nicola's parents were very poor. So Nicola had to leave school early. Now when her children ask her to help them with their homework she feels terrible. Nicola is unable to read or write.

5. Gerard was injured in a serious accident. He will have to spend the rest of his life in a wheelchair.

3. Margaret's parents have made a rule which requires Margaret to be home by eight o' clock at night, even when she has no school the following day.

6. Ruth lives in a doorway on High Street. She ran away from home six months ago after a family row.

Find Your Group
Discuss

Think of a time when you felt free.

Think of a time when you felt unfree.

In Your Religion Journal

List some words which remind you of being free.

List some words which remind you of being unfree.

It is possible to draw a distinction between the freedom which comes from within ourselves and the freedom which comes from circumstances around us. There are factors which curtail our freedom within us, e.g. fears, inhibitions and so on. There are also factors which limit our freedom in the circumstances which surround us, e.g. the time and place where we live, etc.

Some of these limitations can be overcome and there are others over which we have no control.

Consider the following.

Claire would love to be able to swim. She watches the rest of her family with envy when they go on holiday to the seaside. Claire's mother thinks that her fear of water dates back to a sea trip which the family made when Claire was four. There had been a storm. The crossing was very rough. Most people were seasick. Claire had been terrified.

Discuss

What is it that takes away Claire's freedom to learn to swim?
Is this something that is imposed on Claire from outside herself or from inside herself?
How do you think it would be possible for Claire to overcome her fear?

Ursula takes part in the marathon each year. Last year she came third in her category. Each evening she can be seen practising in her wheelchair around the neighbourhood where she lives.

Discuss

What factors are limiting Ursula's freedom?
In what ways do you think she has overcome some of these?

Paul would love to be tall. He has always been smaller than the others in his class. He can beat most of them in a race but he would love to play basketball and the taller lads are always chosen for the teams.

Discuss

What can Paul do about his height?
In what way is his freedom affected?

In Your Religion Journal

List some things from inside yourself which you think limit your freedom. List some things in the circumstances around you which you think limit your freedom.

All living things have an urge to grow and develop. If you were an acorn you'd want to become an oak. If you were a caterpillar you'd want to become a butterfly.

Every person has a dream about how they would like to grow. They have an image of the person they would like to become. Unlike the plant or the insect, as human beings, we have the ability and the freedom to choose. We also have the ability to think and to decide.

To a certain extent then, we can choose the type of person which we would want to become. We can decide to do certain things which will ensure that we will actually grow as we would like to. For example, if you decide that you would like to become an air hostess, you can take steps to make that happen by studying languages at school. Or if you would like to become a thoughtful, kind person you can make that happen by trying to be on the look-out for the needs of those around and by lending a hand wherever you can.

However, our choices are also limited. We cannot choose the country in which we are born, the family we belong to or the century in which we live. We cannot choose the colour of our eyes, the size of our feet or the intellectual ability which we have.

However, unlike the acorn or the caterpillar, we can take what we have – the givens – and then the choices which we make will determine the way in which we grow.

In Your Religion Journal

Write a paragraph entitled: I would like to be free to...

The Three Birds

Once upon a time a kind swan found three eggs abandoned on a river bank. She took them into her nest and hatched them out. The first turned out to be an eagle, the second a dove and the third a sparrow. When they were ready to fly the swan took the three fledglings on her broad back and placed them on a ledge up in the mountains.

The three remembered nothing of that flight for the simple reason that they saw nothing. So terrified were they that they kept their eyes closed for its entire duration. Once they had reached their destination the swan informed them that she would have to leave them for a while. But not to worry. She would return again and take them on a wonderful trip to a land where the sun never sets and where there is no such thing as sickness or old age. In the meantime they were to learn to fly.

'Everything becomes possible once you learn to fly,' she told them. 'The sky is the limit. There's nothing to it. It's quite simple. This is all you have to do.'

With that she spread her enormous wings, threw herself into space, and soared off gracefully over the mountains.

Naturally the three were very lonely after the swan left them. They stood there for a long time hesitating. They took turns walking to the edge and peering over. There was nothing below them but space. It was quite unnerving, to say the least.

The eagle was the first to take the plunge. The dove and the sparrow watched with great apprehension as he spread his wings and threw himself out over the void. But they were thrilled to see how after a few moments of great uncertainty, during which he appeared to be falling to earth like a stone, he gained control, flew around in a half-circle and then rejoined them on the ledge.

'The swan was right,' said the eagle. 'There's really nothing to it.'

And with that he flew off again, this time venturing further out over the void. Soon the dove took the plunge, and when she returned to the ledge she echoed what the eagle had said. Soon the eagle and the dove were flying quite freely. But the little sparrow refused to take the plunge. The others tried to coax him, but it was no use.

'It's too risky,' he cried. 'It's all very well for you two. You have both been blessed with sturdy wings. But just look at the size of my wings. They would never hold me up.' 'But then consider how small you are,' said the eagle kindly. 'Of course your wings will hold you up. We'll even support you. But that won't be necessary, you'll see.'

But the sparrow refused. In the days and

weeks that followed, the eagle and the dove flew further and further afield. Yet no matter how far they ventured they always returned home before dark. At first they had no other aim in life than to enjoy the sheer thrill of flying. They ate and slept only that they might have the strength to fly. Each time they returned they related to the sparrow all the wonderful sights they had seen.

But then life got a little more complicated for them, but more interesting as well. The eagle was horrified to discover that all the other birds, and indeed not a few animals, were afraid of him.

On catching the slightest glimpse of him, little birds flew into the woods, and little animals scurried into holes and burrows. He did not like this, so he made a decision to befriend all the little creatures who could not defend themselves. One day he came back with a story of how he had driven off a hawk as he was about to swoop on a sparrow. Another day he told how he had rescued a young lamb from crows that were about to peck its eyes out.

And the dove made a wonderful discovery. One day she alighted on a tree close to where two farmers were engaged in a bitter quarrel. However, on seeing the snow white dove one of them exclaimed, 'Look ! That dove is telling us that we should live at peace with one another. Let's make up.' And they shook hands, and the dove was very happy. Ever afterward she saw herself as a messenger of peace and goodwill. This added a whole new dimension to her flying.

All this time the sparrow clung resolutely and stubbornly to the ledge. He had discovered a patch of soil rich in worms and was growing fatter with each day that passed. The fatter he got, the lazier he got. The lazier he got, the less the idea of flying appealed to him. He built himself a snug nest in a crevice, well out of the wind and rain. His philosophy became, 'Take life easy.' And yet, from time to time, he complained bitterly to his two comrades about how unfair life was, especially on sparrows.

Then one day when the three of them were resting on the ledge, the swan arrived back. The eagle and the dove gave her a great reception.

'Are you ready to come with me to the land of eternal sunshine ?' asked the swan. 'Yes,' cried the eagle enthusiastically. 'Yes,' cried the dove enthusiastically. 'And what about you, little sparrow ? Aren't you coming ?' 'I can't,' said the sparrow glumly. 'What do you mean you can't ?' 'Because I never learned to fly.'

'What ? You never learned to fly ? You mean you neglected the one thing that makes a bird a bird ? And how did you spend your time ? Stuffing yourself with food, and lolling about in the sunshine, I suppose ?'

The sparrow made no reply. 'Well, I'm sorry, but there is nothing I can do for you,' said the swan. And turning to the other two she said, 'Let's get going. We have a long way to go before evening.'

On hearing this the sparrow looked at his two comrades and asked, 'Are you not coming home again ?' 'We're going home,' they replied in unison.

With that the three of them flew away, leaving the sparrow there on the ledge. As they pulled away he walked slowly to the edge, peeped over and then made a half-hearted effort at launching himself into the air. But he didn't succeed and quickly drew back again from the edge.

He stood there watching them as they grew smaller and smaller in the sky until finally a mountain crest took them away from him forever. Then he knew what real loneliness was, for he had no company but the worms. The one who had never left home now had no home to go to.

Discuss

What prevented the sparrow from flying ?

Did the sparrow's lack of freedom come from inside or outside ?

What did the swan mean by saying, 'You mean you refused the one thing that makes a bird a bird '?

List some of the things which you think make us human.

Which of these would you think is the most important ?

In what way can we refuse whatever makes us human ?

Everybody wants to be free. People have given their lives for freedom, for their own freedom and for the freedom of others. People have suffered hardships and have struggled against all the odds in order to one day be free.

Whenever people are unjustly deprived of their freedom, when an innocent person is put in prison or when someone is taken hostage, the whole world responds in outrage and horror.

Research

Martin Luther King, Gandhi and Oscar Romero are just a few of the people who gave their lives for freedom.
Select one of these or another person of your choice and do a project on their struggle for freedom.

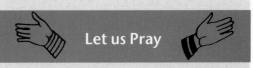

Let us Pray

God, grant us the serenity
to accept the things we
cannot change;
courage to change the things
we ought,
and wisdom to know the
difference.

Lesson Nine

The Road to Freedom

Life Map

We can describe our life as a journey. At this moment we have reached a certain point on the journey. The journey will continue. Some journeys are great adventures. Some end in disaster. Some are simply routine and boring.

We are free to make our own life journey into whichever of these we wish.

Paul has drawn his life map. The direction of the line changes to show when his experience has been good and when it has been bad. He has used symbols to indicate times when something of major importance happened in his life. We have shown a few of them.

The book indicates when he started school at four. The cross comes at a time when he was feeling very sad and lonely because his grandmother had died.

The map of Australia stands for what Paul considers the most exciting thing which ever happened to him. He went with his father to visit his father's sister who lives in Australia. He has used different colours to represent the various stages in his life – pre-school, primary school and post-primary school, etc.

The X indicates where he is at present and the dotted line represents the future.

Every new stage of our life is marked by a 'leaving behind' of a former stage. This can sometimes be difficult, even painful and always involves a decision.

The first step is usually the most difficult and the most terrifying.

Think of the following:

your first day at school;

the first time you ventured into the deep end of the swimming pool;

the first day you took your place on the school team;

your first appearance on stage in a school concert/play.

In Your Religion Journal

Draw your life map.
Show the good times and the bad times.

Choose symbols to represent the things of importance which have happened to you, good things, disappointments, hard decisions which you had to make and so on.

Indicate the different stages which your life has come through. Mark times of decision.

Place an X to indicate where you are at present. Show the remainder of the journey by drawing a dotted line.

Imagine what the line represents. What will you do? What stages lie ahead? What decisions lie ahead?

Think about the direction in which you would really like your life to go in the future.

Sharing

Talk about your life map with one other person in the class.

In Your Religion Journal

Write words which describe how you felt whenever one of the above experiences or something similar happened to you.

Write words which suggest how you felt when you had accomplished what you set out to do.

Draw a picture to illustrate the most difficult first step you have taken in your life so far.

Imagine the following:

you are leaving home to work in the USA;
you are about to enter hospital;
you are about to set off on a voyage around the world.

Imagine it is the night before you undertake one of the above.
Write about how you would feel.

Change and Growth

One night a father decided that his son was now old enough to go out to the barn to feed the horses. The boy, however, told his father that he was afraid of the dark. The father stepped out onto the porch with the boy, lit a lantern, gave it to his son and asked him how far he could see as he held up the lantern.

'I can see half-way down the path,' said the boy. The father directed his son to carry the lantern half-way down the path. When the boy reached that point, the father asked the boy how far he could see now. The boy called back to the father that he could see to the gate.

The father urged the boy to walk to the gate and when the boy was at the gate, the father asked how far he could now see.

'I can see the barn', came the boy's reply. The father encouraged the boy to go to the barn and open the door. When the boy finally shouted back that he was at the barn and could see the horses, the father simply called, 'Now feed the horses', and stepped into the house.

Discuss

Which part of the journey do you think was the most difficult for the boy?
What did he have to do before he could see the horses?
In your own life, how far ahead do you think you can see right now?
How far ahead would you like to be able to see?
What initially prevented the boy from being 'free' to go to feed the horses?
What was necessary in order for him to overcome this?

The Exodus story in the Old Testament is the story of the Hebrew people's great journey to freedom.

In the story we see God's wish for the freedom of all people. God wants people to be free from all the things which prevent them from achieving their highest possible potential as human beings. In the Exodus story we see the difficulties, doubts and fears of the people. They desperately wanted freedom. However, the road to freedom took them through the desert.

Slaves in Egypt

They didn't know what might lie ahead, what dangers, what difficulties. When the chips were down they were more comfortable with slavery in Egypt; at least they were accustomed to that way of life. They knew what to expect. In our own lives we can see similar doubts and fears about unknown, unfamiliar situations.

Joseph, an Israelite, was sold by his brothers and brought down to Egypt. In Egypt he became one of the King's chief advisers. When there was famine in Israel he was joined by his family. The Israelites grew in number. Then more than a hundred years later, a new Pharaoh, Rameses II, who knew nothing of Joseph, came to power.

'We'd better beware,' he said one day to his ministers, 'there are too many of these Hebrews about and they are far too strong for us to feel safe. If we're ever at war they'll go over to the enemy and fight against us.'

So orders were given to break their spirit. They were forced to work as slaves on the building of new store cities in the Nile Delta. Their numbers still increased. Pharaoh then ordered that all the baby boys be thrown into the River Nile. Moses was saved from this fate by the clever planning of his mother and sister.

Can you remember the story? You will find it in chapter two of the Book of Exodus.

Moses is called by God

When Moses grew up he saw an Egyptian beating up an Israelite. He was filled with anger and he killed the Egyptian. After that he had to flee the country for safety and he settled in the tribal territory of the Midianites.

Moses was looking after his father-in-law's sheep. One day he noticed a bush on fire. The fire continued and the bush did not burn out.

'I must go and investigate,' thought Moses, 'I wonder why the bush does not burn out.' God saw what Moses did. God spoke to Moses. 'Stay where you are,' he said. 'Take off your sandals. You are standing on holy ground. I am the God of your ancestors, of Abraham, Jacob and Isaac.' Moses fell flat on the ground and hid his face when he realised that God was speaking to him.

'I have seen the way my people are treated in Egypt,' God continued, 'I have heard their cry for help. I want you to go back to Egypt to rescue them. I want you to go to the Pharaoh and tell him to let the Israelites leave his land and then I want you to lead the people to freedom.'

'But I am not the best person to send,' protested Moses, 'I'm not a good speaker. And in any case nobody, neither the Pharaoh nor the Israelites, will believe me if I tell them that God has sent me to set the Israelites free.'

'Don't be afraid,' God said to him. 'I will be with you. I will tell you what to say. Have confidence in me.'

Moses did as God commanded. But Pharaoh refused. Nine times Moses asked. Each time God punished the Egyptians with a plague.

You will find the story of the Plagues in the Book of Exodus 7-11.

This is the story of the final plague and the escape of the Israelites from Egypt.

The Israelites Escape

God said to Moses, 'I will send one more plague on the Egyptians. After this, not only will the Pharaoh allow the Israelites to leave, he will drive you out of Egypt. Now go and tell the Israelites to ask their Egyptian neighbours for gold and silver jewellery.'

The Egyptians had, by this time, begun to feel some sympathy for the Israelites. Indeed, Moses was accepted as a great leader by both officials and ordinary people.

Moses said to the people, 'This is what God has said: "I will send one more plague on the Egyptians. At midnight every first-born son, from the son of the King to the son of the slave-woman, will die. The first-born of all cattle will die also. All over Egypt there will be wailing such as never was heard before and will never be heard again."

'Now all the people of Israel must carry out these orders. First you must kill a lamb. Then take a bunch of hyssop, dip it in the blood and smear it on the outer door of your house, on the lintel and on the two doorposts. Then stay indoors. God will pass through the land bringing death to the Egyptians. When he sees the blood on your doors he will pass over and everyone in your house will be spared.'

At midnight it happened as God had promised. All over Egypt the wailing of the people could be heard. The Pharaoh summoned Moses to the Palace. 'Take your people and get out,' he said, 'Go and worship your God as you said you wanted to. Take your cattle if you wish. Just get out from among my people.'

The Egyptians were terrified. 'If they stay we will all be dead,' they said. The Israelites left in such a hurry that they couldn't finish baking their bread. They picked up the unleavened dough and wrapped the kneading bowls in their cloaks.

They set out with large herds of cattle and headed towards Succoth.

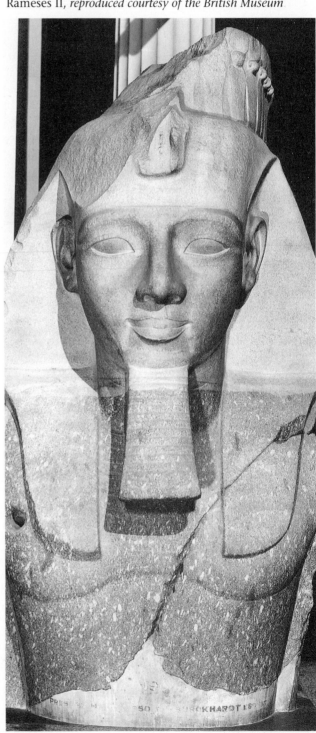

Rameses II, *reproduced courtesy of the British Museum*

The Sea of Reeds

The Israelites travelled day and night. God guided them on their journey. A column of cloud moved ahead of them by day and at night it was replaced by a column of fire. They camped near the Sea of Reeds. Then Pharaoh changed his mind. 'What have we done?' he asked, 'We have let the Israelites go, and we've lost our slaves.' He ordered his chariots out in pursuit of the escaping Israelites. When the Israelites saw what was happening they were in a real panic. They turned on Moses.

'Why did you bring us out here to die in the desert ?', they demanded of Moses. 'Were there not enough graves in Egypt ? Is this what all your talk of freedom has come to ? Why didn't you just leave us alone ?'

But Moses remained calm. 'Don't panic,' he

said, 'God is on our side, all you've got to do is stand your ground.' With that the column of cloud moved from in front of them to behind them and stopped between the camps of the Egyptians and the escaping Israelites. God told Moses to hold his hand over the waters of the Sea of Reeds. A strong east wind blew, drove back the water, and made a dry path. The Israelites walked through on the dry path and the Egyptians went after them with all their horses and chariots and drivers. The wheels of the chariots began to sink in the mud and the Egyptians became frightened. God told Moses to hold his hand over the water again. The water returned to its normal level and the Egyptians were drowned. The Israelites praised God and when they saw what happened they had faith in their leader, Moses. Exodus 12 -14

Discuss

What finally prompted the Egyptians to let the Israelites go?
Why then did they change their minds?
Why do you think the Israelites turned on Moses in anger for having brought them out of Egypt?

Activity

Conversation in the desert.

Joshua: I wish he'd left us alone. At least we knew where we were in Egypt. I'm not at all sure that this fellow Moses knows where we are going to end up.
Nathan: Well, I trust him. I believe what he told us.

Finish off the above conversation.

In Your Religion Journal

Draw a picture to illustrate the Exodus from Egypt.

Pyramid Hill
Nile Delta
Egypt

Dear David,

Greetings once again, from the scorching sands of Egypt. The sun seemed even hotter today and I could see the drops of perspiration on the backs of my fellow workers glisten in the sunlight. I knew we dare not stop. The whips are never far away.

It's evening now and slightly cooler. Work is over and there is nothing to do but wish that this would end. What we wouldn't give to get out of here once and for all !

There's this Moses man who is causing quite a stir at the moment. He says that God has told him to lead us out of here, back to our land.

He's about to go to the Pharaoh and demand our freedom. I'm not so sure that that will achieve anything. And, in any case, though I'd just love to be back in my own land again, to be free from the Egyptian taskmasters, and of course, to be among my own people, the thought of the awful journey through the desert is almost as bad as the thought of having to stay here.

There'd be several weeks, maybe even years, in the desert. Would we find food and water? Would we all be dead before we'd reach home?

Then the Egyptians would have a real laugh !

For the moment, in any case, things will just continue as they are. Tomorrow will bring more work, more harsh words, more beatings, more longings for home.

Can you ever see any good come out of all this?

Best Wishes,

Absalom

In Your Religion Journal This is a letter written in Egypt by one of the Hebrew slaves to his kinsman David. Write David's reply.

In Your Religion Journal

The Israelites experienced a very particular kind of slavery in the course of their life journey. There are many kinds of slavery! Most people at one time or another experience some kind of slavery. Almost always escape is difficult. In today's world there are many forms of slavery which imprison people, for example: hunger; racism; poverty; loneliness; pressures of all kinds from fashion; from the media; from the expectations of others; from addiction; from one's own selfishness and greed and so on.

Can you add to this list?

Write about a time in your life when the attitudes of others helped to enslave you.
Write about a time in your life when your own selfishness or greed helped to enslave you.

Now consider the following situations:

A

Donal's friends have all bought new boots recently. They're the latest fashion and they can be seen when lads of Donal's age get together. Donal's parents can't afford to give him the money for a pair. He feels awful. He wants to be like everyone else. He thinks that he must appear like the odd one out. He doesn't even want to go to the match on Friday in case he's laughed at.

B

James would really like to be friendly with Anne Marie. She lives on the next road. James, however, is black. Anne Marie is white and James feels sure that his friendship with Anne Marie would definitely be frowned upon.

C

All of Margaret's friends smoke. Margaret really would prefer not to smoke. Her father has already had surgery for lung cancer. He is convinced that it was caused by the cigarettes he smoked. Margaret, however, is afraid that if she doesn't join her friends in smoking she will be laughed at. She doesn't even like cigarettes. But she has decided to continue smoking nevertheless.

D

Anita is eighteen. She has recently left school. She's been answering advertisements in papers, attending interviews, contacting employment agencies, but all to no avail. She still hasn't succeeded in getting a job. She hates having to queue each week at the dole office. She'd love to be able to leave home and live in a flat. She just wants to be independent.

E

Thomas is a traveller. He is twenty and works in the local factory. He lives with his family on a halting-site outside the town. Last night he went with his mates for a drink in the pub outside the factory gates. When it came to his turn to buy a drink the bartender refused to serve him.

Discuss

In what ways are each of the above people enslaved?
What would have to happen before they could escape?

In Your Religion Journal

What are the factors which are causing you to be enslaved right now?
What would you have to do to escape from this slavery?

The wall and the ivy

Everybody agreed that I was splendidly built. Sound and solid and rooted in a bed of concrete. Not one of my bricks was out of place. People stood back and admired me. They said I would last forever, well, at least for a century or two. I myself felt I was unshakeable, invincible, immortal.

From the very outset I proved my worth. In wintertime I protected the garden from the onslaughts of the wild west wind. My life was full of meaning. Though my feet were firmly on the ground, my head was in the air. I felt on top of the world.

But then I began to change. I grew discontented. It's hard to explain it. In one sense I was completely self-sufficient. But what began to bother me was the very sameness of my life. I looked around me and saw how the trees and shrubs swayed and danced in the wind. They seemed so utterly happy. And here I was stuck in the same spot, unable to move in the slightest way.

There was something else about the trees and shrubs that I envied. That was the way they changed with the seasons. In the spring they put forth fresh buds and fragrant blossoms. In the summer they filled up with leaves and berries. In the fall they reproduced all the colours of the rainbow. And while it was true that winter stripped them bare, it did so only that spring might renew them once more. As for me, my life was utterly colourless. I had nothing to show but the same old grey bricks that were getting duller with each passing year. But then something happened which changed my whole life.

One spring morning I noticed that a tiny ivy plant had wormed its way up out of the earth right at my feet. It lay there on the ground unable to raise itself. On seeing how small and weak and unsure of itself it was, I was moved with pity. My heart went out to it.

Then it looked up at me, and in a timid voice asked, 'Would you be so kind as to give me a little space? The tiniest bit will do'. How could I refuse? I felt it would be unworthy of great big strong me.

So I answered, 'Sure ! Just grab hold of me'. Up it came. Straightaway I noticed that for all its apparent tenderness, it was a sticky little creature. It didn't just lie against me. It clung to me. It stuck to me so that I did not have to hold it. But in my foolishness I looked upon this as an act of trust in me. Far from resenting it, I took pride in it.

That was the first spring. By the end of that summer I was amazed to see how it had grown. As it grew it naturally occupied more space. However, once it had established a secure hold, it never again asked my permission for anything. It just acted as if it had a right to be there and to do as it pleased. But I did not object. I took the fact that it was thriving as a compliment to me. I did not see it as a threat. Not in the least.

Next spring it put out a number of shoots. I noticed that these too had the ability to cling

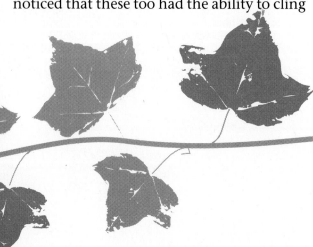

and to stick. Once they had established their grip, they were there to stay. Not even a gale force wind could dislodge them. Again, by the end of that summer, they had all grown, claiming more space for themselves. And once again I congratulated myself.

The truth is, at first I took but little interest in the growth of the ivy. It was more of a distraction to me than anything else. But as time went on I gradually became engrossed in its progress. Its creepy movements and sticky qualities were a continual source of wonder to me.

The same pattern was repeated during the years that followed. Soon the ivy was half-way up my side, and expanding in all directions. When I realised how greedy it was, I confess that there were moments when I felt uneasy. From time to time I heard people remark that I was being 'taken over' by the ivy. I deeply resented such remarks. The thought of being taken over by a miserable little ivy plant was repugnant to my pride.

But then I thought, 'Well, the ivy isn't doing me any harm. In fact, it's doing me quite a bit of good. It has added a considerable amount of colour to my previously colourless life. In the spring and summer I am green. In the fall I am all sorts of oranges and reds. I have even drawn gasps of astonishment from passers-by.'

But there came a spring when the growth of the ivy really alarmed me. The original wisp of a plant, so tender and supple, had now become a snake-like rope, hard and thick. As it crept upward it released, quite literally, a myriad offshoots. It was no longer just a couple of new shoots, but an entire army of them that was let loose on me, every single one of them demanding space for itself. One day as I watched them at work I took stock of my position for the first time. I got an awful shock.

I suddenly realised that I was indeed going to be taken over completely by the ivy. The real horror was knowing that I was powerless to resist its advance.

Well, all this happened quite a few years ago. It seems like an eternity. Now the inevitable has happened. I've been taken over. I'm now covered from top to bottom in ivy. I've completely disappeared underneath it. Not a brick or even a part of one is to be seen. Just one tangled mass of ivy. I'm lost. I'm imprisoned. I feel as if I'm being slowly smothered.

When the full reality of my situation hits me I think back to the day it all began. The simplicity of it all. The innocence of it all. Who could have foreseen that it would come to this?

People say to me, 'It's your own fault. You should never have given the ivy a foothold in the first place'. This kind of talk doesn't help me. It merely annoys me.

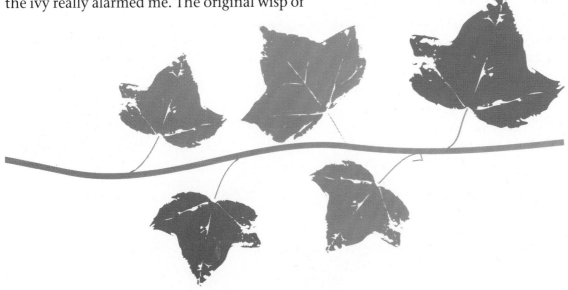

70

Can I be saved? One thing is certain. I cannot save myself. But then do I want to be saved? The question will no doubt surprise you. But let me tell you something. The ivy has come to mean a lot to me. If someone were to come along and suddenly strip me of it, I'd feel naked. I'd die of cold. In fact I'll go further. If you took that ivy away right now, I'm convinced I wouldn't be able to stand up. That's how much I have come to depend on it for warmth and support. To an outsider all this probably sounds unreal. To me it's very real.

And yet there are times when I long to be free of it, when I long to be myself again. The result is I am divided within myself. I am like a child torn between two parents, between what I know is good for me and what I know is harmful for me but which I still want.

So there I am. In need of help. Wanting that help and then not wanting it. Crying out to others and yet desperately wanting to be left alone. Full of self-will and fiercely independent, yet a compliant slave. Me, the great solid mass of bricks and mortar, reduced to this sorry state. Not by the blows of a sledgehammer, but by the subtle, creeping advances of a simple ivy plant.

Discuss

When did the wall begin to be worried about the effect the ivy was having on it?

What prevented the wall from doing something about the ivy?

In what way does the story of the wall remind you of the story of the Israelite slaves in Egypt?

What was causing the wall to be enslaved at the beginning of the story? At the end of the story?

The wall considered the ivy harmless at first. In what way is this similar to the person who smokes just one cigarette and believes that it is harmless?

In what way did the wall end up like a person who is addicted to cigarettes, drink or drugs?

Are there any situations in your own life where you feel torn between two different possibilities: what you would really like to do and what you feel would be the best thing for you to do?

A Time to Pray

In spite of the power and might of the Egyptians, God was always with his people the Israelites. God made it possible for them to escape and promised to continue to be with them in the desert.

As God's people, we too can be confident that God is always with us to protect us from all danger.

This is what the psalmist wrote about in Psalm 27.

Read the following paraphrase of the psalm, slowly and thoughtfully.

With God as my guide
I need never be anxious or afraid.
All the evil in the world cannot destroy God
nor can it destroy those whom God loves.
And so, if enemies surround me,
I will not be afraid.

The one thing I desire most of all
is to live always in God's love and care.
God will shelter me in times of trouble
and guide me in times of uncertainty.

When I call out for help
God does not ignore me.
Even if my family should turn against me,
God will never let me go.
God will guide me through all
the dangers and pitfalls of life.

Glory be to the Father,
And to the Son,
And to the Holy Spirit;
As it was in the beginning,
Is now and ever shall be,
World without end. Amen.

The prophet Isaiah also urges the people to have confidence that God will look after them and protect them.

Israel, the Lord who created you says:
'Do not be afraid – I will save you.
I have called you by name – you are mine.
When you pass through deep waters,
I will be with you;
your troubles will not overwhelm you.
When you pass through fire, you will not be burnt;
the hard trials that will come will not hurt you.
For I am the Lord your God who saves you.
I will give up whole nations to save your life,
because you are precious to me and because
I love you.
Do not be afraid – I am with you!' (Isaiah 43).

Walking with God

Speech bubbles in cartoon:
IF I'M REALLY CAREFUL WITH IT, CAN I BORROW YOUR NEW WALKMAN?

SURE... IF I CAN BORROW YOUR RECORD!

People often make agreements, or contracts, or covenants with one another. There are always two sides involved. Both sides agree to certain things happening provided certain conditions are fulfilled.

Sometimes these agreements are simply made by word of mouth and sometimes they are made in a more solemn manner. Sometimes there are written documents to prove that the agreement has been made. Sometimes the documents are signed by the two parties concerned and there is a witness as further proof that this agreement has been entered into. Sometimes people spend a lot of time bargaining before they agree on a contract.

Discuss

Talk about an agreement you made with someone.
Talk about times when you broke an agreement which you had made with someone.
Talk about times when someone else broke an agreement which they had made with you.

Activity

In groups of two, act out a situation which might happen between yourself and a friend where you are finding it difficult to reach an agreement.

'Well, how much are you hoping to get for it?'

'I've had it for three years and it's in very good condition. I wouldn't want to sell it for any less than £4,000.''

'That's outlandish, I'd expect a share in a garage for that. I'll give you £2,500.'

'Forget it. I'll give it to you for £3,500. It's my last word and that's only because you've bought cars here before.'

Activity

Finish off this cartoon.

Strongbow's Tomb, in Christ Church Cathedral, Dublin where many contracts and deals were made in medieval times.

When the Israelites were rescued from Egypt God was with them. When they were wandering through the desert as free people on their way to the Promised Land, God was with them. Escape from Egypt was only the first step. God knew that they would have many difficulties.

They would have to deal with the threats of the desert – heat, lack of food, lack of water. They would have to learn how to live as free people. They were used to having others control their lives. Now they could make their own decisions.

God made a covenant with the people of Israel. God told them that if they obeyed him and kept his laws, then they would be his people and he would look after them safely as they journeyed through the desert and afterwards when they settled in the Promised Land.

This is how it came about that God entered into the covenant.

Walking with God

After the Israelites had safely crossed the Red Sea they were overjoyed and gave thanks and praise to God.

Thirsty in the Desert

Then, however, they had to journey out into the desert. In fact they had to travel through the desert for forty years before they reached the Promised Land. They walked through the sands for three days without finding any water. Then they came to a place called Marah where they found some water but when they tasted it, it was bitter and they could not drink it.

The people were angry and they complained bitterly to Moses.

Moses prayed to the Lord and the Lord showed him a piece of wood which he threw into the water and the water became fit to drink.

Hunger and Thirst in the Desert

Then they came to Elim where there were water springs and palm trees and they camped there by the water.

Eventually they had to set out again into the desert.

Again they began to complain to Moses.

'We wish that the Lord had killed us in Egypt', they said, 'at least we had water and food; as much of it as we wanted. Out here we will starve to death.'

The Lord Provides

The Lord told Moses, 'I will send food down from the sky. In the morning they will have bread to eat and in the evening they will have water.'

Moses and Aaron called the people together and said,

'It is the Lord who brought you out of Egypt. It is the Lord who will give you food to eat. When you complain, you complain against the Lord'.

In the evening flocks of quails flew in over the camp and in the morning dew covered the earth and when the dew evaporated, the ground was covered with something thin, white and flaky which looked like frost. The people knew that this was the food that the Lord was sending them.

They collected it; it was like seed and tasted like biscuits made with honey. They called it manna.

More Trouble in the Desert

The people moved on. They camped at Rephidim, but again there was no water to drink. The people were thirsty and they started to complain. Again they said to Moses, 'Why did you bring us out of Egypt? Both ourselves and our children will die of thirst'.

Moses said, 'Why are you complaining? Why do you put the Lord to the test?' The people said, 'How do we know that the Lord is really with us?'

Moses didn't know what to do with them. He prayed to the Lord.

'What can I do? The people are so angry that they are ready to stone me.' The Lord said, 'Take some of the leaders of Israel with you. Go ahead of the people. Bring with you the stick with which you struck the Nile. Strike a rock which I will show you at Mount Sinai and water will come out for the people to drink.'

A Desert Battle

They were attacked by the Amalekites at Rephidim. Moses told Joshua to take some men with him and to go and fight the Amalekites. 'I will stand on top of the hill, holding the stick which the Lord gave me,' he said.

As long as Moses held up his arms the Israelites won the battle, but when he put his arms down the Amalekites started winning, so when Moses' arms grew tired, Aaron and Hur brought a stone for him to sit on and they stood beside him and held his arms high until the sun went down.

By then Joshua had completely defeated the Amalekites.

Moses said, 'The Lord will always fight with us against our enemies.'

He built an altar and praised and thanked the Lord.

Covenant with the Lord

Then the Israelites came to the Desert of Sinai and they set up camp at the foot of Mt Sinai. Moses went up the mountain to meet the Lord. The Lord said, 'You saw what I, the Lord, did to the Egyptians and how I carried you as an eagle carries her young on her wings, and brought you here to me, now if you will obey me and keep my covenant, you will be my own people. The whole earth is mine but you will be my chosen people, a people dedicated to me alone'.

Moses went down and told the people all that the Lord had said.

The people answered, 'All that the Lord has said we will do'.

Moses conveyed this to the Lord and the Lord said to Moses, 'Go and tell the people to spend today and tomorrow purifying themselves for worship. They must wash their clothes and be ready the day after tomorrow. On that day I will come down on Mt Sinai where all the people can see me'. Moses did all that the Lord had told him.

On the third day there was thunder and lightning and a very loud trumpet blast. The people went to the bottom of Mt Sinai and God called Moses and Aaron up the mountain.

God spoke, and these were his words:

I am the Lord your God.

Worship no god but me.

Do not make for yourselves images of anything in heaven or on earth or in the water or under the earth. Do not bow down to any idol or worship it, because I am the Lord your God and I tolerate no rivals. I bring punishment on those who hate me and on their descendants down to the third and fourth generation. But I show my love to thousands of generations of those who love me and obey my laws.

Do not use my name for evil purposes, for I, the Lord your God, will punish anyone who misuses my name.

Observe the Sabbath and keep it holy. You have six days in which to do your work, but the seventh day is a day of rest dedicated to me. On that day no one is to work, neither you, your children, your slaves, your animals, nor the foreigners who live in your country.

In six days I, the Lord, made the earth, the sky, the sea and everything in them, but on the seventh day I rested. That is why I, the Lord, blessed the Sabbath and made it holy.

Respect your father and your mother, so that you may live a long time in the land that I am giving you.

Do not commit murder.

Do not commit adultery.

Do not steal.

Do not accuse anyone falsely.

Do not desire another man's house.

Do not desire his wife, his slaves, his cattle, his donkeys, or anything else that he owns.

Discuss

What happens in the story to show that God was walking with the people?
Did the people always find it easy to walk with God?
What in the story shows that this was so?

Gospel of St Luke, *papyrus, 3rd century*.

The ten commandments were guidelines for the Israelites, showing them how to live if they wanted to keep God's covenant. Sometimes they lived according to the commandments but many times they failed to do this.

God never left them or abandoned them. So whenever the covenant or agreement was broken it was always the people who broke it.

Today, we are the people of God.

We too are called to walk with God.

In the ten commandments we also find guidelines which tell us how we should live.

Sometimes we find it just as difficult as the people of Israel did.

Activity

Read the following adaptation of the ten commandments.

The Ten Commandments

1. Honour God. Adore God. Praise God. Love God. God is more important than anything else in your life.

2. Always use God's name with deep respect and reverence; never in anger.

3. Keep the Sabbath day free to worship God in prayer and to take care of the needs of your body by resting from the work which you do during the week.

4. Treat your parents or those who are in charge of you with respect.

5. Always treat human life with respect and reverence. Never do anything which would damage your own life or that of anyone else.

6. Keep sexual love only for the person you are married to.

7. Do not take or keep anything that does not belong to you. Be honest and fair in your dealings with others.

8. Never tell lies about another person.

9. Do not be envious about the marriage partner someone else has.

10. Do not be envious about the money or property someone else has.

Write down ten guidelines which you would give to people who want to walk with God.

In Your Religion Journal

God had brought the Israelites into freedom. The commandments were meant to help them to remain truly free. Choose three of the commandments and say how observing each one of them could help someone to be really free. What would it give him/her freedom from?

T he Lord had freed the Israelites from slavery in Egypt. He had led them through the desert. He had provided them with food and drink. In the ten commandments he had outlined for them how they should live if they wished to be his people and walk in his ways. Still they had doubts about whether or not God was really on their side.

Act out the following drama.

Groups seated around camp-fire at the foot of Mt Sinai.

Benjamin: Well, I suppose it's good to be alive. There have been many times when I thought I was about to meet my end during the past few weeks.

Martha: Me too, it was bad enough being without food but I thought the thirst was the worst thing that I ever experienced.

Lot: I still say that fellow Moses wants his head examined. He should have left us in Egypt. We might have had to work hard, but sure hard work never killed anyone and at least we had clean water to drink and as much food as we could eat.

Rebecca: Come on, there's no need to be so negative. We're free. We can go where we want and make our own choices for the first time in years. The Lord is with us. We did get food and we did get fresh water to drink. I know we're in the desert but I must say I still feel safe because I have confidence in the Lord. If we want to be his people, he will be our God and we need have no fear.

Leah: Rebecca is right. Some of you are so ungrateful. I just don't understand you. The manna that fell on the desert was a real miracle, and it tasted delicious, like biscuits made with honey.

Rebecca: Not to mention the quails which flew in over the camp and made wonderful stew.

Benjamin: Oh all right, all right, so we didn't die! We just came very near to it.

Rachel: Well, where's Moses now ? He's been gone for ages. Aaron is with him too. I wonder what they're up to and what new and wonderful schemes they're drawing up. I just want to get out of this desert as fast as I can.

Joab: The Lord called Moses to the top of the mountain, we'll have to wait till he returns.

Moses enters. Silence falls on those around the camp-fire.

Moses: The Lord has spoken to us. This is what he said:

Moses shows the two tablets of stone with the commandments written on them and reads them out to the people.

I am the Lord your God, you shall not have strange Gods before me.

You shall not take the name of the Lord your God in vain.

Remember that you keep holy the Sabbath day.

Honour your father and your mother.

You shall not kill.

You shall not commit adultery.

You shall not steal.

You shall not bear false witness against your neighbour.

You shall not covet your neighbour's wife.

You shall not covet your neighbour's goods.

Lot: What is the thunder and lightning saying to us? Is the Lord trying to terrify us ?

Moses: Don't be afraid, the Lord is just showing us how we must live if we are to be his people.

Martha: Well, we do want to be his people, don't we?

Chorus: Yes, we want to be his people.

Benjamin: We don't really have much choice do we ? Who wants to spend the rest of their life stuck in the middle of the desert ?

Rebecca: Stop it, Benjamin. All that the Lord has said we will do.

Chorus: Yes, all that the Lord has said we will do.

Activity In groups, make up your own drama about a situation in today's world where there are some people who are finding it very difficult to believe that God has not abandoned them.

If we want to walk with God, the ten commandments offer us guidelines about the things we should do and the things we ought to avoid. Sometimes we choose to ignore these guidelines.

Will I or Won't I?

Margaret's mother asked her to slip out to the shop-next-door for some milk. John, the shopkeeper, had run the shop for several years and before that his father had done so. He knew everybody in the area and the local residents hoped that he would not be forced out of business by the supermarkets.

As Margaret went in John said, 'Margaret, will you do me a favour? My young lad is home from school with flu, my wife is out and I would like to slip into the house and see if he's OK. Will you stay here and look after things for a few minutes ?'

Margaret agreed immediately. She looked around. Cigarettes, gas lighters, sweets, chocolates, money in the till, they were all available, all inviting.

Something small, a quick action, John would never notice.

Discuss

What is there in the story to indicate that John and Margaret knew one another quite well?

What could Margaret have done when she was left alone in the shop?

What do you think you would have done or been tempted to do?

What's most important ?

Peter: I'll meet you on the way to the youth Mass in the parish tonight, John.

John: Oh, I forgot to tell you, I'm not going.

Peter: Not going ! Why ?

John: I've just started an evening paper round. I need the money. I want to buy a new track suit.

Peter: But surely the youth Mass is more important and it's only one night.

John: Youth Masses won't get me a new track suit. I'll see you tomorrow, Peter.

Standing out in the Crowd

Margaret: Here comes Anne and we've just one cigarette left.

Elizabeth: Just in time, Anne. Here you are (*handing Anne the cigarette*).

Anne: Phew, the air in here is thick with smoke. I hope you realise what you're doing to your health.

Margaret: Oh shut up, Anne, and have the cigarette.

Anne: I'm serious. I saw another programme on television lately. I don't think anyone except a fool would even sit in a room like this, not to mention actually smoke the filthy things.

Elizabeth: Well, I never heard such a sermon in my life. What a goody-goody !

Margaret: Come on, Anne, you've had your joke. Now, have a cigarette and sit down.

Anne: Look, I'll see you tomorrow. I'm off for a jog.

The Best Picture

Margaret: He really makes me sick. He's so full of himself. He thinks he's God's gift to the world.

John: The real problem is that the teachers all seem to agree with him. They think he's God's gift to the world as well.

Laura: Well, let's see if we can find a way to change their minds.

Michael: Change their minds about Paul ! You must be joking.

Margaret: No, it must be possible. All we have to do is think of something that would really annoy them, do it, and then make it look as if it was Paul who did it.

John: We'd better be careful. It could backfire. We might end up in bad trouble ourselves.

Margaret: Not at all. Remember, we did it before ! When we were in first year we fixed it so that Joseph Power got suspended for a week. That kept him quiet for the rest of the year.

Michael: Margaret is right. All we need is a bit of imagination. Let's get together after school and see what ideas we can come up with.

Activity

In the situations you've just read, the people involved might have thought differently about what they were doing if they had remembered the guidelines that are given to us in the commandments.

Can you say which commandment might have influenced them in each of the situations ?

In Your Religion Journal

Write about a time in your life when a choice you made was influenced by what one or other of the ten commandments teaches.

Write also about a time when you refused to be influenced by the teaching of the commandments.

Think about the area of your life where you find it most difficult to do what is right.

A Time to Pray

Help us, Lord, to walk with you always.
Give us the courage to keep your commandments.
Help us to recognise that true freedom can only be found when we live in your way.
There are many things which threaten to enslave us, unhealthy friendships, unhealthy habits such as drinking, smoking or taking drugs.
Sometimes it's easy to be fooled, just as the Israelites were, when they told Moses that they had been better off as slaves in Egypt.
Help us to believe that you are with us always.

Our Father

Our Father, who art in heaven,
hallowed be thy name.
Thy Kingdom come.
Thy will be done on earth, as it is in heaven.
Give us this day our daily bread,
and forgive us our trespasses,
as we forgive those who trespass against us;
and lead us not into temptation,
but deliver us from evil. Amen.

Test Yourself
Do the Looking Back exercises on page 225

Unit Four
Sin and Recon- ciliation

Lesson Eleven

Evil & Sin

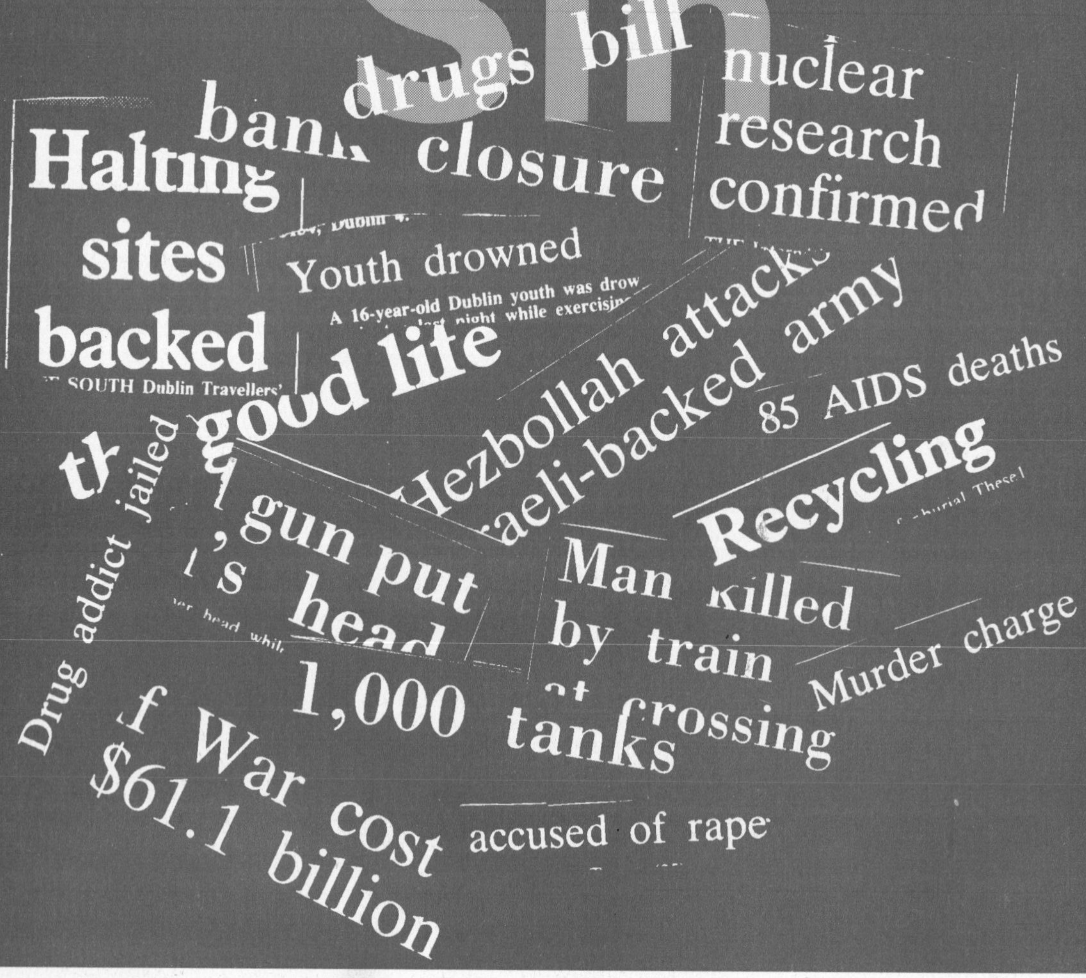

drugs bill

nuclear research confirmed

bank closure

Halting sites backed

Youth drowned

A 16-year-old Dublin youth was drow
last night while exercisi

SOUTH Dublin Travellers'

good life

Hezbollah attacks

Israeli-backed army

85 AIDS deaths

Drug addict jailed

gun put

head

Recycling

Man killed by train at crossing

Murder charge

1,000 tanks

War cost $61.1 billion

accused of rape

When we look around us at the world we live in we see lots of good things happening. There are many things going on which show us the goodness of people in action.

We can see people caring for others in homes, in institutions, in the Third World; we can see people working for peace in the troubled parts of the world; we can see some people who are prepared even to give their lives to bring freedom and hope to others.

We can see the developments that have come about because of the way in which people have used their intelligence: developments in the area of science; in industry; in computers.

We can see the efforts that people are making to make the earth a more beautiful place to live in.

In our own homes, in school, in the locality where we live we can see people making efforts to care for others, to make the world a happier and healthier place to live.

Activity

Find cut-outs from newspapers and magazines which illustrate the good that is in the world.
Make a number of collages to display on the classroom walls.
OR
Interview people you know about the good things which they see happening in your local area. Find a way of presenting what you have discovered to the class. You could also find pictures and cuttings in local newspapers.

In Your Religion Journal

Write about something which you saw happening in the last week which showed some of the good that is going on in the world.

82

There is also evil in the world; in fact, when we look at the newspapers it sometimes seems as if goodness does not exist. There are headlines which speak of earthquakes, famine, war, car crashes, rape, overdose and abandoned babies etc.

As well as the evil that makes the newspaper headlines there is also the evil that is part of everyone's daily life, in every home, in every village, in every town and in every city.
We meet it in the jealousy, the dishonesty, the laziness, the greed, that occur in the human relationships that are part of all our lives.

Some of the evil in the world is outside the control of human beings, for example, an earthquake. We call this **physical evil.**
Then there is also the evil which is caused by the things people do, the choices they make, the way in which they relate to one another. We call this **moral evil.**

Activity

Find as many newspaper headlines as you can depicting evil in the world.
Make a collage using the cuttings.

In Your Religion Journal

Write about something you saw happening last week which pointed to some of the evil that is in the world.

Activity

Make two posters, one with the caption, 'Physical Evil', the other with the caption, 'Moral Evil'. Illustrate the captions.

All evil causes suffering:
- It causes physical pain;
- It causes bitterness;
- It causes loneliness;
- It causes destruction of the environment;
- It causes death.
Can you list other effects of evil?

Cut out some headlines from the newspapers showing the different kinds of evil that are in the world. In each case see if you can also show what effects the evil has on people and on the environment.

The Mystery of Suffering

Most suffering seems to be pointless. It's very difficult, for example, to see any reason why thousands of people have to suffer pain, loneliness, even death as the result of an earthquake. However, some suffering is necessary and eventually good comes from it.

Read the following story.

The Guitars

A folk group didn't seem to be enjoying much success until one night a member of the audience suggested the guitars needed tuning. On reflection, this seemed wise advice, since all these guitars had been bought second-hand and were usually stored in either very damp or very dusty rooms.

Various tuners were contacted through the *Yellow Pages* and the least expensive one was given the job. He arrived within minutes and eagerly set about the work.

Taking hold of the first guitar, he began pulling and tensing its strings.

'Ouch ! Hey ! Ow ! Ooh !' yelled the unfortunate victim. The other guitars heard and saw what was happening and they all became terrified. One of them whispered to his friends, 'Just look at him. He's a sadist ! He seems to enjoy making people suffer.' All the guitars were now shaking with fear but the tuner took no notice and continued working with an apparently pitiless lack of concern.

Meanwhile, in the far corner, half-hidden under a cushion, Adolfo, one of the smaller guitars, remained frozen with fear, deliberately trying not to move, 'Please God! Don't let him find me. Save me from this torturer and I'll do anything you ask !'

Adolfo's prayers certainly seemed to be answered. The tuner failed to notice him as he lay still and motionless underneath the cushion. 'Thank you, God, for sparing me,' gasped the grateful little guitar.

In the evening, the musicians arrived, ready for their next engagement. As soon as they began trying them out, they were delighted: 'These are fantastic now! I can hardly believe they could ever sound so good.'

The guitars, of course, felt very flattered and proud of themselves.

Then, one of the guitarists noticed Adolfo sticking out from under the cushion. As soon as his strings were pulled, everyone groaned. Then they all started laughing, 'What a croak ! It's a right duff guitar, this one. I think we'll give it a miss for tonight at least.'

They all picked up the other guitars and went back downstairs. Poor Adolfo was left alone. He felt insulted and began crying, 'Nobody likes me. I'm useless.'

Moral Evil

I do not understand what I do;
For I don't do what I would like to do
but instead I do what I hate.
I don't do the good that I want to do;
instead I do the evil that I do not want to do
(*Romans 7:15,19*).

In these words St Paul says something that is probably true for all of us.
Can you remember a time when you did something which you knew was wrong because of pressure from your friends, because of fear of being laughed at, or because of your own selfishness?

In Your Religion Journal
Draw a picture to illustrate how you felt before and after you did it.

Conscience

When we think about an action and decide whether it is a good action or a bad action we are using our conscience.

Our conscience helps us to see the difference between right and wrong.

We can use our conscience before we do something. Our conscience will help us to decide if it is right or wrong. Sometimes even if our conscience tells us that something is wrong we will still do it.

Sometimes after we have done something our conscience helps us to understand that what we did was wrong.

A Quick £20

John was walking home one night after the disco. It was a badly lit part of the city and he could barely make out the shape of the old lady who was walking in front of him on the footpath.

As he drew nearer he noticed that she was carrying a bag under her arm.

'Old Age Pension day' flashed through John's mind in red letters. He also thought of the new CD discs he wanted so badly. It would take forever saving his pocket money every week. Then something inside him said, 'Don't be daft. She's an old woman. Leave her alone.' Even while these thoughts were in his head John had raced up behind her. She jumped with fright at the hurrying feet. It was easy to force the bag from under her arm with just a quick movement of his fist. John ran, opening the bag as he did. He found £20, took it, and threw the remainder on the pavement.

Discuss

What is your response to what John did ?

Did John listen to his conscience?

What excuse might John try to offer for what he did?

In Your Religion Journal

Imagine John came face to face with the old lady. What might he say ?

Write a story to illustrate a situation where someone follows his or her conscience.

How many of the following statements do you agree with?

Sometimes I don't follow my conscience because:

I'm afraid I'll be laughed at.

I want to be one of the crowd.

My parents wouldn't like it.

I want to do what seems to make life easiest for me.

I don't think of others.

I want to become a better person.

It's not fashionable.

I don't want to be a good person.

Some things which help our conscience to develop.

We get help and guidance from our parents, teachers, priests and other adults who have more experience than we have.

Discuss

Talk about a particular incident when someone older than you helped you to understand why something was wrong.

As we grow older our understanding develops. We come to see more clearly how the things we do affect others. We can see why some of the things we do are wrong.

Discuss

Can you think of some things which are acceptable behaviour for a four-year-old or a five-year-old but which would not be acceptable for you?

We hear and understand the guidelines in the Bible for good living.

Discuss

Can you remember some of the things Jesus said which show us how to make life more worthwhile for ourselves and for others?

We hear the teachings of the Church which tell us how we should live if we want to be followers of Jesus.

Discuss

Can you think of something the Church says which helps us to know how we should live?

As followers of Jesus we have a duty to inform our conscience. We should find out about right and wrong. We should try to examine all that is involved in the decisions we have to make so that we will be aware of the consequences of our actions.

Sin

When our conscience tells us that something is wrong and we still decide to do it, we sin. If what we do is seriously wrong, if we know that it is seriously wrong and we still do it, simply because we want to, we commit a mortal sin. There are three things which make a sin mortal:

The action involved is seriously wrong ;

We know that it is seriously wrong ;

We still decide freely that we want to do it.

A mortal sin is very serious. It breaks our relationship with God. It shows that we do not want to live as God has called us to. Usually it causes serious harm to another person or maybe even a number of people. It also damages our relationship with that person. The person knows that we want to hurt them.

Activity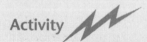

Give examples of mortal sins which you or the people you know could be guilty of.
Think of ways in which you may seriously fail in your duty to God, or seriously harm or fail in your duty to someone else.

If you want to follow your conscience the following questions will help you to make good decisions.
What is being done?
Why?
What is my reason and intention in doing this ?
How is it being done?
Who is it going to affect?
How will it affect them?

Is there anything I have heard from the Bible or in the teachings of the Church which will help me to decide if it is good or bad?

Read the following two stories.

The art room walls were covered with pictures of all kinds. The room was alive with colours and shapes. Tomorrow the judging would take place and the winners in the competition would receive their prizes.

Everyone thought that they knew already who would come first. Margaret just seemed to have a knack with her art work that the others couldn't get hold of. Everything she did looked so perfect. It was hard for her classmates to imagine how she could ever be any better than she already was.

Mostly they admired Margaret's work, but sometimes it was difficult not to feel a bit jealous. Why did one person have so much while others seemed to have so little?

John and Anne were walking around the room having a last look before they went home. They stopped in front of Margaret's picture. 'Well, it looks as if she's done it again !' said Anne. 'Oh, she makes me sick,' said John. 'It's really unfair that anyone should find it as easy as she does to do work like this. Let's get the paint brushes and make a mess of it.'

'Are you sure, John?' asked Anne, 'It would be a terrible thing to do. She'd be so disappointed. Though I must say I'd love to see her name at the bottom of the list for a change.'

'Well, come on then, let's do it,' said John.

In a few minutes Margaret's picture, which had taken hours to paint, was truly unrecognisable.

The art room walls were covered with pictures of all kinds. The room was alive with colours and shapes. Tomorrow the judging would take place and the winners in the competition would receive their prizes.

Everyone thought that they knew already who would come first. Margaret just seemed to have a knack with her art work that the others couldn't get hold of. Everything she did looked so perfect. It was hard for her classmates to imagine how she could ever be any better than she already was.

Mostly they admired Margaret's work, but sometimes it was difficult not to feel a bit jealous. Why did one person have so much while others seemed to have so little ?

John and Anne were walking around the room having a last look before they went home. They stopped in front of Margaret's picture. 'Well, it looks as if she's done it again,' said Anne. John wasn't listening. He was looking at his own picture which was hanging above Margaret's.

'What are you looking at, John?' asked Anne. 'I know your picture is OK but it doesn't compare with Margaret's.'

'Maybe it will when I've finished,' replied John, as he went off for a can of paint and a brush. Anne watched as he pulled over a table and climbed up to reach his painting.

'Just a little dab at the top will give a totally new look to the picture.'

'Be careful, John,' shouted Anne, as he held the dripping brush over Margaret's picture. 'You could destroy Margaret's picture.'

'Oh don't be such a fusspot,' said John. With that a big blob of paint fell on Margaret's picture and dribbled right from the top to the bottom of the painting.

Discuss

What is the difference between what happened in each of these stories?
Which is more serious? Why?

We can also sin in our thoughts. Deliberately to wish someone harm is wrong. Deliberately to wish someone serious harm is seriously wrong. However, many thoughts come into our minds without our having much control over the matter.

These are temptations rather than sins. It is only when we deliberately make these thoughts our own that the possibility of sin arises. Full consent is always necessary for a sin to be serious and it is normally obvious to us when we have given this.

Therefore, if you have any doubts about the matter, it is usually safe to conclude that you didn't give full consent, and therefore there is no question of serious sin.

Of course , whenever we set out to judge our own actions we should be careful not to deceive ourselves into thinking that our own actions are either better or worse than they actually are.

Less serious sins are called venial sins. They may be less serious:

–Because the action itself, while wrong, is not seriously wrong (for example, an action which might cause slight harm to someone but not serious harm);

–Because a person does something on the spur of the moment without appreciating how serious it is, or without intending to do it, or in a moment of panic or confusion.

It is important to remember that a sin can only be a mortal sin if we know at the time that it is seriously wrong. Small offences can damage our relationship with other people but usually not to breaking point. In the same way venial sins damage our relationship with God but do not break it.

Activity

Give examples of venial sins which you or the people you know could be guilty of.

From the beginning human beings have at times chosen to do certain actions which fulfilled their own selfish needs and did not take into account their relationship with others or with God.

The Fall

Scene One

Narrator:	Now the snake was the most cunning of all the animals that the Lord God had made. The snake asked the woman:
Snake:	Did God really tell you not to eat the fruit of any tree in the garden?
Woman:	We may eat the fruit of any tree in the garden except the tree in the middle of it. God told us not to eat the fruit of that tree or even touch it; if we do, we will die.
Snake:	That's not true; you will not die. God said that because he knows that when you eat of it you will be like God and know what is good and what is bad.
Narrator:	The woman saw how beautiful the tree was and how good its fruit would be to eat, and she thought how wonderful it would be to become wise. So she took some of the fruit and ate it. Then she gave some to her husband and he also ate it. As soon as they had eaten it they realised they were naked; so they sewed fig leaves together and covered themselves.
	That evening they heard the Lord God walking in the garden and they hid among the trees.
God:	**Where are you ?**
Man:	I heard you in the garden. I was afraid and hid from you because I was naked.
God:	**Who told you you were naked? Did you eat the fruit that I told you not to eat?**
Man:	The woman gave me the fruit and I ate it.
God: (*To the woman*)	**Why did you do this?**
Woman:	The snake tricked me into eating it.

Discuss

To what extent do you think the man and woman took responsibility for what they had done ? Why do you think they did not obey God?

In Your Religion Journal

Pretend you are the woman, or the snake, or the man and write the story of what happened. Illustrate your story.

Scene Two

God:
(To the Snake)

You will be punished for this. From now on you will crawl on your belly, and you will have to eat dust as long as you live. I will make you and the woman hate each other; her offspring and yours will always be enemies. Her offspring will crush your head and you will bite their heel.

(To the woman)

I will increase your trouble in pregnancy and your pain in giving birth.

(To the man)

You listened to the woman and ate the fruit which I told you not to eat. Because of this you will have to work hard to make the ground produce food. It will produce weeds and thorns. Only by sweat and hard labour will you be able to make the soil produce food. You were made from soil and you will return to soil.

Discuss
How did the sin of Adam and Eve affect their relationship with nature, with one another, with God?

Have You Noticed ?
The snake said that if they ate from the tree they would become like God, knowing what was good and what was bad. They would take God's place and they, instead of God, would decide what was good and what was bad. This tells us something important about sin. When we sin, we are really saying, 'I know that God is telling me through my conscience that this is a bad thing to do but I know better and I'm going to do it.' When we sin we are trying to make ourselves into our own God, but all we actually achieve is to become less like God and less like his image in the world.

Activity
Form groups of four. One person takes the role of God, one of Eve, one of Adam, one of the snake.
Talk about what happened in the story of 'The Fall' expressing your feelings about what you did and what the others did.

90

God had led the Israelites from the slavery of Egypt and had given them all they needed as they travelled through the desert. They had agreed to keep the covenant which God had made with them. They said they would keep God's laws and God promised to look after them. Even so they were prepared to damage their relationship with God.

The Golden Calf

After the people had heard the ten commandments, the Lord called Moses up the mountain again so that the covenant could be sealed.

Before Moses came back the people became impatient, 'Where has that fellow, Moses, gone ?' they asked. 'We don't know what has happened to him'. And they said to Aaron, 'Make us a god to lead us.' Aaron said, 'Take off the earrings, your sons, your daughters and your wives are wearing and bring them to me.'

He melted down the earrings and poured the gold into a mould and made a bull calf. When the people saw it they said, 'This is the god who led us out of Egypt.'Aaron built an altar in front of the bull and they sacrificed animals on it. Then they feasted and danced and sang in front of the altar.

'Go back down the mountain,' the Lord said to Moses, 'Your people have sinned. They have turned away from me. They have made a gold bull calf. They say it is their God. They are worshipping it and offering it sacrifices. I am angry with them.'

Moses went down the mountain. Before he reached the bottom he heard the sounds of the people singing and rejoicing. He was carrying the two tablets of stone on which the Lord had written the ten commandments. He was so angry that he dropped them and smashed them at the bottom of the mountain.

Exodus 32:1-20

Discuss

Why do you think the people made the golden bull calf and worshipped it?
What does this action say about their trust in God?

Activity

Imagine you were a reporter for a local newspaper. You might use one of the following headlines for an article describing what you saw happening.

MELTED GOLD IN THE DESERT

BROKEN COMMANDMENTS

PEOPLE FIND A NEW GOD

Choose one or find your own headline. In your religion journal write out the article which you might have written for the newspaper.

In small groups act out the scene at the bottom of Mt Sinai.

Discuss

Which of the characters in the story of the 'Golden Calf' might have said the following quotations ?

'I was really angry. I couldn't believe that the people would be so fickle.' "All that the Lord has said we will do," they told me. And then they go and do exactly what they had promised not to do. I was just shocked.'

'Well, how were we to know where your man Moses had gone? Several times we nearly died from hunger and thirst in the desert. And for all we knew he might not have come down the mountain again. We had to look after ourselves, you know.'

'You've no idea what these people are like when they're angry. To tell you the truth, I was afraid when they said to me, "Make us a god." They might have killed me had I not done what they had asked. And so I made them a god out of melted gold.'

'I have kept all my promises. I said that I would deliver them from Egypt and I did. I said that I would lead them safely through the desert and I did that too. I made a covenant with them. I promised that I would be their God and that I would always be with them guiding and protecting them. They promised that they would live as I had asked them and now look at what they have done.'

Activity

In small groups decide on one particular phrase from the passages from St Paul's letter to the Romans which you think you would like to use as a guide for doing good.
Make a poster to illustrate the phrase.
Write the phrase underneath your illustration.

It is very difficult to turn away from evil and do good. St Paul gives us some guidelines.
These are taken from *Romans 12:1-21.13:8.*

ourselves

Don't try to do 'what everybody does'; let God keep your mind alive and ready to think new thoughts, and you'll be a very different person from what you were. In this way you will be able to find out what God wants you to be and to do – what is worthwhile and right and grown up.

ourselves
as friends of Jesus

Each of us has different gifts; God has seen to that. We must use them. For example: some of us are able to understand God's Way more clearly than others; some of us deal with business better; some of us are teachers; some of us are speakers. Let us use our different gifts with God's help.
If we give, let us be generous givers; if we are leaders, let us be energetic leaders; if we are helping others, let us be cheerful helpers.

ourselves
and other people

Remember the words of Jesus:

'Bless those who treat you badly; bless them – don't curse them.'

Share other people's happiness and other people's sadness. Learn to respect everybody.

Don't be proud. Mix with ordinary people.

Don't talk as if you know all the answers.

As far as you can, be friends with everybody. Never try to get your own back, my friends, leave that in God's hands. You know what the Bible says...'I will see justice done,' says God, 'punishment is in my hands.'

Remember what the Bible also says: if your enemy is hungry, give him food; if he is thirsty, give him drink.

If you do this, you will make him ashamed of himself.

Don't be beaten by evil; beat evil by doing good.

Lesson Twelve

Forgiveness and Reconciliation

Maria: I feel very hurt. I trusted Anne. I thought she was a true friend. If somebody else had done it I mightn't feel so bad. It's just that I really looked upon her as a friend. I don't know why she did it.

Jennifer: Never mind. You have lots of other friends and she's not worth bothering about. Anyone who would treat a friend in that fashion is not worth bothering about.

Maria: It's not as easy as that to forget about it. I feel silly because I did trust her. I should have seen through her earlier. I don't know how I will ever be able to face her again.

Discuss

What do you think Anne did?
When have you ever felt as Maria does?
What will Anne have to do if the relationship between herself and Maria is to improve in the future?
What will Maria have to do?
Is it easy?

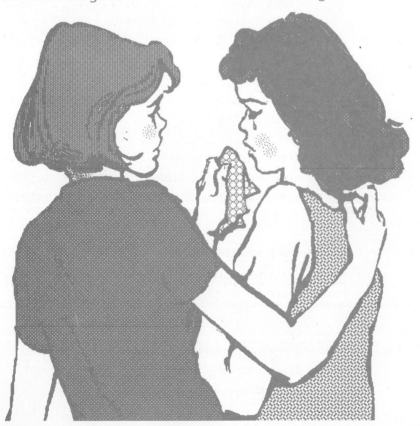

Spend some time, perhaps in your bedroom before you go to sleep or perhaps in the church, thinking about the things you do which cause hurt and pain to others.

Think of one time when you hurt your parents or one of your family.

Think of one time when you hurt one of your friends.

Try to decide what things you would need to avoid in order to prevent the same thing happening in the future.

When a broken relationship comes together again we call what happens

Reconciliation

There are a number of steps which must take place before reconciliation can be achieved.

1. A person realises that they have done wrong.

2. They realise that someone has been hurt.

3. They admit that they have done wrong by saying so to the person who has been hurt.

4. They tell that person that they are sorry for what they have done.

5. They do whatever they can to put things right again for the other person.

6. The other person tells them that they forgive them.

In our human relationships reconciliation does not happen easily. We find it difficult to say sorry. We would prefer not to have to admit that we are wrong and when somebody else has hurt us, we often find it difficult to forgive. We also find it difficult to say, I forgive you when someone else has hurt us.

When we damage our relationships with others we also damage our relationship with God. God calls us all to live with love, truth, peace, respect and justice towards those around us and towards the world we live in. When we fail to do that, when we hurt another person, physically or by doing or saying something which causes lack of trust between us, we not only damage our relationship with that person, we also damage our relationship with God.

Jesus shows us in his life how God wants us to treat those around us. Jesus also shows us that when we fail to do that, God is always ready to forgive us. Sometimes, because we may find it difficult to forgive others, we can find it difficult to really believe that God is always ready to forgive us.

If we are not reconciled with God it is because we have failed to carry out some steps which are necessary for reconciliation, not because God is not ready to forgive us.

God is also ready to forgive us when we break our relationship with him by failing to say our prayers, not going to Mass or by using his name in vain.

Jesus also told many stories which show us how God forgives us. This is one of the best-known of these stories.

The Two Sons

A MAN AND HIS TWO SONS were farmers. The younger son came one day to his father. 'Dad,' he said, 'it's time you handed over the farm to the two of us. Give me my share.'

That's what the father did. He divided up the farm between his two sons and handed it over.

The younger son quickly packed his things and went abroad. There he threw his money away having 'a good time'.

At last, his pockets were empty. Then the harvest failed all over the land.

There he was – no money and no food. He took a job with a farmer there, and the farmer sent him off to feed the pigs in the fields. He felt like swallowing the pigs' food himself. Nobody lifted a hand to help him.

Then he knew what a fool he'd been. 'How many of the labourers on my father's farm have more food than they want,' he thought, 'and here I am starving to death ! I'm going home to my father. I've wronged God, and I've wronged my father. I'll tell him so. And I'll tell him, too, that I don't deserve to be called a son of his; he can take me on as a labourer.'

He got up and went home.

When he was still quite a long way from his father's farm, his father saw him coming. He felt very sorry for him; and he ran out to meet him, threw his arms round his neck and kissed him. 'Dad,' the boy began to say, 'I've wronged God and I've wronged you. I don't deserve to be called a son of yours....'

'Quick !' his father called to his servants, 'Go and get his best clothes out. Get a ring and sandals and dress him properly. And kill that calf we've fattened. We'll have a feast and a grand time tonight. My boy was dead and lost; and here he is alive and back home again !'

And they began to celebrate.

Now the older son had been out on the farm. He was coming home and had almost reached the farmhouse when he heard the sound of bagpipes and dancing. He called one of the farmhands out, and asked him what was going on.

'Your brother's back,' said the man. 'Your father's killed the calf because he's safe home again.'

The older son was furious and he wouldn't even go inside the house. His father came out and begged him to come inside. 'Look,' he answered back, 'I've slaved for you all these years. I did everything you told me to do. But what do I get? Not even a kid to have a good time with my friends. This son of yours can throw his money away on girls, if he likes, and come home again and you go and kill a calf for him. 'My dear boy,' said his father, 'we're always together. All the farm is yours, you know that. We had to celebrate tonight. It's your *brother* who was dead and lost; it's your *brother* who's alive and back home again !'

Discuss

What words would you use to describe the younger son?

How do you think the father felt when his son left?

Why did the son decide to go back to his father's house?

What words would you use to describe the father?

Why was the Father prepared to welcome back his son in spite of everything?

The story says, 'When he was still quite a long way from his father's farm his father saw him coming'.

What does this suggest about the father?

How did the younger son feel when the father welcomed him home?

How did the elder son feel when his brother came back?

Why did he feel like this?

When have you ever acted as the younger son in the story did?

When have you ever acted as the older son in the story did?

Have you ever been treated in the same way as the father treated the younger son?

How did you feel when that happened ?

What did the younger son have to do before he could be reconciled with the father?

What did the older son have to do before he could be reconciled with his father and with his brother?

It is Jesus who helps us most clearly to understand the forgiveness of God.
When he forgave people Jesus showed us what the forgiveness of God is like.

Read the following stories:
Luke 5:17-26;
Luke 7:36-50;
Luke 19:1-9.

Discuss

How do you think the people in the stories felt:
-before they met Jesus?
- after they met Jesus?
What do you think of the way in which those who were watching reacted to what Jesus had done?

Activities

Make a comic strip to illustrate the story of the Prodigal Son.
Act out the story of the Prodigal Son. You could have four scenes.

Scene 1: Leaving Home
The younger son leaves home.

Scene 2: Having a Good Time
Imagine what life was like for the younger son when he was away from his father's house.
In this scene you could act out the dialogue that might have taken place between the younger son and his friends and between the younger son and the farmer who gave him work feeding pigs.

Scene 3: Welcome Home
The son comes back.

Scene 4: What About Me?
Show the reaction of the older brother;
the dialogue between the older brother and the father;
the dialogue between the older brother and the younger brother.

Activity

Write your own version of the Prodigal Son story set in today's world.

When we have done something which damages our relationship with God there are many ways in which we can be reconciled.
We can tell God in our own words that we are sorry.
We can say an Act of Sorrow.
We can remember that we have done wrong and tell God we are sorry at the Penitential Rite in the Mass.
We can celebrate the sacrament of Reconciliation.
Mortal sin destroys our relationship with God and cuts us off from the reception of Holy Communion. The sacrament of Reconciliation is God's merciful welcome where he comes out to meet his prodigal sons and daughters. The person who is truly repentant, who knows his or her need for forgiveness, ought to appreciate that gift. The Church requires that a person who has committed mortal sin should receive the sacrament of God's mercy before receiving Holy Communion.

The Sacrament of Reconciliation

In the sacrament of Reconciliation we have the opportunity to experience and celebrate God's forgiveness.

In the sacrament God forgives us, through the words and actions of the priest, for whatever wrong we have done.

The priest represents Jesus Christ, who offers us reconciliation, but in doing so he also represents Jesus' body, the Church. The risen Jesus acts through the Church, and he is always closely united with the Church. When we damage our relationship with God through sin, we damage our relationship with the Church as well. By failing to live as true followers of Jesus, we fail to play our part as members of the Church.

In the same way the reconciliation which Jesus offers in the sacrament, through the ministry of the priest, is reconciliation both with God and with the Church. The priest helps us to clarify if or to what extent we have sinned. The priest also speaks the words which assure us of forgiveness.

But Jesus has identified himself with the whole human race, for whom he died, and especially with those who suffer injustice and oppression. Any offence against them is an offence

against him as well. Therefore, in acting as Jesus' representative, the priest symbolically represents anyone at all whom we may have harmed. When we tell the priest the story of the wrong we have done, we are, in a symbolic way, confessing our guilt and expressing our sorrow to the community at large, and especially those we have wronged.

Sometimes the wrong we do injures someone with whom we have no contact. For example, if we vandalise a public park or public property of any kind we are causing disruption for many people whom we don't even know and may never meet. We cannot, therefore, apologise to them, but we can do so in a symbolic way through the priest.

Before we go to celebrate the sacrament of Reconciliation we should spend some time thinking back over our lives trying to discover how we have at times lived up to God's call and at times failed to do so.

It is a good opportunity for us to make decisions about the areas of our lives which we need to change and also about the areas of our lives where we are already succeeding in living up to God's call. We call this examining our conscience.

The following questions may help you to do this.

1.

Do I show respect for God?

Do I use the name of God or of Jesus in disrespectful ways?

Do I act disrespectfully in church?

Do I pray?

Do I remember to thank God for all the gifts I have been given?

Do I go to Mass when I should?

2.

Do I show respect for myself?

Do I take care of my body?

Do I get involved in activities which will damage my body or my health?

Do I abuse any of the gifts God has given me?

3.

Do I show respect for others?

How do I show respect for my parents?

Do I show respect for others who have authority over me?

Do I help out at home?

Do I hurt or damage people or others in any way by what I say or do ?

Do I tell the truth?

Am I honest?

Am I jealous?

Am I spiteful?

Am I pure?

4.

Do I show respect for the environment?

Do I damage buildings or plants or animals or any public property or property belonging to someone else?

Do I use substances which damage the environment ?

History of the Sacrament of Reconciliation

Part One

From the beginning new members were received into the Church through the sacrament of Baptism. Their baptism was a sign that they were prepared to turn away from all the evil that was in their lives and to begin to live as followers of Jesus.

Some of the new members of the Church occasionally slipped back into their pagan ways and so cut themselves off from the community. As time went on some of them wanted to come back to the Church. They regretted what they had done and wanted to rejoin the community.

Those who wanted to rejoin the Church spent a period of time doing penance. During this time they were called penitents.

They came to the church for Mass but left after the homily since they were not allowed to receive Holy Communion. Other members of the Church community prayed for them and encouraged them.

Particularly during Lent the penitents prayed and fasted. This was a public form of reconciliation since everyone in the community knew who was doing penance. On Holy Thursday, the bishop presided over a special Mass where the penitents were once again admitted to Holy Communion. They also found reconciliation in other ways by taking part in the Mass, giving to the poor, or by looking for forgiveness from the people they had offended.

Italian Penitent in Lent Procession, 1861

In the sixth century the practice of private confession began among the Irish monks. The monks spent their entire lives trying to rid themselves of their faults and to become more pleasing to God.

They would regularly confess their faults to one of the other monks. The monk who was listening would try to help by suggesting some ways in which the other might overcome his faults. Some of the monks became well known because they were very good at helping the other monks come closer to God and they became very popular confessors.

People who lived outside the monasteries began to come to the monks for help and advice.

Thus there were two forms of reconciliation available in the Church. One was public and available only once and it took place in the community. The other was private and available as often as desired.

Gradually confession, followed immediately by absolution/reconciliation and by the private carrying out of the penance given by the priest, became the only way in which the sacrament was celebrated in the Church. It is worth noting that in the earlier practice, while people did carry out penance in public and while the ceremony of reconciliation was a public ceremony, there is no evidence that sins were ever confessed in public.

In 1970 the Church looked again at the manner in which the sacrament of Reconciliation was celebrated. Whenever we sin our action usually damages not only our relationship with God but also our relationship with other people. The Church decided, therefore, that people should have the opportunity to celebrate reconciliation not only privately but also in the midst of the community.

Now there are three forms of the sacrament of Reconciliation available.

1   A person goes to celebrate the sacrament privately with a priest. Through the priest, the person experiences the love and forgiveness of God. The priest also represents the community. When the person expresses his or her sorrow to the priest it is a sign that they wish to be reconciled with the community.

2   A person celebrates the sacrament in a community celebration which also provides the opportunity for each individual to confess his or her sins to the priest.

3   The third form is a community celebration where there is no private confession but where it is presumed that people will confess individually as soon as possible. This form is reserved for emergency situations, for instance, where there is a danger of death and not sufficient time to hear the confessions of all those who wish to receive absolution; or in a situation where there are so many people wishing to receive absolution that there are not enough confessors to hear them all and they would be deprived of absolution or of the possibility of receiving the Eucharist for a long time.

When you go to celebrate the sacrament of Reconciliation

1. Make the sign of the cross with the priest.

2. The priest may read or say some words from the gospel.

3. The priest will invite you to say how long it is since your last celebration of the sacrament.

4. Say the Confiteor (if customary in your country).

I confess to almighty God,

And to you, my brothers and sisters,

That I have sinned through my own fault

In my thoughts and in my words,

In what I have done,

And in what I have failed to do;

And I ask blessed Mary, ever virgin,

All the angels and saints,

And you, my brothers and sisters,

To pray for me to the Lord our God.

5. Tell the priest about the times when you have failed to live as God calls you to.

The priest will listen and may give you some advice.

6. The priest will give you an act of penance.

He may ask you to say some prayers or perhaps to do a certain action. This is to show that you intend to try to do better and that you wish to make amends for any harm you have done.

7. Say the Act of Sorrow.

O my God, I thank you for loving me.
I am sorry for all my sins:
for not loving others and not loving you.
Help me to live like Jesus and not sin again. Amen.
OR
O my God,
because you are so good,
I am very sorry that I have sinned against you,
and with your help I will not sin again. Amen.

8. Absolution:

The priest extends his hands and prays:

God, the father of mercies,
through the death and resurrection of his Son,
has reconciled the world to himself
and sent the Holy Spirit among us
for the forgiveness of sins;
through the ministry of the Church
may God give you pardon and peace
and I absolve you from your sins
in the name of the Father and of the Son and of the Holy Spirit.

You respond:
Amen.

9. Dismissal.

The priest then says:
Give thanks to the Lord for he is good.

You respond:
His mercy endures for ever.

The priest concludes:
The Lord has freed you from your sins. Go in peace.
OR
The priest may use another form of words which requires no response.

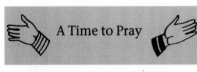

A Time to Pray

There are times in all our lives when we need to stop and take stock of the way in which we are living. Often we will find things in our own lives which we need to turn away from. We ought at times such as these to remember the words of the prophet Joel:

Come back to the Lord, your God.
He is kind and full of mercy;
he is patient and keeps his promise;
he is always ready to forgive and not punish *(Joel 2:13).*
Spend a few moments in silence thinking over areas of your life.

You might ask yourself the following questions:

How have I lived up to my relationship with others at home, at school?

How have I been treating my friends?

How have I shown respect for my own body and other people's bodies?

How have I shown care and respect for the environment ?

Have I been honest and truthful?

You can also be confident that God is listening with love and forgiveness.

I've Done Wrong

Dear God, I see how hard it is to be good without you.

All kinds of people and things help me forget about you.
But now I come back to you, sorry, and not feeling good about myself.
You are the only one who can help me and I know you will.

I will remember that I need your help.
I will try to listen for your voice and do what I know you wish me to do, and be what I know you want me to be.
With your help I will know your love and try to give it to everyone I meet
(Based on Psalm 31).

Test Yourself.
Do the Looking Back exercises on page 225

Unit Five
Celebrating the coming of Jesus

Lesson Thirteen

Advent

Advent is a time of waiting and preparation. It is a time of expectation, hope and joy.

Like the season of Lent, Advent is an opportunity to make a fresh start, to make a renewed effort in the way we live our lives.

The season of Advent begins four Sundays before Christmas Day and lasts for the following four weeks.

Advent is a time of preparation for the birth of Jesus at Christmas and it can mean many different things to people.

Time can pass so quickly that we can easily forget about the real meaning of Advent and we arrive at Christmas Day without preparing ourselves for the celebration of Jesus' birthday.

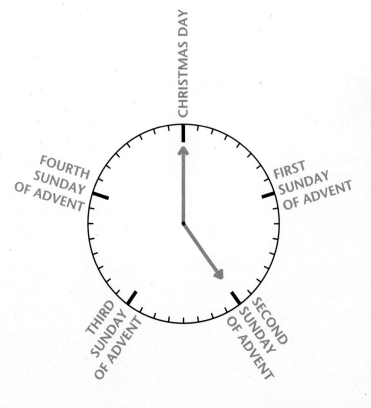

CHRISTMAS DAY

FOURTH SUNDAY OF ADVENT

FIRST SUNDAY OF ADVENT

THIRD SUNDAY OF ADVENT

SECOND SUNDAY OF ADVENT

Discuss

What does Advent mean to you?

If you were a young child, Advent might mean visiting Santa, and going to see the Christmas lights turned on by a local celebrity.

As a student at school, Advent might mean last minute swotting for Christmas tests.

If you were at work, Advent might be a time of parties and late nights.

If you were to work at home and look after a family it might be a long trail of shopping and careful budgeting, and rushing to fill Santa's lists and find the missing bulb from the Christmas tree lights!

Activity

Draw your own Advent clock. Fill it in as each week of Advent passes with your hopes and expectations for each day and your Advent resolution for that particular week.

Resolutions

Early in December Mrs Fitzpatrick said to her pupils, 'Let's write out our resolutions for Advent about how we will make a renewed effort in the way we live our lives. I'll put them up on the board at the back of the classroom.' The pupils agreed and when the resolutions were pinned up on the board, they all gathered around to read them.

One boy, called Michael, suddenly went into a fit of anger. 'She didn't put up my resolution and I gave her mine first. I always knew she didn't like me, and that just shows it!' On and on he ranted and raved.

The teacher, who overheard this from her store room, was embarrassed. She hadn't meant to exclude his resolution. Quickly rummaging through the papers on her desk, she found it and immediately went to the board to put it up. The resolution read:

> I RESOLVE TO BE MORE UNDERSTANDING AND NOT TO LET LITTLE THINGS UPSET ME ANY MORE.

During Advent, at the beginning of a New Year, and during Lent we often make resolutions which we fully intend to keep. But sometimes these resolutions can soon be forgotten about. Advent is a time when we are called by the Church to take stock of our lives, to decide where we need to make changes and to resolve to do whatever is necessary in order to become a better person.

It is very difficult to change ourselves or our habits even when we have decided that we want to do this. We can, in our prayers, ask God to help us to change and to find the courage and strength we need to grow.

Advent is about Waiting

We are always **waiting** for something. Possibly you are waiting for your exam results, or your holidays or maybe even your next birthday.

Discuss

What do you think of the resolution which Michael made?

In Your Religion Journal

Why do we make Advent resolutions ? In what way can our Advent resolutions help us to prepare for Christmas ?

Can you think of other things that you are **waiting** for ? Write about these.

The Jewish people waited many hundreds of years for the birth of Jesus. An air of expectancy built up as they waited for their Messiah to come and free them from their suffering and from foreign rule.

THE JERUSALEM HERALD

| I BC | LATE EDITION | ISSUE No. 345 |

The prophet Isaiah has said:
The Lord himself, therefore,
will give you a sign.
It is this: the maiden is with child
and will soon give birth to a son
whom she will call, Immanuel
(Isaiah 7:14).

In Your Religion Journal

You are a reporter for the *Jerusalem Herald*. The atmosphere in Jerusalem is one of hope and expectancy as the Jews wait for the promised Messiah. Write a report for your newspaper, indicating what it is like to live in Jerusalem at this time. Why do the Jewish people look forward to a Saviour? What do they hope he will achieve?

Find Your Group
Discuss

What are you looking forward to this Christmas? What are your hopes and expectations?

For us as Christians we wait and look forward to our celebration of Jesus' birthday throughout the month of December. We are waiting to celebrate the gift of life and love which God gave to the world in Jesus.

2,000 years ago the world was waiting for the birth of the Messiah.

In parts of the world many people do not look forward to Christmas, for they are still waiting. They are waiting to see some signs of Christianity.

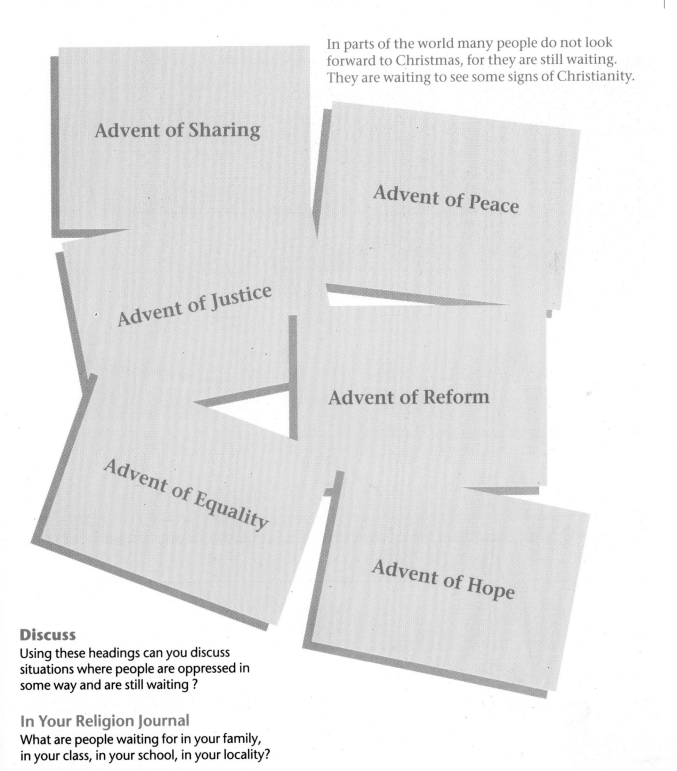

Advent of Sharing

Advent of Peace

Advent of Justice

Advent of Reform

Advent of Equality

Advent of Hope

Discuss
Using these headings can you discuss situations where people are oppressed in some way and are still waiting ?

In Your Religion Journal
What are people waiting for in your family, in your class, in your school, in your locality?

Class Activity

Make a wall map of the world. Using pictures and articles from newspapers and magazines, pinpoint areas in the world which are still **waiting** for some signs of the Advent of Christianity. Think up a suitable title for your wall display.

Decide on a project which you can get involved in, either as an entire class, or in small groups, which will help someone or some groups of people in your locality to experience the joy of Christmas this year.

Find Your Group
Activity

Put up a crib in your classroom. Each group can take responsibility for making some of the figures and for decorating the crib.

During the weeks leading up to Christmas prepare with your groups a short prayer service. You can make posters or banners on a particular aspect of Christmas. You could also include a story, a drama or a reading.

Use the class crib as the focal point when each group in turn leads the class in prayer.

During Advent the classroom crib can be used to focus our attention on the real meaning of Christmas. It gives us an opportunity, through prayer, to come to a better understanding of what we celebrate at Christmas.

The First Crib

In the winter of 1223 Francis of Assisi was staying at a small friary in Greccio, in Northern Italy. A rich man from nearby offered the friars any gift they wished at Christmas. Francis said:

I want to celebrate Christmas with you.
Up in the rocks you have a cave –
there prepare a crib full of hay;
bring an ox and a donkey.
I want to feel and see with my own eyes
how much the Son of God wanted to be poor
when he was born for love of us.

And so that year all the friars and the local people gathered together at the now famous cave of Greccio.

Christmas

During our season of Advent the commercial world is trying to 'sell' Christmas to the shopper. Their interest in Christmas closes with the shops on Christmas Eve. That's when for us Advent ends and we begin to celebrate Christmas — a celebration that continues until the 6th January and the feast of the Epiphany.

However, for many of us, we begin to celebrate much too early. Advent is a time of preparation, a time to look forward to the coming of Christ. In some cases we arrive at Christmas Day, which should be the high point of celebration, tired out from our Christmas shopping and parties and so the rest of the season is left to drift along.

Christmas on Trial

To settle the question of whether or not we should celebrate Christmas any longer it was decided to put Christmas on trial. The time of the trial is shortly before Christmas.

Read and act out the following scene.

Characters:

J = Judge
P = Prosecutor
D = Counsel for Defence

Witnesses:

Mr O'Brien; Mr McCann;
Ms Hughes; Ms Goff;
Ms Carey; Mr Deans.

Jury:

You and the rest of your class.

J: The case before the court is that Christmas should be abolished. The Prosecutor is Mr O'Sullivan. The Counsel for the Defence is Ms Breen, both very distinguished lawyers. I now call on both of them to briefly introduce the case for and against Christmas.

P: Your Honour, my case rests on the fact that the way we celebrate Christmas no longer has any real meaning. It is an insult to the founder of our religion.

D: Your Honour, I agree that our manner of celebrating this great feast leaves a lot to be desired. Still, I believe that it must be kept. I'll give my reasons later.

J: Let us proceed at once with the witnesses. Need I remind them that they are under oath?

Loneliness

P: I call Mr O'Brien to the stand. (*He takes the stand.*) Mr O'Brien, please tell us a little about yourself.

Mr O'Brien: I'm a bachelor of seventy-nine years of age. I live alone.

P: Tell the court how you spent last Christmas.

Mr O'Brien: There's not much to tell. I spent it all alone like I spent the last eight Christmases since my sister died.

P: How did you feel?

Mr O'Brien: Very lonely indeed. The loneliness gets worse at Christmas.

P: Have you a television?

In Your Religion Journal

List five ways in which you can improve your preparation for the Christmas celebration.

Mr Deans

Ms Hughes

Mr O'Brien: No, my sight isn't good enough for it.

P: Are you looking forward to this Christmas?

Mr O'Brien: To tell you the truth I dread the thought of it.

P: My client is typical of thousands who spend Christmas alone.

This is the time when families draw closer together. The sight of this togetherness serves only to make those who are lonely feel their loneliness all the more acutely.

In From the Cold

D: I call Mr McCann to take the stand. (*He does so.*)

Mr McCann, you belong to the Society of St Vincent De Paul.

Mr McCann: That's correct.

D: What is your view of Christmas?

Mr McCann: It seems to bring out the best in most people. We hold a special collection for the poor and we get more in this collection than we get during the rest of the year. Somehow Christmas touches the hearts of everyone.

D: What do you do with this money?

Mr McCann: We provide coal, food and clothes for the needy. We distribute a couple of dozen hampers to people in need and we buy toys for the children of large struggling families. We pay rental for television sets for old people living on their own. That kind of thing.

D: This must take up a lot of time and energy?

Mr McCann: Yes, but I've never heard one of our members complain.

D: What precise value do they see in it?

Mr McCann: Well, when Christ came into the world he came poor. There was no room for him in the inn. We try to make sure that the poor are not left out in the cold at Christmas. We believe that in welcoming them we are welcoming Christ himself.

D: That will be all, Mr McCann.

Much Too Busy

P: For my second witness I call Ms Hughes. (*She takes the stand.*)

Ms Hughes, tell us something about yourself.

Ms Hughes: I work in the home raising our young family.

P: What does Christmas mean to you?

Ms Hughes: A mountain of extra work! There are cards to be written, presents to be bought, wrapped and delivered. The house has to be cleaned and decorated. The Christmas shopping has to be done. With the crowds and the traffic this gets worse every year. Then, of course, there's the cooking. I'm always nervous about the turkey. If the turkey doesn't turn out right then, for some, the whole Christmas is ruined!

P: Spiritually, what does it mean to you?

Ms Hughes: Very little. Don't get me wrong. I consider myself as good a Catholic as the next. It's just that I don't have time to think of that side of Christmas. I'm lucky if I can get three minutes on Christmas Eve to pop in for Confession, and half an hour on Christmas morning to go to Mass. Even then I'm so tired and distracted that I get very little out of it.

P: Would I be right in saying that you don't relish the approach of Christmas?

Ms Hughes: Yes indeed. There are some things that I enjoy about it and I don't deny its importance. But there is too much fuss, too much worry about it, at least for a mother, trying to make everybody happy, making sure no one is left out. Then you see so much of your work is wasted or not appreciated... food left over... toys cast aside.... Honestly, I'm glad when it's all over.

P: Thank you, Ms Hughes.

Mr McCann

Ms Carey

Mr O'Brien

Sharing

D: I call on Ms Goff to stand as my second witness. What do you think of what Ms Hughes had to say?

Ms Goff: I sympathise with her, but I have to say that in our family it's not like that at all. I agree that there is a lot of extra work to be done but we share it out. This sharing helps to unite us. The children do most of the cleaning and decorating. My husband and I do the shopping. We try not to leave it until the last minute. I do the cooking, but when it comes to the washing up, I'm not allowed touch a thing! Then we sit down and enjoy the TV shows.

D: You don't find that these TV programmes spoil the spirit of Christmas?

Ms Goff: Not at all. They are generally very entertaining.

D: As a family do you do anything special for Christmas?

Ms Goff: We invite an old man who lives down the road for Christmas dinner. It gives our children a chance to share.

D: Do you enjoy Christmas?

Ms Goff: I do. Maybe we are lucky. But I don't think we are exceptional. I see the same thing happening in families around us.

D: How about the spiritual side of Christmas?

Ms Goff

Ms Goff: We try not to neglect it as we consider it very important. We all go to Confession and Communion. At the centre of the home is a crib, built by the children. Here, we gather each evening for some family prayer.

D: Thank you, Ms Goff. That will be all.

Peace and Goodwill

P: Now for my third and final witness. Would Ms Carey please take the stand? (*She does so.*)

Please introduce yourself.

Ms Carey: I'm a seventeen-year-old student. There are nine of us in the family, including my parents and granny.

P: Tell us what you think of Christmas?

Ms Carey: Christmas is supposed to be a family feast. But in our home everybody is so busy that we hardly have time to talk to one another. Either that or we are all glued to the TV. Christmas is also supposed to be a time of peace and goodwill. But as far as I can see it doesn't always turn out like that.

It's true that on Christmas morning people go out of their way to salute one another. But the goodwill doesn't survive the day.

We send cards to our friends but never to our enemies. For instance, in our family there is an uncle who never gets a card because of some row that happened ten years or more ago. In my short experience I've never seen Christmas help people make it up if they have fallen out during the year. In fact, if anything, the opposite is true. The door is more firmly shut at Christmas against the unwanted than at any other time of the year. We don't want them to spoil our Christmas!

P: Would you see your family as

fairly typical in that respect?

Ms Carey: Yes, I would. From listening to my friends, it seems to be the same all over.

P: Thank you, Ms Carey. Your witness, Ms Breen.

D: No questions, your Honour.

A Prodigal Returns

D: Mr Deans, please take the stand. (*He does so.*) I understand that last Christmas was a very special one for you. Would you like to tell the court about it?

Mr Deans: Gladly. Like many people in this country I was brought up a Catholic. But in my twenties I drifted away from the Church and for the last fifteen years I had given up the practice of my religion.

D: And then?

Mr Deans: Well, last Christmas Eve I was passing a church when suddenly I felt the urge to go inside. I did so and before I knew it I was queueing for Confession. I made my peace with God and had the happiest Christmas of my life.

D: Do you think your conversion had anything to do with the fact that it was Christmas Eve?

Mr Deans: I'm certain that it had a lot to do with it. In fact, I'm quite sure that had it not been Christmas Eve it would not have happened.

D: Would you say that there are others who have similar experiences at Christmas?

Mr Deans: I'm certain there are. I think if you were to speak to any priest you would find that many prodigals like me return home at this time. There is an enormous spiritual attraction about Christmas. In my view it would be a tragedy to do away with it.

D: Thank you, Mr Deans. You can step down now.

J: We've heard the witnesses. I would now like Mr O' Sullivan to sum up the case against Christmas.

P: Christmas has become a big spending spree for those who can afford it. It encourages excessive eating and drinking in grown-ups as well as selfishness in children. More people are killed on our roads at this time than at any other. Christmas raises the hopes of the lonely and the depressed but never fulfils them.

It does not break down any barriers because we only share our goodwill with our friends. Enemies are never guests at the Christmas banquet. As for the religious meaning, I am convinced that it does a disservice to our religion. Instead of preparing a way for the Lord, as the Gospel urges us, we prepare a way for the commercial vultures. We should not use the excuse of Christ's birth to be selfish, to waste money, or to over-eat. It turns my stomach to see a crib in the local supermarket. This is a Christian country. Christmas should reflect our Christianity. Christmas should be abolished. It is beyond redemption. Christ hardly gets a look-in. The headlines are dominated not by his birth but by the price of turkeys!

Yes, to celebrate Christmas without Christ is like celebrating a wedding without the bride and groom.

J: I call on Ms Breen to sum up her case for saving Christmas.

D: When all is said and done, Christmas still recalls the greatest event of all time — the Incarnation.

Jesus is Immanuel — God with us.

Even if there is loneliness, let us not forget that at the first Christmas there was no room in the inn for Christ himself. People go out of their way to be friendly to one another. There is an outpouring of goodwill. Friends we have forgotten during the year are thought of. Bonds are strengthened. Scattered families are reunited. Nor are the poor left out in the cold. More is done for them at Christmas than during the rest of the year. The Scrooge, the miser in us all is put to flight.

I admit that there are some excesses in eating and drinking. Still, Christmas is a time for joy and it is right that people should celebrate. And I don't for a moment agree that it is without religious meaning. The churches are overflowing. Many return to God at this time. I know that the commercial vultures are very active but this commercialism can be a challenge to us Christians.

There will always be those people, no matter what circumstances exist, who will try and make a quick profit, and in a lot of cases this is what happens during the Christmas season.

Christmas offers us the opportunity to shine with the light of Christ and to set an example for others to follow. It is for these reasons that I think our celebration of Christmas should be saved.

J: The court will recess and the jury must now decide whether or not our Christmas celebration should be abolished.

Choose one of the following reasons why you celebrate your birthday:

(a) you'll get lots of presents;

(b) you're going to have a party with all your friends;

(c) because twelve/ thirteen years ago you were born;

(d) you're another year older and you'll soon be considered an adult.

Find Your Group
Discuss

Each person is to think of *one* reason why we celebrate the birth of Jesus.
Use these reasons to illustrate a poster or banner entitled:
We celebrate the birth of Jesus because...

In Your Religion Journal

You are spokesperson for the jury. Now that you have heard all the evidence **for** and **against** Christmas, write your verdict, giving reasons for the decision you make!

Here is the story of the birth and childhood of Jesus according to the Gospel of St Luke. You will notice that each scene is one of the joyful mysteries of the rosary. The story begins when the birth of Jesus is announced to Mary.
Read and act out the following.

Characters:

God; Angel Gabriel; Narrator; Mary; Elizabeth; Innkeeper; Shepherds; Simeon; Jesus.

Scene One

The Birth of Jesus is Announced

God: I think it's time, Gabriel, that I sent you to tell Mary the Good News.

Gabriel: Yes, I know Mary, she's going to marry Joseph next year. Well, when do you want me to go and tell her the news ?

God: You can go tomorrow, you'll find her in Galilee in a town called Nazareth.

At Mary's Home

Gabriel: Greetings, Mary, don't be afraid, I have come to tell you some Good News. You are the person whom God has highly favoured. You have been chosen to be the mother of Jesus, the Son of God.

Mary: But how can this happen? I am not yet married to Joseph.

Gabriel: God has blessed you, and the power of the Holy Spirit will come upon you. You will become pregnant and give birth to a son and you will call him Jesus.

Everything is possible to God, for even your cousin Elizabeth who is very old is already six months pregnant.

Mary: I am afraid of what you are telling me, Gabriel, but I will put my trust in God so let what you have said be done to me.

Scene Two

Mary Visits Elizabeth

Narrator: Shortly after Gabriel left, Mary got ready and hurried off over the hill-country to visit her cousin Elizabeth. She knew that Elizabeth would need some help around the house and in preparing for her baby to arrive. Because of her great faith, Mary believed the things that Gabriel had said to her. When Mary arrived in the small village, she went directly to Elizabeth's house. Elizabeth's husband Zechariah opened the door to Mary.

He was unable to speak to her and had to make signs with his hands. Zechariah had been told by the angel Gabriel that Elizabeth would have a son, but because he didn't believe that this promise would come true, since both he and Elizabeth were quite old, he was told that he would be unable to speak until the birth of the baby. Using sign language, Zechariah welcomed Mary into the house and asked her how she was and he also asked about Joseph.

Mary: Joseph is very well, Zechariah, he is very busy these days in the carpenter shop. Is Elizabeth about ? I heard the great news, I'm sure you are both delighted.

Elizabeth enters the house.

Mary: Congratulations, Elizabeth, you're looking very well. I have come to stay with you for a while.

Narrator: When Elizabeth heard Mary's greeting, she could feel her baby move within her and she began to welcome Mary by saying:

Elizabeth: Of all women you have been specially blessed and blessed is the child which you bear. This is a great honour having you come to visit me, now that you have been chosen to be the mother of Jesus.

Narrator: Mary was delighted to see Elizabeth and she began to say:

Mary: My soul glorifies the Lord,
My spirit rejoices in God, my Saviour.
He looks on his servant in her lowliness;
Henceforth all ages will call me blessed.
The Almighty works marvels for me.
Holy his name!
His mercy is from age to age,
On those who fear him.
He puts forth his arm in strength
And scatters the proud-hearted.
He casts the mighty from their thrones
And raises the lowly.
He fills the starving with good things,
Sends the rich away empty.
He protects Israel, his servant,

Remembering his mercy,
The mercy promised to our fathers,
To Abraham and his sons for ever.

Elizabeth: I'm so pleased, Mary, that you can stay with me for the next three months.

Scene Three

The Birth of Jesus

Narrator: After three months, Mary returned home to Nazareth. Both her mother and Joseph had missed her while she was staying with Elizabeth, but they were delighted to hear that Elizabeth had given birth to a boy called John. It was a short time after Mary had returned home that the Emperor Augustus decided to take a census of the people throughout the Roman Empire. This meant that everyone had to go and register in their own home town.

Joseph: I know it is going to be a long journey for you, Mary, but we will have to go down to Bethlehem in Judaea to register for the census. I will borrow my friend's donkey and this will at least help to make the journey more comfortable for you.

Mary: Don't worry about me Joseph, I am only worried about the child I am carrying. When we arrive in Bethlehem it will soon be time for me to have the baby, but I have put

112

my trust in the Lord and so everything will work out the way he wants it.

Narrator: It was late when Mary and Joseph arrived in Bethlehem. Joseph went around Bethlehem looking for somewhere to stay. He came to an inn.

Joseph: Would you have a room, even for one night? My wife is going to have a baby and we have nowhere to stay.

Innkeeper: The town is packed with people from all over the country; it's the census. I have no room and I don't believe you'll get a room anywhere in the town.

Narrator: The Innkeeper's wife had noticed Mary and realised she would soon have her baby so she showed them to a barn at the back of the inn.

Mary gave birth to her baby. She called him Jesus. She wrapped him in strips of cloth and laid him in a manger.

That same night there were some shepherds who were spending the night in a field nearby, taking care of their sheep.

An angel appeared to them saying:

Angel: Don't be afraid, I am here with Good News.

Tonight in Bethlehem a baby was born, he is your Saviour, Christ the Lord! You will find him wrapped in strips of cloth and lying in a manger.

Shepherd 1: I wonder why we were told that Christ has been born, after all we are only shepherds.

Shepherd 2: Maybe because we have always put our trust in God. Come on, we must go to Bethlehem and visit the baby.

Narrator: Mary and Joseph were delighted to see the shepherds, for having no close family nearby they wanted to show their child to someone. When the shepherds saw the baby they told Mary what the angel had told them,

that he was Christ the Saviour. The shepherds began to sing and praise God for all they had seen and heard.

Scene Four

Presentation of Our Lord in the Temple

Narrator: It was time for Mary and Joseph to take Jesus to the Temple in Jerusalem for the ceremony of purification. It was the custom that every first-born male child was dedicated to God in the Temple.

Joseph: I am just going out to the market to buy a pair of doves and two young pigeons, to offer as a sacrifice in the Temple.

Mary: Try not to be too long, Joseph, we have to be at the Temple by this afternoon.

Narrator: A man by the name of Simeon who was living in Jerusalem had been waiting for many years to see the promised Messiah.

When Mary and Joseph arrived at the Temple, Simeon was waiting for them. He took the child in his arms and said:

Simeon: Now, Lord, you have kept your promise, with my own eyes I have seen my Saviour. This child will decide the fates of many in Israel. He will be accepted by some people and rejected by others.

Narrator: And Simeon turned to Mary and said:

Simeon: Your heart will be broken by great sorrow.

Scene Five

Finding in the Temple

Narrator: When Mary and Joseph had finished all that they had to do in Jerusalem, they returned home to Nazareth.

Each year, however, they would return to Jerusalem for the Passover festival.

When Jesus was twelve years old , they went to the festival as usual. It lasted for about a week. When the festival was over they would start back for Nazareth. Usually the women and men would walk in separate groups, so that it wasn't until the first night of their journey that Mary and Joseph met each other again.

Joseph: How are you finding the journey, Mary? Only another couple of days and we'll be home.

Mary: Yes, every year the journey does seem to get shorter. I hope you are looking after Jesus all right.

Joseph: But I haven't seen Jesus since we left Jerusalem. I thought he was travelling with you.

Mary: And I thought he was travelling with you; so where could he be?

Joseph: I'll ask some of my friends, maybe they've seen him.

Mary: I'll ask some of the other women from Nazareth if they've seen him.

Narrator: After a night of searching Mary and Joseph decided to go back to Jerusalem to look for Jesus. It took them three days before they found him, sitting in the Temple with some of the Jewish teachers, listening to them and asking them questions. The teachers were amazed at his intelligent answers.

Mary and Joseph were both very relieved to have found him.

Mary: Why have you done this, Jesus? Joseph and I have been terribly worried trying to find you.

Jesus: Why did you have to look for me ? Didn't you know I had to be in my Father's house ?

Narrator: But Mary and Joseph did not understand fully what Jesus meant by his answer.

Jesus returned with Mary and Joseph to Nazareth, and lived there until he was thirty.

Read this story from the Bible.

You will find it in Luke 1:26-2:52.

While reading through the account of Jesus' birth and child-hood in Luke's gospel, we notice the very important part played by Mary.

At the Annunciation scene we see how completely God's plan depended on Mary co-operating and saying '*Yes*' when she was asked to be the mother of Jesus. By listening to God and by answering '*Amen*', so be it, Mary freely chose to allow God's plan to be fulfilled in her.

Mary probably had made plans for her own life, to live quietly in a town called Nazareth and marry the local carpenter, Joseph. God's plans probably took her by surprise. She probably thought that she was not worthy to be the mother of Jesus, she probably wondered if she could cope, and asked herself why she was chosen. But Mary was a woman of great faith and humility. She was not sure what to expect, she was afraid and a little worried but she put her trust in God. This was a great challenge for Mary, but through putting her trust in God, Mary found the strength to cope with what was ahead of her.

The prophets had been telling about the promised Messiah. People had waited for generations and looked forward to His coming. Now when it happened it seemed as if God's becoming man and being born of a woman was ordinary. He came as a child born into the poorest circumstances; a child whose mother and foster father could not even find somewhere to stay for the night; a child who was welcomed into the world by a group of shepherds.

But Jesus was no ordinary child.

Mary cared for and nurtured him, she watched him grow and eventually she watched him suffer and die for all people. He was not only a human child, he was also truly God; when we say the 'Hail Mary' we call Mary the 'Mother of God'.

The arrival of a first born baby is an exciting time. The genuine joy and expressions of love from everyone around the couple make the occasion extra special. A young couple look forward to showing their new baby to family and friends, and to telling everyone their good news.

In Bethlehem Mary and Joseph had no close family or friends nearby. They showed Jesus, first to the shepherds and then to the Kings or Magi.

We celebrate the occasion when Mary and Joseph *showed* the baby to the Magi, on the 6th of January. It is called the feast of the Epiphany which means 'showing or revealing'.

This is a significant feast because it was the showing of the infant Jesus to the non-Jewish kings. Traditionally one of the kings is shown as European, one as Asian and one as African emphasising that Jesus came to all people, not just to the Jews.

Since very early times tradition has had it that there were three visitors to the infant Jesus. This probably arose because three gifts were brought. They were usually thought of as kings, possibly because of Psalm 72:10 which says:

'The kings of Spain and of the islands will offer him gifts; the kings of Sheba and Seba will bring offerings ....'

At some time in the past they were given the names of Caspar, Melchior and Baltassar.

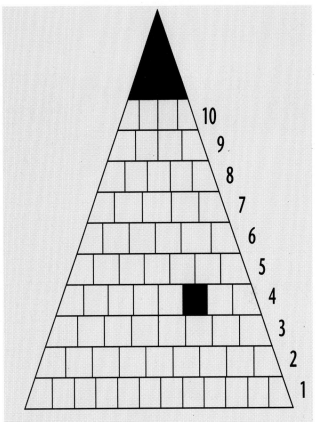

Using the clues complete the

Pyramid

1. Type of incense brought as a gift.
2. They got there before the kings.
3. Name given to this feast of the three kings.
4. Which psalm are the kings mentioned in?
5. Meaning of the word Epiphany.
6. Name of one of the kings.
7. A type of perfume offered as a gift.
8. The day in January when we celebrate this feast.
9. Another name for the kings.
10. This guided the kings to Bethlehem.

Test yourself.

Do the Looking Back exercises on page 226.

Lesson Fifteen

We Are All Different

There are many factors which make people individuals and different from one another, nationality, colour, age, sex, language, religion and so on. In the following activities we will explore some of these differences. Copy and fill in the charts below in your religion journal.

Personal Profile

Surname

Christian Names

Address

Date of Birth

Nationality

Colour of Eyes

Colour of Hair

Height

Shoe Size

These are further details which make you different from other students in your class.

Preferences

Favourite Group

Favourite Food

Favourite Colour

Favourite TV Programme

Favourite Sport

Favourite School Subject

Person I Most Admire

Find Your Group
Discuss

Share these details about yourself with the group. Listen to others in your group.
What do you notice about each person's list?
Can you think of any reasons why each person's list is different?

In Your Religion Journal

Imagine that you could become the kind of person you would ideally like to be. Write about this.

Jesus showed us how to accept and respect everyone with all their individual differences. He accepted and respected people when nobody else showed respect towards them.

At the beginning of his ministry he proclaimed that he had come to bring the Good News to everyone:

The Spirit of the Lord is upon me,

because he has chosen me to bring

good news to the poor.

He has sent me to proclaim liberty to the captives

and recovery of sight to the blind;

to set free the oppressed

and announce that the time has come when

the Lord will save his people (Lk 4:18-19).

Discuss

Which group of people referred to in the passage might not have been accepted and respected by people in Jesus' time ?
Are there situations in the world today where there are similar groups of people who are not respected?

Jesus always looked for the good in other people. He encouraged his followers to use their own gifts and talents to the best of their ability.

He appreciated each person as an individual.

Jesus cared for and showed respect for everyone in society. He welcomed the outcasts – those who had been crippled by illness, women and Gentiles. He judged no one from hearsay or by the class they belonged to. He did not dismiss anyone because they had a different religious outlook. He was free from prejudice. He openly welcomed everyone.

He was ready to listen to other people's point of view. At the same time Jesus Christ made it clear that truth was very important. He didn't pretend that any one belief was as good as any other. He wasn't afraid to disagree with other people's attitudes and opinions or in some cases to oppose what others said or did. Jesus Christ had come to proclaim the truth and it is that truth which he told his Church to proclaim.

So, for example, he disagreed with those who denied that there would be a resurrection of the dead. He opposed the idea of divorce and he was often shown as opposing and criticising some of the religious ideas and teachings common at that time. Jesus Christ always respected people and was free from prejudice against them.

He also respected the truth. He teaches that we must love and respect everyone whatever our differences but that we must also remain faithful to the truth he has given us. While some points of division involve remaining faithful to the truth, even when others disagree, many are due to misunderstanding, prejudice or fear.

Scripture Research

Read the following extracts from Luke's gospel. What do they tell us about the attitudes Jesus had towards others who differed from him in some way ?
5:27-31
6:27-36
7:1-10
7:36-50
11:37-46

Discuss

Have you ever tried to change someone because they were different from you?

Read the following story.

The Red Rose Clan

I grew up in a lovely garden in the company of thousands of other roses, all of which were red like myself. The garden was surrounded by a high wall. Thanks to this wall I lived a very sheltered life. When I was little I got many a lecture from older roses. I was left in no doubt that it was a very big privilege to have been born into the Red Rose Clan. It was made equally clear to me that very high standards were expected from a red rose. It will come as no surprise then when I tell you that my life was very strict. I had to obey a lot of rules. I can still recall some of them: keep your stem upright; keep your head modestly cast down at all times; never forget what you are – a red rose.

On no account must you climb over the wall. I was continually being warned to be on my guard against bad example. An elder, wishing to be helpful, would say: 'All the roses in this garden are red. But don't be deceived by this. Sadly, there are some roses that are not the same as our clan and who don't belong. Rosaleen, you must avoid them, for they will attempt to lead you astray with their strange ideas.'

Though my life was strict, I was not unhappy. In fact, things went pretty smoothly for me until I reached the half-way stage in my growing. Then, something happened to me which suddenly robbed me of my peace of mind. I was bitten by a very strange bug — the bug of curiosity. All at once I realised that there were so many things in my life that I didn't understand. Why for instance, were we all the same colour? Why was our life so sheltered? What lay on the other side of the wall?

As I tossed these questions around in my mind a wild idea came to me. I looked up at the top of the wall and I said, 'I wonder, if I stretched myself, could I reach the top? If I could, then maybe I might take a quick peep over. Just a peep!'

Up I crept, inch by inch. It was difficult, yet marvellously exciting. By stretching myself to the very limit I just managed to reach the top. I hesitated for a moment and then I saw what appeared to me to be lots of other roses, like myself in every aspect but colour! Even though I cast only the briefest of glances at them, I noticed that some of them were pink, some white and some even yellow.

'How can this be?' I asked myself. 'Have I not been taught that there is only one kind of rose – a red rose?'

After much hesitation I finally decided to confide in one of the elders. It happened that this particular elder was very close to me and had sheltered me from many a storm.

'Please could you tell me,' I began hesitatingly, 'but those flowers on the other side of the wall...are they really what they seem to be...are they really roses?'

'How did you find out about them?' he asked

sternly. 'I...I saw them myself', I said. 'You know you shouldn't have done this', he replied. 'I'm disappointed in you. You, Rosaleen, above all. We had such high hopes for you. Let me give you a bit of advice for the future. Forget those flowers you saw on the other side of the wall. They don't belong to our clan. The only true rose is a red rose. Do you understand that?' 'Yes', I answered timidly.

Not long after this a new Chief Elder was appointed. It was summer when he took office and the weather was stifling. At first we didn't know what to expect from him. Then one day the Chief Elder did something very surprising. He abolished some of our long-cherished rules. We began to realise that many of the rules which we had observed so carefully had served only one purpose – to protect us from the 'hostile' world beyond the wall. The Chief Elder seemed to be suggesting that we had nothing to fear from that world. That, in fact, we had much to learn from it.

One day I caught a glimpse of two faces peering at me from over the wall. Without thinking twice, I threw caution to the winds and climbed the wall. I saw that one of them was white and the other pink. 'Hello,' I said in a friendly voice.

'Hello,' came the reply in an equally friendly voice.

'My name is Rosaleen,' I said. 'That's funny,' the white one answered, 'because my name is Roseanne and this is Pinky,' nodding to her companion. There was a pause, for we were a bit tense.

'Lovely day, isn't it?' I ventured next. 'Yes, indeed, though I think we could do with a little rain,' answered Pinky.

'Yes, I suppose we could. It hasn't rained in ages,' I said.

'Have you noticed those lovely cool breezes that have been around of late?' Roseanne asked, 'Indeed I have,' I said. 'In fact they have brought new life to our garden. I thought we were going to suffocate until they came along.' 'Strange that you should say that,' Pinky remarked, 'because Roseanne and I had been saying exactly the same thing.'

We continued to chat for some time more. At the end of our conversation Roseanne said, 'We must meet again.' 'Yes, we must,' I agreed.

For my part, I was truly amazed when I discovered that they knew as little about us as we did about them. Gradually the tension and the fear that had existed between us evaporated, and this made our meetings all the more enjoyable and fruitful.

Slowly a great transformation took place. After having come to acknowledge one another's existence, we gradually came to accept our differences. We learned to see ourselves as members of one great family – the Rose Family– a family of enormous variety and beauty.

The wall still stands between us. It may be that we still need it to protect us from the winter weather. However, we have grown up and have learned to communicate with one another in spite of it.

That is my story. But, as you can see, it is not just my story. In a sense it is the story of the entire Rose Family. All of us roses, red and white, pink and yellow, are better and richer since we discovered one another.

In Your Religion Journal

Imagine you were Rosaleen and had climbed to the top of the wall. How did you feel when you looked over and saw all the other roses just like yourself?

Why do you think there was tension and fear between the two sides of the wall?

Why was Rosaleen a bit tense when she first met with Roseanne and Pinky?

What helped to make their meetings more enjoyable?

Can you think of a time when you ignored someone just because you thought they were different from you? Describe the incident.

Communication helped Rosaleen and her friends to see themselves as members of one great family – the Rose Family.

What can the Christian family learn from this story?

Activity

Make up a cartoon strip which illustrates a story of two people who are suspicious of each other. They misunderstand each other's point of view. They finally become friends.

Differences among the Christian Churches

Jesus Christ founded only one Church, which he entrusted to his apostles, under the leadership of Peter. He wanted all his followers to remain united in this one Church. The Church established by Jesus with the apostles is to be found in the Roman Catholic Church, that Church has preserved the full truth which Jesus has entrusted to us.

Through the ages divisions have arisen among Christians, and from time to time groups have broken away to form separate Churches. This is a great tragedy and usually there were faults on both sides.

The Catholic Church does not pretend that it is perfect. It knows that sometimes its members live lives that do not follow the example of Jesus, and it freely accepts that very many Christians outside it lead good and holy lives. It teaches that other Christian denominations are closely related to it in many ways, and that God uses them in his work of salvation. Above all, it teaches that all Christians are united by the common bond of Baptism, and are all, therefore, children of God.

In the past there have often been bad relations between Catholics and other Christians, and this has been the result of faults on both sides. Today there are determined efforts to understand each other better, to get rid of prejudices, to co-operate with each other and to live in friendship and mutual respect. The leaders of the Catholic Church have urged all its members to play their part in working for the unity of all Christians.

Divisions among Christians

There have been two major schisms in the course of Christian history. The first happened in 1054. The Eastern and Western communities of the Church had been drifting apart for many years, partly because of political divisions and rivalries which had come about after the fall of the Roman Empire in the West. Most of the Eastern part of the Church split away from Rome under the

leadership of its most important bishop, the Patriarch of Constantinople. It became what is now known as the **Eastern Orthodox Church** with its headquarters in Constantinople.

The second schism, which took place in the sixteenth century, is known as the **Protestant Reformation**. Its first leader was Martin Luther, an Augustinian friar who at first set out to correct what he saw as abuses in the Church, and there were many abuses which needed correction.

There are many things that Catholics can admire about Martin Luther. He was courageous in protesting against many wrong practices in the Church of his day and against the lack of action by the clergy to correct the widespread religious ignorance and superstition found among ordinary people. He rightly stressed the importance of Christians having faithful trust in God and the uselessness of human efforts without God's grace. He did a great service by pointing out the importance of the Bible as the Word of God and by his concern to ensure that ordinary people should be able to read it and get to know it. All of these were things which needed to be said, and not one of them was opposed to the Catholic faith.

Conflict with the Church

On a number of points, however, Luther did propose doctrines which contradicted long-established Catholic teaching, and it was this which brought him into conflict with the Church. We cannot mention them all here, but on the following page there are a few important examples.

Apart from Luther, other Protestant leaders emerged, such as Zwingli and John Calvin.

These and others produced teachings which differed in some respect from those of Luther. Because these early reformers placed a great emphasis on private interpretation of the Bible, the Protestant Reformation led to the formation of many different groups, each with its own interpretation on certain issues. It is because of this that there is such a variety of Protestant Churches.

The Road to Unity

The split was not simply religious. It suited political rulers to have no connection with Rome, because it gave them greater control over the Church in their territories. There has been bitterness between the Catholic and Protestant Churches for centuries. It was a matter of 'them and us'.

Now, however, with the Ecumenical movement, there is a new search for unity among Christian Churches. The road to unity is a long, long road. It means we must begin to leave behind years of ignorance, suspicion, prejudice and fear. Dialogue, sincere talking and listening will begin to build bridges.

In Your Religion Journal

How many Christian Churches can you list?
How many of these Churches are in your area?
Do you know people from other Churches?
How could the statement, 'We will agree to differ', help the Christian Churches come closer together on the road to unity ?

Catholic Church's Teaching	Martin Luther's Teaching
The Catholic Church teaches that each person is free to accept or reject God's gift of Grace (which includes Faith, Hope and Love) by which we are reconciled with God and brought to heaven.	Luther agreed that carrying out good works and living a good life was desirable. But he denied that carrying out good works or living a good life helped people to achieve eternal salvation. He taught that people were saved by having faith alone. According to Luther, faith in God was all that mattered.
The Catholic Church teaches that it is not faith alone which enables us to please God and reach the happiness of heaven. We need a faith which is made living and active by God's gift of love, a faith which, with God's help, is expressed through living a good life and carrying out good works.	Luther himself (though not all his followers) taught that people were not free to accept or reject God's gift of faith but rather God decided who to grant this gift of grace to, and who was denied it. According to Luther this means that people go to Hell not because they reject God's grace but because he has chosen not to grant it to them.
The Catholic Church considered that Luther had gone too far by attempting to deny human freedom. The Catholic view is that God's power is above all shown in his ability to achieve his purposes by working through human freedom rather than suppressing it.	Luther was very concerned to stress God's absolute power and to point out how people are utterly dependent on him. By doing so, Luther was denying that God has given us the freedom to accept or reject his gift of faith.
The Catholic Church teaches that the Bible is the Word of God, entrusted to the Church which is guided by the Holy Spirit. In the Church the Pope and bishops, as successors of the apostles, have a special God-given authority to interpret its message and to make binding decisions on matters of faith.	Luther asserted that the Bible itself was the only source of Christian teaching. He denied that the Pope and bishops had any special teaching authority.
The Catholic Church teaches that there are seven sacraments.	Luther accepted only three of the seven sacraments: Baptism, Eucharist and Reconciliation, but even here he denied much of the traditional teaching concerning them. For example, he denied that the Eucharist was in any way a sharing in Christ's sacrifice.
The Catholic Church teaches that human beings share in Christ's resurrection so that there is 'no longer male nor female, slave nor free' but that all are renewed in Christ.	Luther taught that human nature is damned because of original sin and that forgiveness is possible only when Christ stands between God and the person who is seeking forgiveness.

The following letter is from a student at St Patrick's Post-Primary school. She is doing a project on Christian Unity, and has written to members of the Church of Ireland, Presbyterian and Methodist Churches, to find out what it means to be a member of each of their communities.

Activity

Read the following three replies from members of the Churches Kathy wrote to for information for her project.

St Patrick's Post-Primary
Slaters Hill

Hi,

This week at school our RE teacher has asked us to do a project on Christian Unity. I thought you would be able to answer some of my questions about your Church.

Do you read the Gospel?
Is it important in your Church?

Who originally founded your Church?

Who is the Leader of your Church?

Do you have other ministers?

How many sacraments does your Church celebrate?

At what age are members of your Church confirmed?

Could you describe your Sunday Service ?

I would like to know what it means to you to be a member of your Church.

Thanks for all your help.

Best Wishes,

Kathy

Dear Kathy,

Thanks for your letter. I am happy to answer your questions on the Methodist Church.

Reading the Gospel is a very important part of our faith. Indeed within the Methodist Church, the Bible holds a unique and special authority for its members. We rely exclusively on the Bible to guide us in our daily lives, and we look to the Bible as our rule of faith.

Under the leadership and inspiration of John Wesley in the eighteenth century, Methodism began as a new way of preaching and proclaiming the Christian message within the Church of England. However, soon after Wesley's death in 1791, Methodism broke away from the Church of England to form a new Church called the **Methodist Church**.

The chief representative or the Leader of my Church is the **President**, who is elected every year at a conference. Within each church parish or **Society** as we call it there are two types of ministers. **Ordained** ministers preach, administer the sacraments and guide the people in their faith, whereas the **local** ministers are trained to conduct worship and preach, but they cannot administer the sacraments.

We celebrate two sacraments – Baptism and Holy Communion. However, unlike the Catholic Church we do not recognise that the Eucharist is actually Jesus Christ's Body and Blood, only that Christ is present in a special way in the bread and wine.

There is no fixed age for members of our Church to be confirmed. It is a matter of choice. Those who have chosen to have their baptismal vows 'confirmed' are called **full members** and they make a serious commitment to lead a Christian life and accept the duties of membership of the Methodist Church. **Adherents** are those who have chosen not to be confirmed. They are welcome to take part in the Sunday Service, but they are not prepared to make a full commitment to the Methodist Church.

Unlike the Mass, our Sunday Service is free in form – that means it does not have a fixed pattern of liturgy every week. The form of the service depends upon the particular preacher. He can choose the prayers, hymns, scripture readings and the theme for the sermon. The focus of the service is on the sermon, which can last up to twenty minutes.

Hymn singing is a very big element in Methodist worship.

We receive the Eucharist once a month, remembering the passion and death of Jesus Christ.

As a Methodist I believe it is important to form a deep personal relationship with Jesus Christ. As a Christian I try my best to follow Jesus in my life. It is a lifelong commitment to the Christian way of living.

I use my gifts and talents to serve God in a number of ways, through caring for other people and being a living witness to the gospel.

I hope this is of some help to you.

Good Luck!

Dear Kathy,

It was great to hear from you. I am always pleased to talk to people about what it means to be a member of the Presbyterian Church.

As a Presbyterian, the Gospel is central to my faith and worship. We believe that the Bible is the Word of God. We believe that Scripture is the sole authority in guiding our faith and it is for this reason that Presbyterian worship is based on listening to the Word of God in Scripture.

The Presbyterian Church separated from the Anglican Church in the sixteenth century under the influence of John Calvin and his disciple John Knox. It is for this reason that it is called a Reformed Church. In England it is called the **United Reformed Church.**

Unlike the Catholic Church there is not one individual who is Leader of the Church, but rather the Church is governed by a group of **elders** and ministers. There are two types of elders: **ruling** elders, who guide people in the faith; while **teaching** elders or **ministers** administer the sacraments and teach the Word of God. Unlike the Catholic Church we do not ordain bishops.

. We celebrate only two sacraments – Baptism and the Eucharist. Baptism is usually administered to children, but we do not believe that Baptism makes the child a Christian, but rather the child must respond in faith before he/she can really be a Christian.

Presbyterian Sunday worship is simple and direct. We congregate in a church, which we call a **Kirk**. We listen to the Word of God from the Bible and the preacher's words of encouragement. Like the Methodist Church the sermon can be quite long since this is the focus of the Service.

We receive Holy Communion less frequently than members of the Catholic Church. In some Presbyterian churches the Eucharist will only be celebrated twice a year. We do not consider the Eucharist as a sacrifice, nor do we consider that the bread and wine become Jesus himself, but we believe that when we receive the Eucharist, we are spiritually nourished by a power which comes from Christ.

To me, being a Presbyterian means making a personal commitment to my faith. I follow the teachings of Jesus Christ in my life, and by following Jesus as best I can, I get to know my Saviour and serve him through daily prayer and bible readings and through caring for and forgiving others.

See You Soon,

Dear Kathy,

This is a great opportunity for you to find out about other Christian Churches, since during this week 18th-25th January, the Churches will celebrate Christian Unity Week.

Perhaps it would be most helpful if I tried to tell you about the Anglican Communion, which includes the Church of England, as well as the Church of Ireland of which I am a member. As a member of the Anglican Communion I have a great respect for the Bible. I believe it is the Word of God and that it teaches me all that I need to grow in a loving relationship with Jesus in order to be saved.

The **Anglican Communion** was established after the Reformation but it has retained a number of features which Catholics will recognise as very familiar. For instance, the Anglican Communion also has bishops. Many people consider it to be a kind of half-way house between Roman Catholicism and the original Churches of the Reformation. Within the Anglican Communion you will find many shades of opinion on matters of doctrine and practice. Some, often called **Evangelicals**, or **'Low Church'**, place a strong emphasis on Scriptures and preaching. Their services are relatively simple and they avoid the use of such things as vestments. Others, sometimes called **Anglo-Catholics** or **'High Church'**, are much closer in their beliefs and practices to the Roman Catholic Church. They put a great emphasis on the celebration of the Eucharist, wear vestments, use incense and have statues in their churches. The Church of Ireland is a member of this reformed family of churches.

Although the Anglican Communion generally and the Church of Ireland in particular accept the ancient teachings of the Christian Church expressed in the Nicene creed, we also accept the changes made at the time of the Reformation; such as the statement that the Old Testament and the New Testament contain all that is necessary to be saved.

Both the Church of Ireland and the Church of England are governed by their own **General Synods** (comprising bishops, clergy and lay people). In Ireland the Arch-Bishop of Armagh is Head of the Synod, but before passing any laws concerning the Church he must consult the other members of the Synod. In England this is done by the Archbishop of Canterbury.

The Church of Ireland, like the Church of England, ordains bishops, priests and deacons. In Ireland both men and women can become deacons and priests.

In both countries men only can be ordained bishops. The parish clergy are called rectors in Ireland. In England they are sometimes called rectors, but more often vicars.

The Church celebrates two sacraments – Baptism and Holy Communion. But it also recognises that Confirmation, Ordination, Holy Matrimony, Ministry of Absolution and Ministry of Healing are ways of obtaining grace and are known as **Sacramental Ministries of Grace.**

The usual age for candidates to be confirmed is fourteen years. Candidates choose themselves whether to go forward and confirm their promises made at Baptism. Candidates who are confirmed by the 'laying on of hands' by the bishop are then free to receive Holy Communion for the first time.

The form of Sunday Service is quite similar to that of the Catholic Mass. We have a structured liturgy, that means we have the **Ministry of the Word** and the **Ministry of the Sacrament.** The Holy Communion service is celebrated on the first and third Sunday of every month and members of the Church who are confirmed are expected to receive Holy Communion at least once a month. In England the practice varies greatly. In many parishes Holy Communion is celebrated every Sunday, and in some High Church parishes, it is actually called Holy Mass.

Being a member of the Church of Ireland helps me to follow the teachings of Jesus from Scripture. It gives me a set of values and allows me to express my faith with others who share the same beliefs. The Church helps me become involved in and create a community spirit.

All the best with your project!

Find Your Group

Discuss

Now you have looked at three other Christian Churches.

What similarities are there between the Churches?

What are the main differences between the Churches?

What can we learn from the other Christian Churches?

Can you name any other Christian Churches which we have not already mentioned ? Tell the class what you know about other Christian Churches.

Someone has written a letter to you asking for information on the Catholic Church. Write a letter in reply answering the following questions.

Dear Student,

I have been asked to do a project on Christian Unity, and I wonder if you could help me answer some questions on your Church.

Do you read the Gospel ?

Is it important in your Church ?

Who originally founded the Catholic Church?

Who is the Leader of your Church?

How many sacraments does the Catholic Church celebrate?

At what age are members of your Church confirmed?

What form does your Sunday Service take?

What does it mean to you to be a Catholic?

In working for unity we should:

– Avoid making untrue or prejudiced statements about those who belong to other denominations;

– Co-operate with one another in social works and in work for the Third World;

– Pray together for unity and on occasions of public prayer;

– Take part in reflection on the teachings of the different denominations in order to discover common ground.

Activity Fill in the following chart which will help you to compare the Churches you have studied.

	METHODIST	CHURCH OF IRELAND	PRESBYTERIAN	CATHOLIC
Origin of Church				
Leader of Church				
How many sacraments are celebrated ?				
Age of Confirmation				
Form of Sunday Service				
How often does one receive Holy Communion ?				

Activity

The following words are all connected with the Church of Ireland, Methodist, Presbyterian and Catholic Churches. Find them in the Word Search and write sentences showing that you understand this connection.

Presbyterian; Kirk; Bishop; Priest; Elder; Pope; Church; President; Unity; Sacrament; Sermon; Mass; Service; Methodist; Catholic; Anglican; Synod; Vow; Adherent; Wesley; Knox; Hymn; Rector.

Class Activity
Is it possible to arrange a visit to the church of another Christian community ?
Report back to the class. In what way does it differ from the Catholic Church ?

S	P	X	P	R	I	E	S	T	V	T	C
Y	K	I	R	K	K	M	A	S	S	N	I
P	O	P	E	V	N	B	R	I	Y	E	L
R	B	I	S	H	O	P	E	D	N	R	O
E	R	C	B	W	X	W	C	O	O	E	H
S	E	H	Y	E	Q	E	T	H	D	H	T
I	C	U	T	S	A	C	O	T	M	D	A
D	I	R	E	L	D	E	R	E	F	A	C
E	V	C	R	E	S	E	R	M	O	N	H
N	R	H	I	Y	T	I	N	U	K	T	Y
T	E	S	A	C	R	A	M	E	N	T	M
L	S	O	N	A	C	I	L	G	N	A	N

A Time to Pray

Leader: **Let us Pray for unity:**

among those from different cultures;

among those with different coloured skin;

among those of different faiths;

among all Christian Churches.

Lord, hear the prayers of your people
and bring the hearts of believers together in your praise
and in common sorrow for their sins.
Heal all divisions among Christians
that we may rejoice in the perfect unity of your Church
and move together as one
to eternal life in your kingdom.
Grant this through our Lord Jesus Christ, your Son, who
lives and reigns with you and the holy spirit, one God,
for ever and ever.

Let us listen again to Jesus' own prayer to his Father
for unity among his followers:

'I have made you known to those you gave me out
of the world. They belonged to you, and you gave
them to me. They have obeyed your word, and now
they know that everything you gave me comes
from you. I gave them the message that you gave
me, and they received it; they know that it is true
that I came from you, and they believe that you
sent me. I pray for them. I do not pray for the world
but for those you gave me, for they belong to you.
All I have is yours, and all you have is mine; and my
glory is shown through them. And now I am
coming to you; I am no longer in the world, but
they are in the world. Holy Father! Keep them safe
by the power of your name, the name you gave me,
so that they may be one just as you and I are one.
While I was with them, I kept them safe by the
power of your name, the name you gave me. I
protected them, and not one of them was lost ,
except the man who was bound to be lost – so that
the scripture might come true. And now I am
coming to you and I say these things in the world
so that they might have my joy in their hearts in all
its fullness (*John 17: 6-13*).

Let us Pray:

Leader: The Lord of peace and unity be with you.

All: And also with you.

Leader: My friends, we are part of a divided family. Today we
pray for understanding.

We ask God to open our minds and our hearts.

We ask God to banish our suspicions and prejudices.

Because we have failed in the past to understand our fellow-
Christians in the Protestant communities we ask God for
pardon and peace. *(Pause)*

Leader: For the times we have lived on prejudice,

Lord, have mercy.

All: Lord, have mercy.

Leader: For the times we have lived on suspicion,

Christ, have mercy

All: Christ, have mercy.

Leader: For the times we have been content with our
ignorance,

Lord, have mercy.

All: Lord, have mercy.

Leader: May almighty God have mercy on us, forgive us our
sins and bring us to everlasting life.

All: Amen.

Leader: Let us pray.

Father, increase our understanding,

inspire us to open ourselves to our fellow Christians,

through Christ our Lord.

All: Amen.

Prayer:

1 We pray that all Christian communities may
renew themselves and draw closer to the will of Christ.
Lord, hear us.
2 We pray for leaders of Christian communities
everywhere, but especially in our own country.
Lord, hear us.
3 We pray for understanding among divided
Christians.
Lord, hear us.
4 We pray that we may follow the path of love,
respecting the truth as we understand it.
Lord, hear us.

The World of Judaism

Throughout the ages people have asked questions about where the world and all it contains comes from, about why it exists at all and about what life is for. They have come to believe in a superior being or beings, and have expressed their belief in religious practices.

Christians believe in God. Christians believe that God made us, and that we can be helped to know something about all that is God through observing creation. Christians also believe that God's self-revelation comes to us in the fullest way through Jesus Christ. Through other religions also, people strive to understand the world and express their God-given instinct to worship a greater being than themselves. Most religions contain elements which Christians would consider true and valuable and some in particular contain much which is very similar to aspects of Christian belief.

In the same way in which Jesus showed us how to accept and respect everyone with all their individual differences, so we should respect the sincere beliefs of others and seek out and value all that is good in other religions.

Judaism and Christianity

One religion for which Christians should have particular respect is Judaism – the religion of the Jews. As Christians our own roots are in the Jewish tradition. These two religions are linked in the person of Jesus and in the Bible. It was from among the Jewish people that Jesus himself was born. The apostles and many of the early disciples who first proclaimed Christianity to the world were also Jews who had been brought up in the Jewish faith. We share the common bond and heritage of the Old Testament Scriptures. In the Old Testament we read that it was to the Jewish people that God's revelation first came.

Judaism is a Way Of Life

The religion of the Jewish people is probably more familiar to you than other religions, since Judaism was the parent of Christianity.

Like all religions Judaism is a way of life. However, the Jews are more conscious than many others of the link between religion and life. The Jewish people practise their faith both in the home and in the synagogue.

The terms Jew and Judaism both come from the word Judaea, which is the name of the southern part of the land in which the people of Israel lived in ancient times. In Jesus' day the Jews were waiting for the coming of the Messiah, the great Saviour who would establish God's Kingdom. Christians believe Jesus is that Messiah, while Jews are still waiting for the coming of the Messiah.

Religious Jews who keep very strictly to the ancient traditions of Judaism are called **Orthodox**. Others, who do not observe all the traditions and who have introduced a number of changes in modern times, are called **Liberal** or **Reform** Jews.

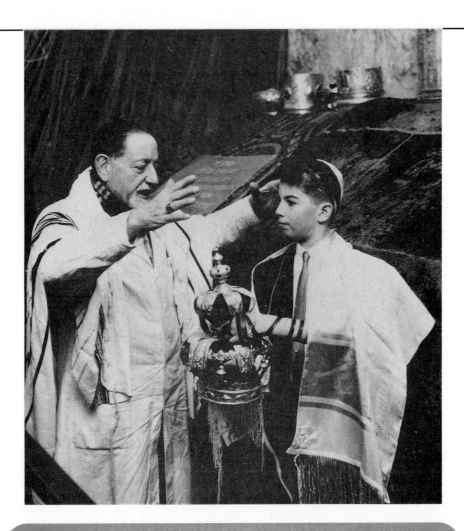

Bar Mitzvah Boy

'Hurry up, Daniel. You're keeping us all late, we have to be at the synagogue for 11.30 a.m.'

Mrs Cohen was in a fluster today. Her son was to become **Bar Mitzvah,** or Son of the Commandment. He had reached the grand age of thirteen, and a special ceremony was to be held in the synagogue, in his honour.

She was proud of Daniel, for he had diligently learnt to read Hebrew from the sacred book—**the Torah.**

For the first time in the synagogue, Daniel would take his place with the other men and he would be invited by the rabbi to read from the Torah and sing the benedictions in Hebrew.

Arriving at the synagogue the Cohen family were met by the **rabbi**, who gave Daniel a warm welcome, and reassured him that there was no need to be nervous, after all he would soon be assuming full adult Jewish responsibilities.

Mrs Cohen and her daughter Hannah took their seats in the gallery, where they could clearly see the **bar mitzvah** ceremony taking place.

Daniel was presented with a skull-cap (**Kipah**) and a striped prayer shawl (**Tallit**) to wear, and he was also given a prayer book (**Siddur**).

Hannah saw her brother getting up on to the raised platform from where the Torah was read from a scroll. Hannah had learnt at school that the Torah included the first five books of the Jewish Scriptures (also known as the Pentateuch) and the laws attributed to Moses, concerning worship and daily life.

After finishing the reading from the prophet Isaiah, Daniel took his seat with the other men and the **Cantor**, who was an expert in music and ritual, led the singing.

The rabbi, who was the chief official and teacher of the synagogue, smiled warmly at Daniel and congratulated him. The rabbi was a very wise man and everyone had great respect for him. Daniel hoped that one day he too would be a rabbi, but he knew that he would first have to go to university and then complete another five years in special training!

The following day Hannah was day-dreaming in class, when she heard her teacher Miss Hurvitz ask her a question. 'I'm sorry, Miss Hurvitz, I didn't hear the question', Hannah admitted quietly. 'Well, not a bit of wonder, you've been miles away all morning, now would you like to share with the rest of the class just what you were dreaming about?'

'I was thinking about my brother Daniel, he became Bar Mitzvah yesterday and I was at the ceremony.'

'This is a great opportunity, Hannah, for you to tell the rest of the class just what happens at a bar mitzvah ceremony,' said Miss Hurvitz, who was now smiling. Hannah gladly told the class what happened in the synagogue, making sure not to leave out any details. She had just finished her story when the bell sounded. Miss Hurvitz

Items from the Jewish Museum, Dublin

hurriedly wished them all a good weekend and '**Shabbat Shalom**'.

It was 12.30 p.m. when Hannah arrived home from school. As was usual on a Friday, the school closed at lunchtime, so that the children could help their mothers prepare the ritual meal for the Sabbath. The Jewish Sabbath or day of rest begins when it gets dark on a Friday evening and lasts until Saturday night. Hannah looked forward to helping her mother prepare the evening meal. The Sabbath meal was a special combination of food and ritual.

Hannah had taken charge of setting the table; this was the one night of the week when she would actually volunteer. The table had to be laid in a symbolic way. She was very careful to make sure that the cloth covering the two small loaves was without a wrinkle. And the wine-cup, with its finely inscribed stem, was polished to the last. 'Only the best will do for Shabbat,' she'd tell her mother.

Mr Cohen had told Hannah that the two specially prepared loaves of bread remind the Jews that they received a double portion of manna for the Sabbath when they were being led through the wilderness by Moses; while the empty cup is reserved for the prophet Elijah whom Jews believe will return to herald the coming of the Messiah.

Sunset was approaching, and this was the cue for Mrs Cohen to light the candles, an indication that the Sabbath had begun.

Hannah waited patiently for her father and brother to return from the synagogue, so that she could fully enter into the spirit of Shabbat, and the family could at last begin the meal.

On their return, Mr Cohen and Daniel touched the **Mazuzah** on the doorpost, as was customary before entering the house to remind themselves that a Jewish home is a holy place. The Mazuzah was a small case containing a tiny scroll with the first two paragraphs of the **Shema** (Deuteronomy 6:4) printed on it.

When all the family had seated themselves the meal could begin. Mr Cohen began with a blessing, the **Kiddush**, before passing the cup of wine around the table. After washing his hands, blessing the bread and sharing it out, Mr Cohen recited some words from the Book of Proverbs in praise of his wife. The formal blessings being over, the meal began.

The specially prepared **Kosher** food tasted better than ever to Hannah, and she thought this was probably because she was enjoying Shabbat.

At the end of the meal Hannah joined with the rest of her family in singing Shabbat songs of thanksgiving. She always looked forward to celebrating Shabbat with her family; in a way it always brought them closer.

She thought about tomorrow: in the morning she would go to the weekly service in the synagogue with her family and in the evening her father would bring the Sabbath to a close with the ceremony of **Havdalah**, at which a blessing is said over wine and in which a candle is extinguished, symbolising the passing of the very special day of Sabbath for another week.

Hannah had already begun to look forward to the **Pesach**, the Passover festival which would begin the following week. She would celebrate with her family and friends for eight days, but the highlight of the festival for Hannah was the **Seder** meal which was held on the first of the eight nights of the festival.

Activity

Compile a dictionary of the Hebrew words highlighted in the story and their meaning.

Look up Deuteronomy 6:4-9. This text is the Shema. It begins the official Jewish morning and evening prayers.

Why do you think the Jews see the message of the Shema as being so important?

In Your Religion Journal

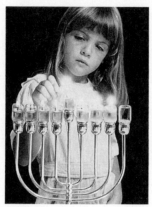

Write out the first three commandments. In what way do you think each of them can help people to put into practice what they are told in the Shema?

Draw pictures to illustrate the meaning of these three commandments.

Imagine that you are a friend of Jesus when he was growing up in Nazareth. Mary and Joseph have invited you to their house for a celebration of the Sabbath. Write about what happens.

Can you think of a time when Jesus attended a synagogue? Tell the story. (Luke 4:16-30)

Discuss

Can you remember the prayers and religious practices you learned from your parents at home?

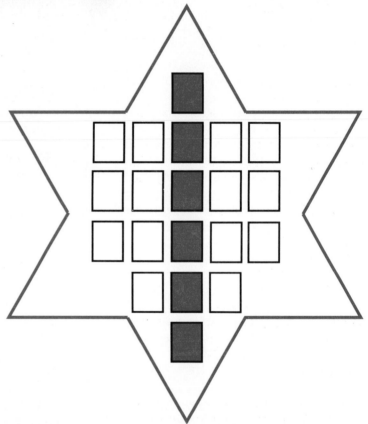

This is the Menorah. It is one of the signs or symbols of the Jewish religion.

Within each synagogue, a candelabrum, or Menorah, burns continually, in remembrance of the one that was used in the Temple in Jerusalem.

Fill in the Star of David by answering the following questions. When the exercise is complete the coloured boxes will give the name of the sacred language of the Jews.
1 Most important prayer for the Jewish people, found in Deut 6:4–9.
2 Chief official teacher and lawyer of the synagogue.
3 Most sacred book for the Jews – the law of Moses.
4 Name given to a person who is born into Judaism.

The Star of David, also known as the Shield of David, was, according to one tradition, used on the shields of David's soldiers. Today it appears on the flag of Israel.

Jewish Feasts and Festivals

Over thousands of years the feasts and festivals observed in the homes and synagogues of the Jewish people have helped to keep them united. Besides the observance of the Sabbath, the yearly festivals are based on the Jewish lunar calendar.

The Sabbath

The observance of the Sabbath, which may date to the time of the patriarchs, is a key element of Jewish worship. It commemorates both the creation of the world and the deliverance of the people of Israel from Egypt. The Sabbath is the day when Jews let go of work and human effort to remind themselves that the world is in the hands of the Creator.

Every Sabbath is a holy day for Jews. It is a day set apart, when they do no work, not even cooking. Meals have to be prepared before the start of the Sabbath. It starts on Friday evening. First, the mother lights the traditional Sabbath candles. This is one of the prayers she says:

Lord of the Universe, I am about to perform the sacred duty of kindling the lights in honour of the Sabbath. Grant that peace, light and joy ever abide in our home. For with thee is the fountain of life. In thy light do we see light.

Then with her hands over her eyes she says a blessing over the light.

Men and boys go to the synagogue, to 'welcome the Sabbath'. Women and girls often do this at home. Later there is a special meal, at the beginning of which the father says a blessing over a cup of wine, and then over special Sabbath loaves of bread. Blessings over bread and wine are also said before the midday meal on the next day. During the meal traditional Sabbath 'table songs', **Zemiroth**, may be sung by the family. The meal ends with a prayer of thanksgiving.

Devout Jews attend morning and afternoon services in the synagogue. The Sabbath ends late on Saturday evening with a ceremony called **Havdalah**. This marks the separation of the Sabbath from the rest of the week. The father says a blessing over a glass of wine, and also over a box of sweet smelling spices in the hope that the sweetness of the Sabbath will continue through the week. He also says a blessing over the candles, as a sign that God created light on the first day, which is now approaching.

> ### Discuss
> The Jewish people celebrate their Sabbath from Friday evening until Saturday evening. What are they celebrating?
> When do Catholics celebrate their Sabbath and what are they celebrating ?
> Do you think it is a good idea to have a special day each week for worship?
> What effect do you think the Jewish way of observing the Sabbath is likely to have on the family ?

New Year and Day of Atonement

In September or October the Jews begin their New Year, **Rosh Hashanah**, with ten days of repentance. They look forward with hope to the future and they repent for the past.

On New Year's Eve the family have a festive meal, at which they eat apples dipped in honey. This is a sign of their hope that the New Year will be sweet for everyone.

On the following two days they remember God's creation of the world, and in the morning service in the synagogue a ram's horn, called the **Shofar**, is blown. They see this as a summons to repent and return to God so that they can start off the New Year in a right way.

This ten-day period of reflection ends with the feast of **Yom Kippur** – the Day of Atonement. It is considered the most holy day of the Jewish year. On the eve of Yom Kippur the prayer called **Kol Nidrei** is recited in the synagogue. In it, God is asked to forgive people who have failed to keep their promises.

Yom Kippur is a day of fasting and prayer. Orthodox Jews eat their last meal before the eve of Yom Kippur and then they may not work, eat, drink, anoint the body or wear leather shoes for twenty-four hours.

Activity

One of the readings used in the synagogue on the feast of Yom Kippur is Isaiah 57:14 – 58:14 (Catholics also use part of this as one of the readings at Mass on Ash Wednesday). Read it, and say what you think is the main message in it.

Some very important festivals celebrate the belief that God specially chose the Jewish people and has a special relationship with them. In these festivals Jews remember the great things God has done for them, and they put their trust in God for the future.

The Passover

One of the most important spring holy days is the **Pesach** – the Passover. It is observed by having special foods served at a **seder**, or ceremonial meal. Unleavened bread, blessed wine and spices and the retelling of the story of the escape from Egypt are part of the commemoration.
They celebrate not just that God set the people of Israel free, but that he chose them to be his own people. This special relationship between the Jewish people and God is called the covenant.

Read the following.

Imagine you are going back in time almost two thousand years – to Jesus' time. Imagine that you are a good friend of Jesus. The two of you are going with Mary and Joseph to celebrate Passover in Jerusalem. This important feast commemorates the events of the Exodus of your people from slavery in Egypt many centuries ago. You and Jesus live in Nazareth, a small town about sixty miles from Jerusalem. Both of you are excited as you begin your journey to the holy city.

For four days your small group walks along dusty roads that people have used for centuries on their journey to Jerusalem. Each evening you rest by the roadside or in an inn. Then one day in the late afternoon, you see from the top of a hill the wonders of the city. The light from the setting sun shines on the Temple. Imagine its beauty. You have never seen anything like it.... Quickly you hurry towards the walls of the city. You will be here for a whole week. What wonders await you ! When you enter the city, you find a room at an inn for the night, and you dream of tomorrow....

The night passes. At sunrise you are up, wide awake, and ready for the adventures of this first day in the city. After a quick breakfast of flat unleavened bread and dates, you enter the stream of pilgrims that are browsing in the market place beyond the door of the inn.

Tourists like you jam the streets of Jerusalem. As you walk along the busy streets, you are surprised to see other Jews from all over the Roman Empire – travellers from Egypt, Rome, Athens, Ephesus – and pilgrims from all over your own country. You hear many languages as the people bustle about the marketplace. Shopkeepers hawk their wares and sell every kind of food and clothing. They argue with you over the price of a hammer for Joseph, a piece of pottery for Mary and a game for you and Jesus....

You push your way through the busy streets to get to the Temple; the biggest building that you have ever seen. You are used to the synagogue in Nazareth, a small dark building. The Temple is enormous ! You watch the priests sacrifice animals in the Temple. The odour of blood and incense fills your nostrils.

The day grows long. Wearily you wander through the narrow streets of Jerusalem on your way back to your lodging. You are pressed against the wall of a building when a huge flock of sheep passes by.

As night falls, Jesus and you talk in excited voices about your experience of Jerusalem – the sounds and sights, the smells and tastes of the city. All your senses have been awakened by the adventures of this day. You have heard the noise of people speaking in foreign languages and laughing out of the sheer joy of being in Jerusalem. You have seen pilgrims dressed in strange and exotic clothes. You have touched the hairy belly of a camel. You have smelled many exotic foods. Some you have even tasted....

The festive air of the city has captured your imagination. Everywhere you look you see signs that the great feast of Passover is about to begin.

Never before has the feast meant so much to you. Never before have you realised what great things God has done for your people.

What a time to be a pilgrim !

What a time to be with Jesus and his family !

What a time to be alive and in Jerusalem !

Now read Luke 2:41-51

The Feast of Weeks

Fifty days later is the feast of Pentecost also known as the Feast of Weeks. This celebrates the establishment of the covenant when God gave the chosen people the ten commandments at Mount Sinai fifty days after the Passover.

This feast is called **Shavout** in Hebrew. The Jews see the ten commandments as a sign of God's covenant with them. In the synagogue everyone stands when they are being read. At lunchtime in a Jewish home, there are often round loaves on the table decorated with a ladder. This is a reminder of Moses going up Mount Sinai to receive the commandments.

The Feast of Tabernacles (or Booths)

Five days after Yom Kippur, the Feast of Tabernacles, **Succoth**, is celebrated. This week-long autumnal feast of thanksgiving commemorates the time when God looked after the Israelite people as they wandered in the desert. During the festival, devout Jews erect outdoor tabernacles or booths (tents) and may decorate them with harvest fruits and eat their meals in the tabernacles and sleep under the stars. In this way they remember how God looked after their ancestors and this encourages them to continue to have trust in God today.

A celebration called **Rejoicing in the Torah** closes Succoth and marks the end of the yearly reading of the first five books of the Jewish Scriptures.

Two other festivals celebrate great events which happened in Jewish history and which Jews remember with thanksgiving and hope for the future.

Purim

The feast of **Purim** celebrates how the Jews in the Persian Empire were saved by the great courage of a woman called Esther. Esther, who became Queen of Persia and who was devoted to her people, successfully foiled a plot to massacre all the Jews in the Persian Empire. In the synagogue the Book of Esther is read to commemorate this event (Esther 9:20 –31).

The Festival of Lights

The festival of lights or **Hanukkah** is celebrated in December and commemorates the restoration of the Temple after it was destroyed by the Syrians in 160 BC. The eight-branched Menorah, called a Hanukkia, is a central symbol in the week-long celebration. To this day synagogues recall the time when the Temple was used for worship with a perpetually burning candelabrum.

Good afternoon,

My name is Rabbi Steinberg. I am delighted to come here today to introduce you to the practices and beliefs of Judaism.

Let me begin by telling you about our worship. The Sabbath service is held in the ————. In Orthodox services the men sit separately from the women and children who sit at the back or in a ————.

In the synagogue men must cover their heads at all times usually with a skull-cap or ————. Many of the men wear ———— or prayer shawls and use a ———— to help them say their prayers.

Presiding over the worship is the ————, the chief official and teacher of the synagogue. He is assisted by the ———— who is an expert in music and ritual. He leads the people in singing.

For Jews the most sacred book is the ———— /the law of Moses. The ———— as it is sometimes referred to contains the first —— books of what Christians call the Old Testament. These books are known as ————; ————; ————; ————; ————.

The language of the Torah and the prayers is ————, the sacred language of the Jews. The service is conducted from a raised platform where the Torah is read from a ————. From an early age children are taught special prayers and blessings for morning and evening. In particular they learn the passage in Deuteronomy 6:4-9 known as the ————.

Very often when you enter a Jewish home you will find a ———— on the right hand doorpost. This is a small case containing a tiny scroll with the first two paragraphs of the ———— printed on it. As a Jew enters the house it is customary to touch the ———— to remind them that a Jewish home is a holy place.

Last weekend my son was thirteen, that meant he became ——- ———— which means ——- —— —— ——-. A special ceremony was held in the synagogue to mark the occasion. At the age of thirteen he now assumes full adult male Jewish responsibilities.

Attendance at the synagogue service is only a part of the celebrations for the Sabbath. The Sabbath meal is an important ———— occasion. It begins with a blessing or ———— before the cup of wine is passed around the table. The table is set in a ———— way. Two specially prepared ———— of —— remind the Jews that they received a double portion of —— for the Sabbath when they were being led through the wilderness by ——. An empty cup is also reserved for the Prophet ———— whom Jews believe will return to announce the coming of the ————. We eat specially prepared ———— food. This is the Hebrew word for 'fit and proper' which refers to the special preparation and rules regarding the eating of animal products. As you may know Jews do not eat —— or shellfish, and meat and milk may not be served at the same meal. The meal ends with a prayer of thanksgiving.

Throughout the year we celebrate different feasts and festivals. Our New Year begins in September or October with ten days of repentance.

This period ends with the feast of —- ————. It is considered the most ———— day of the Jewish year. Five days later we celebrate the feast of ———— or ————. We give thanks to God for the time he looked after our ancestors in the desert.

In December we celebrate the festival of lights or ———— ————. This feast commemorates the restoration of the Temple in Jerusalem.

In spring one of the most important festivals is the ———— ————. We celebrate the freedom of the Israelite people from Egypt and the special relationship between the Jewish people and God.

Fifty days later we celebrate Shavout, otherwise known as the feast of ————. This feast celebrates the time when the covenant was established at Mount ————.

Thank you for your attention.

Peace be with you ————

Test Yourself.

Do the Looking Back exercises on page 226

Unit Seven
Following Jesus

Lesson Seventeen

LUKE'S GOSPEL

Who was Saint Luke?

Luke was a native of Antioch in Syria. He is the only New Testament writer who was not a Jew. His gospel was written for Gentiles. He knew that the people who would read what he had written would not be familiar with Jewish history or customs. Greek was his own language.

He was intelligent and well educated. He was a doctor by profession and this probably accounts, in part at least, for his great compassion, especially for those who were poor and downtrodden.

Luke was not an apostle, though he did become a follower of Jesus. He was a friend and co-worker with St Paul. He accompanied Paul on some of his great missionary journeys which we read about in the Acts of the Apostles.

The evangelist Luke, 12th century

Structure of Luke's Gospel

1. Prologue or Introduction 1:1-4

Luke dedicates his gospel to an official called Theophilus.

2. Infancy narrative 1:5 - 2:52

This part of the gospel tells the story of the events which led up to the birth of Jesus, the Presentation in the Temple, and the story of the boy Jesus with the Jewish teachers in the Temple.

3. Jesus prepares for his work 3:1- 4:13

Here we find the story of John the Baptist and the account of the preparations which Jesus made before he began his work of preaching and teaching throughout the land.

4. Jesus in Galilee 4:14 - 9:50

The next section deals with the time which Jesus spent in Galilee. In this section we read about Jesus calling his disciples. We also find many of the parables which Jesus told and several of the miracle stories.

5. The journey to Jerusalem 9:51 - 19:27

Jesus leaves Galilee and begins the journey towards Jerusalem. Again we find many of the miracle and parable stories that we are familiar with. We also get the definite feel that opposition to Jesus is mounting.

6. The passion and death of Jesus 19:28 - 23:56

In this part of Luke's gospel we find the story of the passion and death of Jesus.

7. The resurrection and ascension Chapter 24ff

Here we find the story of the resurrection of Jesus, his appearances to the disciples and his ascension into heaven.

Activity
(a) In your bible find the beginning and end of each of the seven sections.
(b) Look at the headings in the chapters in each section.
(c) Design in your journal an introductory page for each of the sections.

What did Luke see as important ?

Luke wanted to communicate that the Good News which Jesus brought was for all people, not just for Jews. Luke was a Gentile and the people for whom he was writing were Gentiles. He wanted them to know that Jesus had come to save them too.

His gospel shows that Jesus had concern for all those who were weak and down-trodden; the poor, the out-casts, sinners and women, who were looked down upon in the society of the time.

The incidents and stories related in Luke's gospel show Jesus as one who is compassionate and forgiving, who wants to save people from sin and from anything which oppresses them. He is shown as someone prayerful, who frequently takes time to communicate with his Father in prayer and who urges his followers to pray.

In Your Religion Journal

Design a cover for Luke's gospel.

Listeners respond angrily to preacher.

New Preacher takes to the road in Galilee.

Strange claims from preacher.

No ordinary teacher!

Carpenter's son makes a mark.

Activity

Read Luke 4:16-30. Imagine that you are a reporter for a local paper when this incident takes place. Choose one of the above headings. Write a report about what you saw happening.

With authority and power this man gives orders to the evil spirits and they come out (*Luke 4:36*).

Activity

Find out what it was that Jesus did which prompted the people to make this remark.

In Your Religion Journal

Make a list of your friends. What are the most striking qualities which each one of them has?
Are there any common qualities which they all have ?
What do you think it says about you that you have chosen these people to be your friends?

Find Your Group

Imagine that you are about to set out on an important project. Decide what the project is. You have twelve people to help you. What qualities do you think you would look for among the twelve?
Why did you decide on these qualities?

Looking for Helpers

Show me your friends and I'll tell you who you are.

What do you think this proverb means?

Now let's take a look at what we know about the twelve apostles chosen by Jesus.

Peter

Peter was a fisherman. He worked with his brother Andrew. Peter was married. He was short-tempered and impetuous. He was humble and could admit his faults.

He showed a strength of personality and faith which made him a leader among the disciples. His real name was Simon. Peter was the name given to him by Jesus. It means 'rock' and Jesus said that Peter was the rock on which he would build his Church. Peter panicked when Jesus was arrested and three times denied that he knew him but he repented afterwards.

Andrew

He was Peter's brother, another fisherman. He had already become a disciple of John the Baptist.

James and John

James and John were another set of brothers, who were also fishermen. John was probably Jesus' closest friend. Before he died on the cross Jesus entrusted his mother, Mary, to John's care. Their father's name was Zebedee and they are sometimes referred to as the 'sons of Zebedee'.

Philip

He was the very first to follow Jesus. He was a native of Bethsaida, also the birthplace of Peter and Andrew.

Bartholomew

Bartholomew was a friend of Philip. Jesus said of him that he was incapable of deceit.

Matthew (Levi)

Levi was a tax collector, employed by the Romans. He was a rich man. Because of the work he did he represented Roman authority and so he was strongly disliked by his own people.

Thomas

Thomas was a sceptical person not easily impressed. We can understand the kind of person he was by his reactions after Jesus' resurrection when he refused to believe that Jesus had risen from the dead until he put his fingers into the holes in Jesus' hands and his hand into Jesus' side. Even today if someone shows disbelief in what they are told they tend to be nicknamed 'doubting Thomas'.

Simon

Simon was a Zealot. The Zealots were the group of people who most wanted to rid the country of the Romans and Roman rule.

James

He was called James, son of Alphaeus, to distinguish him from James the brother of John.

Judas Thaddaeus

He is known as the son of James.

Judas Iscariot

He was the treasurer and the others suspected him of stealing money from the group. He betrayed Jesus for thirty pieces of silver. He regretted this and committed suicide.

Discuss

What do you think of the choices Jesus made in choosing his twelve apostles? What causes of friction do you think there might have been among the twelve, for instance between Levi and Simon?
Read Luke 5:1-11; 27-32

In Your Religion Journal

Suppose Jesus was to put an advertisement in a local paper inviting applications for the job of an apostle.

Write what you consider a suitable advertisement giving a job description and stating the qualifications and qualities which you think would be essential.

Pretend you're Peter. Write down your application for the job. Include a copy of your curriculum vitae, saying what qualifications you have, what experience you have which would be useful, your interests and hobbies, and give the name of someone you think would recommend you for the job.

Luke tells of the healing work of Jesus.

It is generally believed that Luke was a doctor. So he would have had a particular interest in the incidents where Jesus healed people.

It is difficult for us to imagine what it would have been like for people living at the time of Jesus who were ill. There were no hospitals and very little medical care. Medical procedures or drugs which are taken for granted today were not available at that time. Illnesses which are easily cured now were capable of causing great suffering, even leading to death, at that time.

There had been absolutely no research done on physical or mental handicap and so, because people could not see any reasons why these should have happened, they were often seen as God's punishment on the person for some wrong they had done or even for some wrong which their parents or ancestors had done. Because of this, handicapped people were viewed as outcasts of society.

Then Jesus came along. He was able to cure people's illnesses. Naturally they flocked to him.

Research

Make a list of places where people go today to look for cures for their sicknesses:
To a doctor or surgeon who has become famous for his work in a particular area , for example, a renowned heart surgeon;
To clinics where they have developed new ways of dealing with disease and handicap;
To places where people have reported that miraculous cures took place.
Find out more about them.

Activity

Make a wall frieze to illustrate the caption: If you want to be healed....
If possible, interview somebody who has been seriously ill and is now better.

In Your Religion Journal

Write an article entitled: Restored to health.

146

Luke was interested in the healing work of Jesus. He may have kept notes of the incidents he had heard about where Jesus had healed people. When he decided to write his gospel, this journal would have been a very useful source of information. The entries in the journal might have looked like this:

Man Healed

His right hand had been paralysed for years. It was in the synagogue on the Sabbath that he met Jesus. Of course the teachers of the Law and the Pharisees were watching like hawks. If Jesus healed the man on the Sabbath they'd have a good reason for accusing him of doing wrong. Jesus called the man to the front and asked him to stretch out his hand. As soon as the man did this his hand was healed.

Of course he knew what they were thinking and he asked them, 'What does our Law allow us to do on the Sabbath? To help or to harm? To save a man's life or destroy it?' I suppose there was only one answer they could give to that! I think he's going to annoy a lot of people with the things he does and says. Read Luke 6:6-11.

Sight Restored

A blind beggar sitting by the roadside heard sounds of a crowd passing by. When he enquired, they told him it was Jesus of Nazareth. He had heard about the many incidents where Jesus had healed people. 'Jesus, Son of David, take pity on me,' he shouted. Even when they tried to silence him, he continued to shout.
So Jesus stopped and ordered them to bring the blind man to him.
'What do you want me to do?' he asked.
'Sir,' answered the man, 'I want to see again.' Jesus said to him, 'Then, see! Your faith has made you well.'
At once the man was able to see.

The crowd were impressed. They gave praise to God. They seemed to recognise that God was at work through the actions of this man.
Read Luke 18:35-43.

A Cripple for Eighteen Years

Once again Jesus was in the synagogue on the Sabbath. There was a woman who had been crippled for eighteen years. She was so bad that she was bent over and could not straighten up. Jesus saw her. He said to her, 'Woman, you are free from your illness.' He placed his hands on her. Immediately she straightened up. She was delighted and gave praise to God.

Once again they were angry. He had cured someone on the Sabbath. However as usual he had an answer. 'You hypocrites! Any one of you would untie his ox or his donkey from the stall and take it out and give it water on the Sabbath.' Of course they were ashamed of themselves! Read Luke 13:10-17.

Activity

(a) Read from Luke's gospel other stories of times when Jesus healed people. You will find them in chapters 5, 8, 14, 17, 18.

(b) Choose one of the incidents. Find a partner. One of you take the role of the person who was healed, the other person take the role of a reporter for a TV station.
Act out an interview for Television.

In Your Religion Journal

What do you think Jesus felt for the people who were cured by him in these stories?

What do you think he felt for those who did not want him to heal on the Sabbath?

Discuss

What do these healing stories tell us about Jesus?

What qualities did he have?

How did he see other people?

Which three of the following words do you think best describe Jesus in the stories you have read?

Honest   **Holy**   **Strong**

Kind   **Caring**

Loving   **Powerful**

Determined

Courageous

Compassionate

In Your Religion Journal

Now that you have spent some time thinking about the sort of qualities which Jesus possessed, list some people in today's world whom you think possess the same qualities.
How do the stories of the healing incidents from the life of Jesus challenge those of us who want to be his followers today?

Collecting Information

When the time came for him to think about writing his gospel, Luke used whatever records he had kept of the things he knew about which Jesus did. As well as this he would probably have interviewed people who had been with Jesus, who had experienced the kind of person he was and the way that he related to those around him. This is an example of what might have happened.

Luke: Are you saying then, that Jesus had a lot of time for the poor, the needy and the oppressed ? Am I correct in thinking that I heard some of you say that he was friendly with sinners ?

Listener 1: Yes, that's it! He was different. That's why he made such an impact. He just behaved in a way that you'd never have expected. And he turned up in places where you'd certainly never expect to see him.

Listener 2: That was also why the authorities were so annoyed with him. They never really knew what to expect next. He always seemed to take them by surprise and he had an answer for everything.

Listener 3: From my point of view the most extraordinary thing about him was the way he treated women. We were used to being looked down upon and belittled in all sorts of ways. He was different. He treated us with respect – with just the same respect as he had for men.

Listener 4: That's why there were so many women among his followers. And, of course, it was really something new to see women following a rabbi. Until Jesus came along that would have been unheard of.

Listener 5: The incident that really sticks out in my memory happened on the day Jesus was invited by Simon the Pharisee to have dinner with him. There was a woman who was well known locally for being a sinner. She came into the house bringing with her an alabaster jar full of perfume. She stood behind Jesus, crying and wetting his feet with her tears. Then she dried them with her hair, kissed them and poured perfume on them. The people around were amazed. They thought that Jesus, if he was a prophet, would surely know what kind of woman this was. They were surprised that he would even stay in the same room with her, not to mention that he would allow her to touch him. Jesus knew what they were thinking.

He said to them, 'I came into your house and you gave me no water for my feet, but she has washed my feet with her tears and dried them with her hair. You did not welcome me with a kiss but she has not stopped kissing my feet since I came. You provided no olive oil for my head but she has anointed my feet with perfume. I tell you then, the great love she has shown proves that her many sins have been forgiven. But whoever has been forgiven little shows only a little love.'

While they were still trying to digest what he had just said, Jesus turned to the woman and said, 'Your sins are forgiven'. Everybody was amazed. Not only had Jesus associated with the woman but he had actually held her up as an example to the others.

Luke: Would you say that this was an isolated incident or was it typical of the concern and respect Jesus had for women?

Listener 1: There were many such incidents. I have no doubt that this one is typical of the way that Jesus related to women. He didn't set out to put them down. He really treated them with the same respect which he gave to everybody.

Activity

Find other stories from Luke's gospel which would support this claim. Read:

Luke 7:11- 17;
Luke 8:40 - 53;
Luke 10:38 - 42;
Luke 13:10 -17;
Luke 21:1- 4.

Discuss

Who are the people who are most looked down upon or discriminated against in the world today? In your own country today? Who do you look down upon? How does the attitude of Jesus as it is shown in Luke's gospel challenge his followers to treat those who are outcasts in our world?

Luke presents the stories of Jesus

Like the other gospel writers Luke must have been fascinated by the stories which Jesus told. In his gospel we find many of these stories recorded.
Those who first heard these stories were challenged by them. They also challenge us today to think about our values and if necessary to change our behaviour.
As you know, these stories are called parables.

The Parable of the Great Feast

Jesus said to him, 'There was once a man who was giving a great feast to which he invited many people. When it was time for the feast, he sent his servant to tell his guests, "Come, everything is ready!" But they all began, one after another, to make excuses. The first one told the servant, "I have bought a field and must go and look at it; please accept my apologies." Another one said, "I have bought five pairs of oxen and am on my way to try them out; please accept my apologies." Another one said, "I have just got married, and for that reason I cannot come."
'The servant went back and told all this to his master. The master was furious and said to his servant, "Hurry out to the streets and alleys of the town and bring back the poor, the crippled, the blind and the lame." Soon the servant said, "Your order has been carried out, sir, but there is room for more." So the master said to the servant, "Go out to the country so that my house will be full. I tell you all that none of those men who were invited will taste my dinner!" ' (*Luke 14:15-24*)

Discuss

How do you think the king felt?
How do you think those who were invited from the lanes and alleys of the town felt?
Have you ever acted as the first set of invited guests in the story acted?
Why did you do so?
Why do you think Jesus told this story?

The pleasure of the company of

....

is requested at a Great Feast which will be held in God's Kingdom and will continue throughout eternity.

R S V P

This invitation is addressed to each of us. All through life we show that we wish either to accept or turn down the invitation.
We show that we want to accept it by the things we do, by the way we treat others, by the kind of people we are.

In Your Religion Journal

Write your answer to the invitation. Write about one of the things you can do now which would indicate that you wish to accept the invitation.

Sometimes we reject the invitation. We make excuses. We travel in other directions.

In Your Religion Journal

Write about some of the things you might do which would indicate that you did not want to accept the invitation.

Find Your Group

In lesson twelve you have already read one of the stories which Jesus told of God's forgiveness.

Read Luke 15:1-10. Here you will find two stories about God's forgiveness.

Which of the two stories do you find most interesting?

Have you ever been like the shepherd in the first story or like the woman who lost the coin in the second story?
What happened?

Imagine you are the lost sheep. What three words would you use to describe how you felt before the shepherd found you?

What three words would you use to describe how you felt after the shepherd found you?

In Your Religion Journal

Draw an image which shows God as described in these two stories.

Sally thinks:
I've been so bad. I cheated, I stole, I was unfair and unkind to others. I've lost my job as a result. I thought that I'd never be found out.
Then one day the game was up. All that I had tried so hard to cover up had been brought out into the open. Now I know everyone is talking about me. Most of them didn't like me anyhow and they're quite glad that I was found out. But even those that I thought were my friends have turned their backs on me.
Now I'm not sure why I did it. I wish I could start all over again. I'd do things differently. But that's not possible. What's done can't be undone. The future, I'm afraid, looks very gloomy. And as for God! I'm sure in God's eyes I look the same as I look to the people who know me – just a very bad person. I really wish I could start all over again.

Discuss

Have you ever felt like Sally? When?
Do you think that this person's image of God is the same as the image of God which is shown in the stories of forgiveness in Luke's gospel?
In what way is it different?
Is your image of God more like Sally's or is it more like that in the story of the lost sheep or the lost coin?

The Kingdom of God

The people who lived at the time of Jesus had been looking forward for some time to the day when a great leader would come and deliver them from their enemies, the Romans. When Jesus spoke about the kingdom of God the people thought at first that he was talking about a territory where they would live in freedom from their enemies. Jesus, however, was talking about something quite different. He was talking about a time when a group of people would live as God wanted them to. Then the kingdom of God would have come.

Activity In Luke 13:18-21 you will find two stories in which Jesus talks about the kingdom of God. Read them. What do you think the two stories are saying about the kingdom of God ?

In Your Religion Journal Write your own parable about the kingdom of God. The kingdom of God is like ...

Jesus and Prayer in Luke's Gospel

Read Luke 18:1-17.

Which of the following statements do you agree with?

If we took seriously what Jesus said in these two stories we would:

believe that God never listens to our prayers;

believe that God listens to those who are good;

believe that God listens to us if we come before him openly and honestly with all our faults and failings;

believe that it is important to use the right words when we pray;

keep praying even if it seems that our prayers are not being heard.

Test yourself on Luke's gospel.

Find the odd one out in each of the following groups.

Peter	The Sower	Mary
Andrew	The Workers in the Vineyard	Elizabeth
Philip	The Rich Young Man	John the Baptist
Jairus	The Good Samaritan	Simeon

What have the others got in common?

Name three people or groups of people who were healed by Jesus.

Which of the apostles was a tax collector?

Who said to Jesus: 'I do not deserve to have you come into my house. Just give the order and my servant will get well'? (*Luke 7:6.7*)

To whom did Jesus say:
'Salvation has come to this house today'? (*Luke 19:9*)
What caused Jesus to make this statement?

Name three people who had their sins forgiven by Jesus.

Who went away from Jesus sad, 'because he was very rich'? (*Luke 18:23*)

To whom did Jesus say: 'Get up and go, your faith has made you well' ? (*Luke 17:19*)

Why did he say it?

Whom did Jesus say was greatest? (*Luke 9:46-48*)

Free to Serve

In Your Religion Journal

Think of some-one you know whom you consider uses the opportun-ities they have to serve others and to live as a fol-lower of Jesus. Pretend you are doing a profile of the person for the local newspaper.

Illustrate your profile with suitable sketches.

Write about a time when you served someone else's needs rather than your own.

Write about a time when you had the oppor-tunity to be of service to some-one else but chose not to.

We all know many people who are followers of Jesus in their lives every day. Some people do extraordinary things and become famous. Most people never become famous and are never asked to do anything out of the ordinary. For most of us it is in doing the tasks of every day that we have the opportunity to put into practice the things which Jesus asks us to do.

Jesus asks us to serve others and to serve God. We are all free to take the opportunities we have in our everyday lives to serve others and to serve God. Sometimes, however, we choose not to do this. We choose to do the sort of things which serve only our own needs.

Being aware of and assuring the needs of others challenges us to be ready to make sacrifices and to put ourselves last.

Sally Trench

Sally Trench was born in 1945 into a very wealthy family. From childhood, Sally was a rebel. She reacted against the lifestyle she saw around her and rejected anything which put money before people.

She was sent to a very prim and proper boarding school which she hated.

She was very unhappy and made herself very unpopular with those in authority to the extent that eventually she was expelled. At the age of fifteen, she went to Africa where she spent some time looking for adventure and excitement.

When she returned to England she saw for the first time the large numbers of people living rough in Waterloo Station. They were dirty, ragged and unhappy. Sally Trench, who felt very much outside of society herself, felt drawn towards them and immediately wanted to do something which would change their reality.

When she was at home she often left the house in the middle of the night. She climbed down a drainpipe and made her way to central London. She visited the railway stations and other haunts of the meths drinkers, addicts and tramps and took them food, blankets, tea and coffee. She was horrified by the conditions she discovered with people dying from the cold, exposure, hunger and addiction.

She enjoyed meeting them and helping them. They knew she cared for them and accepted them as they were; something they had not been used to. In turn, they accepted her, something which Sally had not been used to either.

From an early age Sally was aware of God. At school she was always first in the chapel for Mass. When times were difficult and when most people seemed to be against her it was Sally's faith in God, her belief that God was always with her, that kept her going. She understood that the love which existed between herself and the down-and-outs in London was God's love caring through herself and through other people.

After a year she left home to devote herself totally to looking after the poor and forgotten of London. She didn't want to be anything less than totally committed. This was how she understood her Christian calling.

And so for five years Sally lived among the down-and-outs in London. Each day she walked about twenty miles across central London distributing food and drink. She went from Waterloo, to Charing Cross, to Covent Garden, to King's Cross, to Euston and over to the East End, delivering provisions to the needy wherever she found them, in the Underground, in derelict houses, in stations. She gathered the provisions in whatever way she could. Passers-by gave donations. People who ran restaurants or tea rooms gave her their left-overs at the end of the day, and in the morning she scrounged fruit and vegetable left-overs from Covent Garden. Her vegetable soup became a favourite!

All through this Sally lived rough. She had no income. She often slept in the open. She became a familiar figure in the coffee bars, pubs and late-night haunts of London's teenage drop-outs. Many of the people Sally helped were suspicious of society because society had dealt them severe blows. Therefore, they were suspicious of many of the organised schemes for helping drop-outs. Sally's very personal type of caring, however, was non-threatening. She demanded nothing.

Originally Sally set out to help meths drinkers and tramps who were often middle-aged men. However, as soon as she became aware of the plight of young addicts and drifters she couldn't ignore their needs either. So she often spent the day working among them, snatching a few hours sleep and then later, setting off for her night-time visits to the

154| meths drinkers and tramps.

She had remarkable courage. Once she threw herself into a brawl to separate two junkies. Another time she rushed into a burning house to save an old tramp. She never preached at the people but nevertheless she was not slow to state the values of the gospel when the situation required this. She was nicknamed 'Sally the Christian'. Her form of Christianity took the shape of action much more so than of words.

Eventually the strain became too much and Sally had to spend some time in a mental hospital. She then realised that she would have to change her lifestyle slightly in order to survive. She had no friends other than drop-outs or junkies. She had no life outside of her work. She began to keep a diary. At two in the morning she could be seen in Euston Station scribbling away on toilet paper. It would have remained a private diary but for an incident which took place.

One night Sally was called to a girl who lay dying on a derelict site because she had tried to carry out an abortion on herself with a knitting needle. The girl wanted a priest. Sally brought the priest who was furious with her because at first he thought that Sally was a junkie and was in some way responsible for the girl's death. Sally told him about her life and mentioned her diary. He asked if he could read it. He was responsible for having it published. It became a best-selling book.

Sally became world-famous. But this meant the end of her work with the down-and-outs and dossers who didn't like the fact that she had written a book about them. However, this was the beginning of a new chapter in the life of Sally Trench. She had learned that prevention is better than cure because in a very real way she had experienced how difficult it was for a drug addict or an alcoholic to be 'cured'. She decided to try to help the younger children in need not to become the meths drinkers of the future.

She set up a special education project for difficult children. The school is run like an informal home. The children do English and maths but special emphasis is placed on art, sport, drama, modelling and outings to places of interest.

In Leeds her project 'Spark' tries to help children in need in one of the poorest districts of the city by offering recreation and academic help at the Family Evening Centre.

Sally sees that she is doing God's work. It is her way of answering God's call and of using her freedom to grow and to help others to grow. The challenge of her story is that she saw real religion as religion in action.

Discuss

What words would you use to describe Sally Trench? What do you admire most about her? What questions does her story raise about your own life?

Research

Choose somebody else who you think has served God in extraordinary ways.
Read about his or her life.
What are the qualities which the person has which you consider to be most important?
Write and illustrate a short account of the person's life.

In Your Religion Journal

List some situations which occur in your life at home, in your life at school or with your friends where you choose to either act selfishly and take account only of your own needs, or act with care and concern for the needs of others.
Make a list of at least five areas where you think you could do better.
List some qualities which you think you will have to develop in yourself in order to do this.

Edith Stein

Edith Stein was born in Breslau in Germany in 1891. Edith's family were strict followers of the Jewish religion. Frau Stein insisted on grace in Hebrew at all meals. The walls of the house were decorated with scenes from the Old Testament. Even in her old age she insisted on keeping all the Jewish fasts in all their vigour. Unlike many Jewish families of that time in Germany, Edith's family was outstanding for their loyalty to their Jewish faith. This strict discipline Frau Stein passed on to her youngest daughter Edith.

Edith's father, a timber merchant, died when Edith was two. Her mother had the difficult task of keeping the business going and raising seven children. Edith, being the baby, was her mother's favourite. Edith admired her mother and wished to be like her but soon showed some characteristics which were most unlike her mother's. She was no good at practical things. She was a born rebel. However she was highly intelligent and had absolutely no difficulty at school.

Edith decided to study philosophy. Eventually she studied at the University of Gottingen with the famous Professor Adolf Reinach.

He, like Edith, was a Jew but in 1916 when Adolf Reinach was serving in the army, he and his wife Anna were baptised Christians. Edith spent some time working as a Red Cross nurse's aid with those who had

been wounded in the First World War. She returned to university where she became an assistant to one of the professors and also spent a lot of time translating books and essays. She was looked up to and admired for her work in the world of philosophy. In 1917, as the First World War was drawing to an end, Professor Adolf Reinach was killed in action. Edith went to the funeral and then spent a few days with Anna. This was something that Edith did not look forward to doing as she anticipated that Anna would be devastated with grief, especially since she and Adolf were seen to be the ideal

couple. However, the visit was to mark a great turning point in Edith's life.

When she arrived at the funeral she found Anna, not laid low with grief but busy comforting all those who loved Adolf. Edith later asked Anna how she had been able to cope as she had done. Anna explained that immediately she heard of her husband's death, her grief was so great that she did not want to live. Then some time later she realised that her husband was at peace with God and that helped her to bear her

cross. Edith could not forget that story. She was amazed at Anna's faith.

A few years later in 1921 Edith was staying with some friends who had a large orchard. They spent many hours each day working in the orchard and at night they would sit and read. One night her friends were away and Edith, browsing through the bookshelves, took out *The Life of St Teresa of Avila*.

She became so absorbed that she sat and read all night. Edith's interest in the Catholic religion had been sparked.

She went to the town the next day and bought a missal and a catechism. She began going to early morning Mass. On January 1st 1922 she was baptised into the Catholic Church.

She was also forced to leave the world of Philosophy where she had been accepted as one of the great philosophers of the day. Once she became a Catholic she was no longer trusted and had to give up her position in the university.

She started teaching in a convent school in Spayer run by the Dominican Order. Ever since reading the life of St Teresa she had been interested in becoming a Carmelite nun. But the administrators in the education system did not want to lose her. The Dominican sisters with whom she worked allowed her to join them for prayers. She was always first in the church for Mass in the mornings and she spent several hours each day in prayer in front of the Blessed Sacrament.

In January 1933 Hitler became Chancellor of Germany. The series of events which led to the persecution and attempt at extermination of the Jews and

World War II began. Because of her Jewish background her bosses in the world of education suddenly encouraged Edith to leave and to fulfil her wish to become a Carmelite nun.

Her mother had been forced by the anti-Jewish feelings of the time to give up her business. Edith had continued to support her and to accompany her to the synagogue. Now the final parting of mother and daughter had to take place.

Edith had anticipated her mother's anger when she heard what Edith was about to do. She was completely unprepared for what happened.

Her mother, who had been so strong over the years, raising her children alone and running the family business single-handed, broke down and cried bitterly. She found it very difficult to understand why her favourite daughter was turning away from her in this way. Edith found it extremely difficult to leave her mother who was already suffering acutely from the atmosphere in the country at this time. She was old and afraid. But Edith had made her decision and was not to be put off, though the parting with her mother was extremely painful.

In October 1933 Edith entered the convent of the Carmelite nuns in Cologne. She would henceforth be known as Sr Benedicta. Edith was forty-two. She had now entered a hidden life of prayer among the Carmelite sisters, none of whom had even heard of Edith Stein.

Her cell, with whitewashed walls, had one window which looked out over the convent garden. There was a plank bed covered with a straw pallet, a pillow and a blanket of coarse wool. There was a small table and a low bench. The walls were bare except for a print of the foundress of the Order, Teresa of Avila, a holy water font and a wooden cross.

Although a Christian, Edith was still racially a Jewess and was marked down in official records as such. Because of this she was sent from Cologne to Echt in Holland to be as far away as possible from the persecution of the Jews raging in Germany.

In 1935 Edith's mother died. Her sister Nora, who had become a Catholic, came to live in Holland so as to be near the convent. Nora and Edith were able to meet every day.

In November 1938 synagogues all over Germany were burnt. Jewish shops were looted and any Jews unlucky enough to be on the streets were murdered.

In 1941 one of Edith's brothers and his entire family were taken to a concentration camp. The community began to see if arrangements could be made for Edith and her sister to go to Switzerland. In the meantime a Nazi order was issued that all Catholic Jews were to be seized.

At five o'clock on an August afternoon in 1941 the nuns were in choir when a knock on the door heralded the entry of two SS men. Edith and her sister were taken captive.

A Jewish prisoner who survived wrote of the camp at Westerbrook, *'The distress in the camp and the confusion among the newcomers cannot be described. But Sr Benedicta stood out by her calm and composure, comforting, helping, bringing peace.'*

On 9th August 1942, Edith and her sister Nora entered the gas chamber at Auschwitz.

Discuss

What qualities do you think Edith Stein had?
What do you think would have been the most difficult decision she had to make?

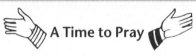

A Time to Pray

Dear Lord,
Help me to find ways in which I can serve you in my own life. Then give me the courage and the strength that I need to do these things even if it is difficult.

Spend some time thinking quietly about some of the ways in which you think you can put into practice the teaching of Jesus in your everyday life. Ask for God's help in the following prayer.

Prayer of St Francis of Assisi

Lord, make me an instrument of your peace.
Where there is hatred, let me sow love;
Where there is injury, pardon;
Where there is despair, hope;
Where there is doubt, faith;
Where there is darkness, light;
And where there is sadness, joy.

O Divine Master, grant that I may not so much seek:
To be consoled as to console;
To be understood as to understand;
To be loved as to love;
For it is in giving that we receive;
It is in pardoning that we are pardoned;
And it is in dying that we are born to eternal life.

Lesson Nineteen

Prayer

When we want to meet our friends we get in touch, maybe by telephone or by sending a letter. We put ourselves out and spend time arranging the meeting and organising a time and place to meet.

When we meet our friends we look forward to talking to them and asking for advice; listening to them and hearing what's happening in their lives. We enjoy their company.

When we pray, we get in touch with God.

All you ever wanted to know about prayer!

Complete the following questionnaire and discover your attitude to prayer. If you have an answer which isn't listed , write it down.

1. How often do you pray?
(a) Never
(b) Every day
(c) In school when prayers are said
(d) At Mass
(e) Only sometimes when things are going wrong

2. Why do you pray?
(a) To ask for something
(b) I don't pray, I don't believe in it
(c) I don't know
(d) To talk to God
(e) To say sorry for something I've done wrong

3. Where do you find you pray most easily?
(a) At Mass
(b) Anywhere
(c) Alone in a quiet place
(d) At school
(e) Other

4. What kind of prayers do you say?
(a) Our Father & Hail Mary
(b) Prayers I learned in primary school
(c) I make up my own
(d) Silent prayers
(e) Other

5. When you pray, do you prefer to:
- (a) Kneel with hands joined?
- (b) Sit and bow your head?
- (c) Stand with open hands?
- (d) Sit with hands joined?
- (e) Other?

6. Which of the following helps you to pray?
- (a) Listening to music/hymns
- (b) Other people
- (c) Silence
- (d) Reading the Bible
- (e) Other

7. Which of the following do you use to help you to pray?
- (a) Rosary beads
- (b) Prayer book
- (c) Don't use anything
- (d) Bible
- (e) Other

8. If a friend was having difficulty in praying and asked your advice, what would you say?
- (a) Use your own words when you pray
- (b) Make time to pray each day
- (c) Get yourself in the right frame of mind – avoid distractions like the TV or radio, preferably a quiet room
- (d) Talk to your parish priest
- (e) Other

9. When you pray, what length of time should you take?
- (a) It depends on the situation
- (b) Ten minutes at least
- (c) I don't time myself when I pray
- (d) As long as it takes to say all I want
- (e) Five minutes at the most

10. In your life would you say prayer is:
- (a) Very important ?
- (b) Has no place ?
- (c) Is important at a time of crisis ?
- (d) Is frustrating because my prayers never seem to be answered ?
- (e) Something you would like to know more about ?

In Your Religion Journal

From the answers you have chosen write an honest conclusion for yourself to the questionnaire, pointing out:

what you have discovered about your prayer life;

what aspect of your prayer life you would like to improve.

What does prayer mean to you ?

Choose *four* words which express what prayer means to you.

Praising

Reflection

Asking

Relaxation

Talking

Thinking

Listening

Alone

Thanking

Saying sorry

Loving

Meditation

Conversation

Your own words

In Your Religion Journal

Your parish priest has asked you to design a Parish Bulletin on prayer, promoting the prayer group which will meet next week.
Using the *four* words you have chosen, you must try to get people interested in prayer by telling them what prayer means to you.
For example, if you feel that prayer is talking in *your own words* to God, then use this expression in a sentence.

Discuss

When you phone your friend how do you start off the conversation?

When two people who know each other meet in the street how do they greet each other?

When you write a letter how do you begin to tell your news ?

These ordinary expressions that everyone uses like, 'Hello, how are you?' are often necessary to start off a more important conversation. They show we are interested in each other. We need a few words to begin with before we begin to tell our friend the latest news or a confidence.

When we get in touch with God through prayer it is rather the same sort of thing. We don't need to look for unusual words, but instead use simple words to begin with – the kind of words we use every day.

In Your Religion Journal

Imagine you are telephoning God; write out a number of ways you might begin a prayer conversation.

This Self-Confidence prayer is a simple straightforward 'talk to God.'

SELF-CONFIDENCE

Lord, I really need your help:
I feel so lonely, so isolated;
I want to make friends, but I can't.
I know I have some friends,
But I sometimes feel that they don't like me,
Or that if they got to know me well, they would stop liking me.
I'm like a wave thrown up on the seashore
That can't get back into the flow.

My best friend seems to like my company, after all;
We make a difference to each other's lives.
Thanks for that.
Thanks, too, for my sense of humour.

Help me, Lord, in times of doubting my worth.
Remind me of my good qualities,
Let me see in myself what others admire in me,
Let me give you thanks for what's good in me,
Rather than moping about what might be.

Thanks, Lord, for me
Thanks for shaping,
Moulding,
Bringing to birth
What's good in me.
Nurture me and build me up.

Help me to encourage others in their goodness.
Let me rejoice in the belief that we are made in your image.
Give us confidence in our own goodness,
So that we can grow in our friendships.

In Your Religion Journal

Using your own words, compose and decorate a prayer on a theme close to your heart.

Class Prayer Board

Tape a large piece of paper along the wall. Each day this week compose your own prayer. Display all the prayers which have been composed by the class on the prayer board.

****

Sometimes there are days when we might not find words of our own to say to God, so we can make use of other people's words. For instance we could say the well-known prayers like the Our Father and the Hail Mary or read a psalm out of the Old Testament, or even read a poem which we like.

However, what is important, when we are saying well-known prayers, is that we think about what we are saying and understand their meaning. There is always the danger that we will rattle through those prayers which are familiar to us.

Mike's conversation with God

Read and act out the following.

Mike said his prayers twice a day. He always said the 'Our Father'; well, it was an easy one to remember and he knew what it meant, that is until one day...

Our Father, who art in heaven.

Yes.

Did I hear a voice?

You did.

Who are you? Look, whoever you are, will you please go away? Can't you see I'm praying ? Now you've put me off. I'd better start all over again. Our Father, who art in heaven.

Yes.

You've interrupted me again!

But you did call me, didn't you?

Call you? I didn't call you. I was just saying my prayers. Our Father, who art in heaven.

There! You did it again.

Did what?

You called me. You said: 'Our Father, who art in heaven.' So here I am.

Oh my God! I didn't really expect you to answer. I mean, I didn't really think you listened to us when we pray.

Oh, so that's how it is! Is that all the faith you have in me? Anyhow, now that we have made contact, what's on your mind?

To be quite honest I haven't given it much thought. You see, I was just saying my prayers for the day. I always say the Our Father every day. It makes me feel good.

Oh, so that's what prayer is for - to make you feel good, I see. Go on.

Hallowed be thy name.

Hold it! What do you mean by 'Hallowed'?

It means... let me see... Hallowed?...Good heavens! I don't know what it means. It's a word I seldom use. In fact, apart from this prayer I never use it.

Tell me something. Do you normally use words you don't understand when you're talking to people?

No.

Well then, why do you do so when you're talking to me? After all, that's what prayer is – a conversation between me and you.

Good point, lord .... By the way, what does it mean?

It means 'Honoured' or 'Holy'.

So what I'm really praying for is that your name might be honoured and respected by everybody.

That's the general idea.

Can I go on now?

By all means.

Thy kingdom come.

What kind of kingdom have you in mind?

I'm not really sure. All I know is that the world is in a mess. All you see in the television news is fighting and killing.

So what would you like me to do?

I'd like you to take control over things down here as you do up there.

Have I control over you?

Some of the time.

I see. What kind of world would you like to see?

I'd like everybody to be able to live in peace.

Do you live in peace with everybody?

Well, nearly everybody but there are some people I find it hard to get on with. In fact I'll be honest. There are a couple of people I'd like to strangle. There's this fellow in my class and he's so mean, he'd make Scrooge seem like Santa Claus. And then

there's my brother. I haven't spoken to him in two months, he just gets on my nerves. I wish he'd leave me in peace.

But what about the rows you start yourself? You're no angel, you know.

This is starting to hurt, Lord. Aren't we taking it a little too seriously?

Well, you did pray for my kingdom to come. So why not let it come in that small corner of the world for which I made you personally responsible? What I mean is - why not begin with yourself? You do want to belong to my kingdom, don't you?

Of course, but I'm not sure what I have to do.

The poor in spirit, the humble, the merciful, the peacemakers, and those who suffer for what is right ... all these belong to my kingdom. In a nutshell – all those who try to do my will.

Your will ... that's the next part of the prayer. Can I go on then?

Certainly.

Thy will be done on earth, as it is in heaven.

Do you realise what you've just said? You've just prayed that my will be done on earth. 'On earth' presumably means in your life too?

Of course.

And what are you going to do about it?

How do you mean, what am I going to do about it. Haven't I just prayed about it?

So you have. But I repeat: What are you going to do about it?

Nothing, I hadn't thought of doing anything.

Oh, so that's how it is! You pray for my will to be done. Then you sit back, fold your arms, and do sweet nothing about it. You know something? You've got a very poor

understanding of prayer.

What do you mean, Lord?

Well, you seem to think that prayer is me doing things for you, instead of me helping you do things for yourself. Let's be practical for a moment. Is my will done in every part of your life?

I go to Mass regularly.

That's part of it. But when, for instance, did you put yourself out to help another person? And what about that tongue of yours? You're well known for your sarcasm, you know.

Wait a minute! I'm no better or worse than anyone else. Still, I really would like to be a better person.

Good! Things are beginning to look up. Praying can be dangerous, you know. If you took it seriously you could end up a changed person.

(*Mike looks at his watch and says...*)

This is taking a lot longer than I expected. Normally I'm finished my prayers in two minutes flat. What's worrying me is that I was due to meet a few of my friends, half an hour ago. Couldn't we finish this another time?

Finished in two minutes flat! Sounds like a slot machine job to me. So you can't wait for my will to be done. Now it's your will that must be done.

Oh well, I suppose I might as well go on. Give us this day our daily bread.

What are you praying for now?

For bread — at least that's what the prayer says, isn't it?

Yes, but bread for whom?

For myself of course.

For yourself? You don't look undernourished to me. In any case I thought you said '*our* daily bread', not *my* daily bread?

I knew you'd bring up those starving people.

What people?

Surely you've heard of Ethiopia?

Of course I have. I was just testing you. So you do know then that millions of my children are literally starving to death. And what, may I ask, are you doing about them?

I give a few pounds now and then.

I see. But maybe you could do more. For instance, maybe you might think of them the next time you are tempted to complain that your dinner isn't properly cooked. However, for the moment let us leave those starving people and return to yourself. You're not hungry, are you?

No, but...

So what more do you want?

Don't get me wrong, Lord. I'm not complaining. I'm grateful for what I have, my family and friends, I go to a good school.

Let's move on then.

I'm afraid of what you'll say. Forgive us our trespasses, as we forgive those who trespass against us.

What about your friend Mark ?

I knew you'd bring him up. It's all his fault. I found out he was laughing at me behind my back, so I fell out with him.

But what about your prayer? ... 'As we forgive those who trespass against us'.

Ah, Lord, be reasonable. I would

look stupid if I made friends with him again. In fact I think I'll have a go at making a fool out of him and see how he feels.

I take it then that you're not going to forgive him?

Honestly, Lord, I couldn't promise you that.

And yet you expect me to forgive you. You're not going to forgive him. Is that final?

That's final.

Well then, for goodness sake go off and meet your friends and don't be wasting my time.

Don't cut me off, Lord. Wait a minute. Are you still there, Lord?

(*No reply*)

Looks like I've been cut off. I was just going to say, Lord, that maybe we could work something out. Maybe I can forgive him after all... I can... I will forgive him ... I will... Are you there, Lord?

I am.

Oh good! You really had me scared for a minute. Thought you'd cut me off.

I take it that you don't like to be cut off.

You bet I don't.

Well, that's exactly what you do when you don't forgive. You cut the other person off from you, and you cut yourself off from me. People who refuse to forgive break down the bridge over which they themselves must pass. So you are willing to forgive him?

I've already forgiven him.

Good, let's get on with the prayer.

Lead us not into temptation.

You know that one always makes me smile.

Why do you say that, Lord?

There are two reasons. The first is this: if you're asking me to save you from all temptation then

you're asking the impossible. You might as well ask me to stop the rain from falling on you.

But you could help me to overcome it?

I could and I will. Temptation is not necessarily a bad thing, you know. It's a test of your loyalty. It's an opportunity for you to grow. Now do you want to know the second reason?

I might as well hear it, though I've a feeling that I won't like it.

Tell me, when did you need me, or anyone else for that matter, to take you by the hand and lead you into temptation? Do you not walk into it of your own accord and with both eyes open? I mean, no one makes you cheat in your exams, or watch a TV programme which you know you shouldn't... Do you want me to go on?

Stop, Lord. I've heard enough.

You insist on putting yourself into situations where you know you're going to be tempted, then you cry to me for help. Now does that make sense?

You remind me of a boy who can't swim a stroke who insists on going in beyond his depth.

I think I'm out of my depth right now.

No, you're doing all right. Go on.

Deliver us from evil.

Evil? What have you in mind?

I feel very insecure at times. I worry about a lot of things ... my school work... my family. I wouldn't like anything to happen to my family. My neighbour's baby died as a result of a cot death. Another family in the street had a child killed in a car accident.

Go on.

Could you not have prevented these things from happening? I mean you're supposed to be able to do anything you want. And you're posed to love everybody. So how can you just stand there and watch these tragedies happen?

In a world where people have free choice, in a world where things interact, where seasons change and things grow and fade, where there are tides and winds and rain, there has to be suffering. A world without suffering would be one in which people could not show their love through courage and self-sacrifice. You should pray when you are suffering - trust me, I will be there to see you through.

Thank you, Lord. I'm finished. That's the end of my prayer.

Don't be rushing off. I hope you've learned something from our little conversation.

Oh, I have, I know where I've been going wrong when saying my prayers.

I used to just rattle through them, and never thought about one thing I was saying. I never even thought of putting my prayers into action. Maybe it would be a good idea if you had this little conversation with a lot more people I know. But I can guarantee you one thing, you'll be hearing from me a lot more, and at least you'll know from here on in I mean what I say.

Thanks Lord. I'll be talking to you soon!

Find your Group Discuss

What was the most important thing Mike learnt from his conversation with God?

What have you learnt from Mike's conversation with God?

Mike was told that, 'Praying can be dangerous. If you took it seriously you could end up a changed person!' In what ways could prayer change you?

Mike seemed surprised when he was told that he should be putting his prayers into action; in what ways can you put your prayers into action?

Five types of prayer

There are times when you have to *ask* your friend for something you need. Or your friend might *ask for help* in some way.

There may be times when you want to *thank* your friend for helping you out.

Friendship means that there are times when you will have to say *sorry* to your friend for something you have done, but at the same time you know your friend will forgive you.

And then there are times when you will want to show your *love* and appreciation for your friend.

In Your Religion Journal

Write down five examples where you had to:
Ask your friend for a favour;
Help your friend in some way;
Thank your friend for something they did for you;
Say sorry for something you did to your friend;
Show your love to a friend, who had been good to you.

Prayer Search

In pairs find these references from the Book of Psalms and decide which type of prayer each one is. Put the reference on the appropriate line.

Asking

Intercession

Adoration/Love

Sorrow

Praise/Thanksgiving

6:2. 9:1. 17:1-2. 18:1. 29:1-2. 30:12. 36:7. 51:1. 51:4. 55:1-3.

At different times of each day, and indeed throughout our lives, we say different types of prayer, depending on how we feel or on what we have to say to God.

We can use four headings for the different types of prayer we usually say.

1
Asking Prayer Petition

When we ask God for something we need or want or to help someone else.

2
Thanksgiving Praise

When we pray and thank God for all we have been given and give praise for all creation.

3
Sorrow

When we say sorry to God for something we have done and ask forgiveness.

4
Adoration Love

When we tell God of our love.

Prayer Box   Draw this prayer box in your religion journal. Compose five short prayers under the headings.

Petition	**Thanksgiving/Praise**
Sorrowful	**Adoration/Love**

In Your Religion Journal

Imagine yourself sitting in a bare room facing an empty chair. The door opens and Jesus enters to take his place on the chair. After some time of quiet and reflection, you begin a conversation with Jesus. Write out your conversation using these headings as guidelines to help you.

You ask Jesus for something that is important in your life.
You ask Jesus to help someone you know.
You thank Jesus for something important in your life.
You say sorry and ask Jesus to forgive you for something you have done in your life.
You tell Jesus how much you love him.

God doesn't hear my prayers!

People often pray to God when they want something or when they face some kind of difficulty in their lives. Every time we ask God for something we hope our prayers will be answered.

A great danger in prayer is taking God for an automatic machine. Press the button and your prayers are answered!

Lord help me get a summer job....
Lord help my mother to get better, she's very ill....
Lord help me get to the disco on Saturday – my parents won't allow me out....
Lord let me pass my exam....

Someone once said that God has four answers to prayer ...
Sometimes God says – **Yes**
Sometimes God says – **No**
Sometimes God says – **Wait**
Sometimes God says – **If**

Discuss

Why did the man think his prayers weren't answered?
What could he have done to save himself?
In what ways did God try to help the man?
What did you learn from this story?

In Your Religion Journal

Write about a time when you asked God for something you wanted.

165

There was a man who one time insisted that when he asked God for something, God was going to give it to him. The dam had flooded and broken its banks and there was a tidal wave on its way down into the village. The police came by with sirens, calling on the people to get out of the house, 'Get out, move quickly, the floods are coming!' But this man ignored the call. Why? Because he asked God to help him. Then the floods came roaring down and burst his front door and he went upstairs and out on the windowsill. Somebody came along with a boat and asked him to get in. Oh no, he wouldn't. He trusted in God. God was going to look after him.

And of course, the floods rose higher and he climbed up on the roof, and when he was on the roof a helicopter came along and lowered a winch for him to grab. No, he refused. God was going to look after him. And of course the guy was drowned.

He arrived up to the gates of heaven and he was very annoyed. Peter realised there was something wrong with him.

'You're grumpy, what's wrong with you?' 'What's wrong? I prayed. I asked God to save me and, after all my trouble, I wasn't answered and I drowned.' And Peter said, 'We did send you the police, didn't we? And somebody in a boat, and then we sent somebody to you with a helicopter! Surely we did answer your prayers?'

When we pray God always listens to us. God's answer is not always what we would like it to be. When God answers our prayers he gives us the gifts which we most need. God gives us these gifts not because we deserve them but because God loves us.

Sometimes people say:

God doesn't answer my prayers because I'm not good enough!

The non-answer of a prayer doesn't mean that you're not as good as somebody else.

Find Your Group

Sometimes we ask God to do something which we could solve quite easily ourselves. For each of these examples suggest ways in which individuals or governments can contribute to the solution in each situation.

If you ask God to help stop the famine in Africa.

If you ask God to help get jobs for those who are unemployed.

If you ask God to help stop terrorist activity and wars throughout the world.

If you ask God to help the black people in South Africa obtain equality with their white neighbours.

If you ask God to help the poor in your city.

If you ask God to remove the threat of nuclear weapons.

These situations could be solved with human effort. It's important to remember that if we use the resources of the world properly, we could feed everyone. The poverty and lack of jobs can often depend on the way the resources and money are distributed in a country and between countries.

If we pray we can be sure that God will give his help and guidance in some way. It might be to aid our efforts or the efforts of others, to awaken the consciences of people who hadn't bothered until now or it might be in a way that we least expected or hadn't thought of.

If we pray, God will be with us, helping us and guiding us in our own efforts to solve our problems.

Sometimes we may be asking God for the wrong thing. For instance if a husband prays to God to save his wife from cancer, and his prayer is not answered, he might wonder what sort of God this is.

Even though God has not intervened miraculously in the laws of nature in order to save his wife's life, this does not mean that the man's prayers have gone unheard. God gives him the strength to cope and to hope, to live in faith that he will meet her again. He can give his wife the courage and faith to come through her time of trial and perhaps become a better person through it.

Sometimes we may be praying for something which is not for our good or the good of others. Many people remember times when they desperately wanted something and didn't get it. Sometimes it is only years later that they realise it was really a good thing that they hadn't obtained what they wanted. What we want is not always what we need or what is best for us. If we pray sincerely and don't obtain what we ask for, we can be sure that God will give us something better in answer to our prayer.

In Your Religion Journal

Write about a time when you prayed to God and your prayer wasn't answered the way you wanted it to be. How did you feel? Looking back, did your prayers help you in any way?

When we pray, it gives us a sense of God's care and love in our lives and a way of looking on the struggles we face throughout life.

If we pray over failure or success, love or hurt, illness or death, we can come to understand it and accept it in a different way.

What God gives us in prayer is not always a quick answer nor a solution to all the social or personal problems. Prayer gives us a sense of trust in God's care and love, and a knowledge that all the time he is working for our good.

Jesus used two parables to encourage us not to give up praying or to lose heart when it seems as if our prayers are not being answered.

The Widow and the Judge (Luke 18:1-8)
A Friend in Need (Luke 11:5-13)

Ways of Praying

Just as we use gestures and actions to help us to express our innermost feelings in conversation, so too when we want to express ourselves in prayer we can use different ways of praying to help us.

Find Your Group
Which way do you prefer to pray?

Alone
With another person
In a group
As a community

Discuss
In each of the above situations prayer can be: silent; shared; scripture-based; formal; informal; through dance; music; mime or drama; using art; using signs & symbols; based on poetry or prose.

Think of times and places when it would be helpful to pray in each of these particular ways.

Jesus Prayed All Ways and Always

We know that prayer was important to Jesus during his life on earth.

Prayer was essential to the religious life of the Jewish people.
Every Jew was encouraged to pray often during the day. Every young Jewish boy was taught the words of the *Shema* as soon as he could speak and he was expected to pray the *Shema* at the hours of prayer each day.

We learn from the Gospel of St Luke that Jesus was reared in a devoutly religious household. He would have learned to pray with Mary and Joseph in their home, and so from early childhood Jesus would have found time to pray every day as it was central to his life.

Jesus constantly turned to his Father for help, strength and encouragement throughout his life. His way of asking for assistance was through prayer. The disciples noticed how Jesus would often go away alone to pray. He used prayer as a source of strength and spiritual renewal. He prayed before all the important events of his life on earth:

before his baptism (Luke 3:21);

before choosing the disciples (Luke 6:12-13);

before and during the miracles (Matthew 14:19; Mark 7:34; John 11:41-42);

during the transfiguration (Luke 9:28-36);

before his crucifixion (Luke 22:44).

The stories about Jesus' prayer life tell us about when and why he prayed, how he prayed, for whom he prayed, and where he prayed.

Class Activity
Look up each of the above occasions in your bible and design a wall frieze illustrating the prayer life of Jesus.

In Your Religion Journal

Look up the *Shema* (Deuteronomy 6:4-5). Write it out and decorate.

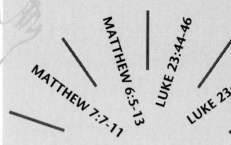
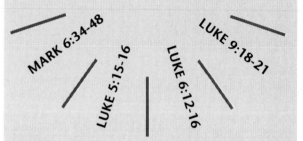

MATTHEW 7:7-11
MATTHEW 6:5-13
MATTHEW 23:44-46
LUKE 23:33-34
MATTHEW 26:36-44
LUKE 10:1, 17, 21-22
MARK 6:34-48
LUKE 5:15-16
LUKE 6:12-16
LUKE 9:18-21

Find your Group

Look up each of the stories on the Prayer Wheel in your bible and decide for each reference, when and why Jesus prayed; how Jesus prayed; for whom Jesus prayed and where Jesus prayed.

In Your Religion Journal

Imagine you are a disciple of Jesus, write a letter to a friend at home telling them about how Jesus prayed.

Places of Prayer

When you want to meet a friend you arrange a time and place where you'll both be able to talk to each other. You don't leave these arrangements to chance. More than likely you'll arrange a place which isn't too noisy and without too many distractions.

Likewise the first step in getting to know God better is to find a good place for prayer.

Some people can pray in any place, on a beach, waiting for a bus, or in the middle of a crowd, but if we want to pray without interruption and distraction we usually need privacy.

The important thing about a place is that it helps us to pray. The best way to find the right place is to experiment to see what works best for us.

Sometimes we find we need to pray alone, sometimes we need to pray with family and friends and at other times we need to pray with the community.

In the gospels we find that Jesus often prayed in different places. Sometimes he prayed alone, or with his disciples, or he would pray with the whole community in the synagogue.

Activity

Look up the following references, write out and decorate the quotations: Mark 1:35; Luke 9:28; Luke 4:16.

Places of Prayer and Pilgrimage

Many people like to go on pilgrimage to the Holy Land of Palestine where Jesus lived and died, and over the years many others have visited one of the shrines dedicated to Our Lady or some great saint. These places have become great centres of prayer and devotion.

Postcard from Knock

Hi there,
I've just arrived in Knock in Co. Mayo to visit Ireland's principal shrine to Our Lady. On 21st August 1879, fifteen people stood spellbound, gazing at an apparition of Our Lady, St Joseph and St John the Evangelist which appeared on the wall of the small parish church. Since then Knock has come from being an obscure village to one of the world's greatest centres of prayer and devotion to Our Lady.
The last time I was in Knock was when Pope John Paul II visited Ireland in 1979 and attended the celebrations to mark the occasion of the 100th anniversary of the apparition at the shrine. I can remember him saying, 'Here I am at the goal of my journey to Ireland: the shrine of Our Lady at Knock. Since I first learned of the centenary of this shrine, which is being celebrated this year, I have felt a strong desire to come here, the desire to make yet another pilgrimage to the shrine of the Mother of Christ, the Mother of the Church, the Queen of Peace.'
The ceremonies for the pilgrim at

Knock consist of making the stations of the cross, reciting the rosary and then walking in procession around the grounds of the basilica.

I'll write again soon.

I. Pilgrim.

Postcard from Walsingham

My journey has taken me to Walsingham, a small village in East Anglia.
Since 1061 Walsingham has been the most famous shrine in England dedicated to Our Lady. A lady named Richeldis di Faverches is said to have received a vision from Our Lady. She was asked to build a house similar to the one in Nazareth where Mary was told she was to be the Mother of God. The house was constructed of wood and in it was a wooden

statue of Mary with the infant Jesus on her knee. It was not long before the shrine became a centre of pilgrimage.

About a mile from Walsingham pilgrims would stop to pray at a small chapel known as the Slipper Chapel. Here they would take off their shoes before walking the last mile to the shrine barefoot.

However, during the Reformation in England, many of the shrines were destroyed. Walsingham did not escape. The holy house was burned and the statue taken to London to be destroyed.

In 1894 Charlotte Boyd restored the Slipper Chapel as a centre of pilgrimage once more. A new statue of Our Lady and the child Jesus was installed and once again pilgrims came flocking to Walsingham.

I took part in the pilgrimage procession which now starts in the village of Walsingham itself. We walked behind a flower-decked statue, reciting the rosary and singing hymns as we made our way to the chapel.

The quiet beauty of the surrounding countryside helped us all pray.

Bye for now.

I. Pilgrim

Postcard from Taizé

My journey wouldn't be complete without visiting Taizé, a small village in Eastern France. I've been here almost three days now and it

has been a wonderful experience. Let me tell you how Taizé was put on the map. In 1940 Brother Roger bought an old house in Taizé. He renovated it and used it to shelter refugees during the war and the more deprived people in the area. He wanted to gather a community of brothers who would live and pray together in a spirit of love and reconciliation and who would live out the values of the Gospel. On Easter Sunday 1949, under the leadership and inspiration of Brother Roger, seven brothers committed themselves for life to live and pray together in the community. Today there are eighty brothers or more from different countries and from several different religious traditions, who

live in the community at Taizé. Every year young people from every denomination and origin come to Taizé on pilgrimage, attracted by its prayer and community spirit. It is a place which has a welcome for everyone, young or old, those who are unemployed or deprived, those who are sick or lonely. Everyone is given the opportunity to pray and deepen their faith. I have met people from many different backgrounds and outlooks on life. We have shared our experiences together and I've enjoyed hearing their points of view on a variety of topics. Throughout the day we have opportunities to join in prayer and sing the Taizé chants in different languages. It is a place of great hope for Christian unity and ecumenism.

Wish you were here!

I. Pilgrim

Test Yourself.

Do the Looking Back exercises on pages 227

Unit Eight

The Passion and Death of Jesus

Lesson Twenty

The Death of Jesus

In Your Religion Journal

Give reasons why you chose the words you did when you thought of death.

In Your Group

Recall the death of a friend, relative or neighbour.

What were your feelings at the time?

What did it say to you about your own life ?

People want to live, but every day newspaper headlines and TV reports bring us news that people die.

Life is fragile. A sudden accident or an illness can end it. Youth or greatness does not guarantee life. Death is a part of life and all living things die eventually.

Which of the following words would you use to describe what you think about death or dying:

Nervous · Afraid · A Waste · Happy · Worried · Sad · Disillusioned ·Despair · Lonely · Unknown · Curious · Abandoned · Anticipation ·

The cycle of life and death in nature continues throughout the world.

Living things change and grow and as each stage of growth dies it makes way for new life. In the same way a baby grows into a young child and then changes and grows into a young adolescent – childhood dies to make way for adolescence and so on.

Two brothers drown in fishing expedition

University student dies instantly in head-on collision with vehicle

House fire claims the lives of a family of four

Great Oak Trees From Little Acorns Grow

Archie the acorn could feel his grasp grow weaker each day. He had clung to the great oak tree for the whole season. He knew it was only a matter of time before he would fall, like the other acorns that had gone before him. And then one day it happened. Archie could feel himself falling. He landed with a heavy thud. As he lay in a daze beneath the leafy canopy of the oak tree he wondered what his new life would bring. Now that he had left the safety of the lofty branches he was nervous about entering the world of the unknown.

He could feel himself being moved. He could see a great hole being dug for him. He wanted to shout out and ask them to stop. He didn't want to be buried. He belonged up in the great oak tree from where he once came. But it was too late. The next thing he knew was that he was being covered with damp cold soil and then everything fell silent. He lay quite still. What else could he do ? The soil was heavy and it was pressing against his shell. He was lonely and he missed the other acorns.

Weeks, maybe even months, passed. Archie had lost all track of time. But he sensed it was winter outside as the temperature had dropped below zero.

He could feel the life drain out of him and he grew weaker by the day. His heartbeat was very faint and he knew that there was a chance he would die if somebody didn't come and rescue him quickly. His beautiful shell which had always protected him began to decay and rot. As winter continued Archie began to lose the will to live, he could feel himself drifting off into a deep coma.

Meanwhile nature had decided to step in and rescue the dying acorn. The earth was beginning to thaw out and rain-water was allowed to seep through.

Archie slowly became aware of the changes in his surroundings. He wakened from his deep coma. At first he didn't recognise himself, his tough shell had softened and died. He felt naked. He didn't know what to expect next. Slowly as spring began to take a hold, Archie could actually feel himself growing. He was overcome with emotion. 'It's happening!' he shouted out, 'I'm not going to die after all, my shell may be dead but I'm alive and I'm going to grow into a great oak tree just like the one I fell from. I'm no longer going to be known as Archie the acorn. One day when I'm fully grown people will call me Archie the oak tree.' But there was no one to hear him or congratulate him on his success. Archie knew, however, that it wouldn't be too long before he was poking his nose above the earth.

A tiny root appeared and dug its way down deep into the earth and at the same time a fragile stem sprang up and began pushing itself upwards.

Archie looked back at his tattered shell, and said, 'Farewell, old shell, thanks for looking after me during the winter months. I have to leave you now, I'm growing to greater things, I'm going to be an oak tree.'

Archie now stands thirty-five feet tall in the local park. He often thinks to himself of the days when he was buried underground, when his shell died to make way for his new life as an oak tree. Now he is holding little acorns on his branches and they'll stay there until the time is right. And Archie smiles to himself when he thinks of the wise old saying, 'Great oak trees from little acorns grow'.

Discuss

When Archie first fell from the oak tree why was he worried about starting a new life?
While Archie was buried underground, how could you have given him hope of a bright future?
In what way did Archie have to die before he could grow into a great oak tree ?

Class Activity

Make a wall display by illustrating the cycle of life and death in nature.

Facing Death

When a friend or relative dies we find ourselves looking closely at our own lives. We often take life for granted but death reminds us of the fragility of life. Facing death prompts people to ask questions about their own life such as: Is this the end? Is there anything more?

In Your Religion Journal

Imagine you have been sentenced to death. You will face a firing squad in the morning. What questions would you ask yourself and what would you think about during the few hours you have left in your cell ?

Through Jesus' death and resurrection we can find comfort and hope that in death everything is not ended. Through his death and resurrection Jesus has answered these questions for us.

It wasn't easy for Jesus to face death, any more than it is for us. Yet at a certain point in his life of preaching he decided that he must leave the quiet of Galilee and proclaim his Father's message in Jerusalem. He knew he would be walking into the hands of his enemies. But he had his work to do. He would go through with it even if it meant death.

In Jerusalem things turned out as Jesus and his friends had feared. Jesus had to face the condemnation and humiliation, the suffering and death, which he prayed he might escape from: 'Father, if you will, take this cup of suffering away from me. Not my will, however, but your will be done' (*Luke 22:42*).

Naturally, his friends regarded his death as a tragedy. His death left them disappointed and dispirited. And then the totally unexpected happened. Jesus who died, whom they buried, whom they thought they would see no more, was risen from the dead.

He was present among the apostles. He had shown that there is a new life, a greater life beyond death.

Perhaps we, his followers, take for granted what Jesus' life, death and especially his resurrection tell us about our own lives and deaths. The resurrection of Jesus assures us that what we have always longed for – eternal life – is possible. It shows us that at death, life is not ended or taken away. It is changed, not for something less, but for something greater.

It is for this reason that in the Preface of the funeral Mass we pray:

In him, who rose from the dead, our hope of resurrection dawned.

The sadness of death gives way to the bright promise of eternal life.

Lord, for your faithful people life is changed, not ended.

When the body of our earthly dwelling lies in death we gain an everlasting dwelling place in heaven.

In Your Religion Journal

Write a letter to a friend, relative or neighbour who has been bereaved. What words of comfort and hope would you offer them?

Activity

This poster was found nailed to a tree in Jerusalem. Work out the secret message using the decoder below.

23, 1, 14, 20, 5, 4

1, 4, 1, 14, 7, 5, 18, 20, 15

19, 15, 3, 9, 5, 20, 25

3, 18, 9, 13, 9, 14, 1, 12

1, 14, 4

2, 12, 1, 19, 16 ,8, 5, 13, 5, 18

1 = A	6 = F	11 = K	16 = P	21 = U
2 = B	7 = G	12 = L	17 = Q	22 = V
3 = C	8 = H	13 = M	18 = R	23 = W
4 = D	9 = I	14 = N	19 = S	24 = X
5 = E	10 = J	15 = O	20 = T	25 = Y
				26 = Z

Find a Partner

Design a poster with a secret message that the disciples might have nailed to a tree in Jerusalem during Holy Week. Get your partner to decode the message.

The Five Sorrowful Mysteries

Read Luke's account of the passion and death of Jesus in chapters twenty-two and twenty-three of his gospel. Read the following adaptation of the five sorrowful mysteries and imagine the agony and suffering Jesus endured on his way to Calvary. Pretend that you are Peter as you accompany Jesus on the road to Calvary.

The Agony in the Garden

Father, if you are willing, take this cup of suffering away from me
(Luke 22:42-43).

It is getting dark when Jesus suggests you go with him to the Mount of Olives to a garden called Gethsemane, to pray a while. You had accompanied Jesus to the garden on other occasions but you have a feeling tonight will be different. You sense that Jesus is worried and anxious about something. When you arrive at the garden you can smell the familiar scent from the olive trees and you can feel the cool night breeze against your face.

He asks you and your two friends to pray that you will not fall into temptation. At first you don't understand fully what he means by this. You can see him a short distance away on his knees praying to his Father. You can see that his face is full of anguish. You hear him say, 'Father, if you are willing take this cup of suffering away from me. Not my will but your will be done.' You can see his sweat falling like drops of blood. You want to help him but you are feeling tired and fall asleep. You are wakened when Jesus returns and asks you, 'Why are you sleeping?'

Again he asks you to pray that you will not fall into temptation. You are annoyed with yourself for falling asleep, because you know it is important to Jesus that you pray with him. On two more occasions Jesus returned from praying to find you asleep.

Lord, teach us to pray. Keep us faithful to you in time of temptation and in suffering.

The Arrest

You can hear talking in the distance. You see a crowd approaching, they are carrying swords, clubs and lanterns. Among the crowd you can see Roman soldiers, Pharisees and elders of the Temple and you recognise Judas, a fellow disciple, who is leading them.

You wonder what Judas is doing with this crowd. He kisses Jesus. It is only when you hear Jesus say, 'Is it with a kiss that you betray the Son of Man?' that you realise Judas has betrayed Jesus to the authorities. You feel angry with Judas because he has been a trusted colleague for three years. You want to protect Jesus so you reach for your sword and cut off the right ear of the High Priest's servant. Jesus reprimands you, saying, 'Enough of this, put your sword back in its scabbard.' He touches the man's ear and heals him.

You regret falling asleep. If you had stayed awake, watching, listening, you might have been able to prevent Jesus' arrest.

You hear Jesus asking the crowd, 'Did you have to come with swords and clubs as though I were an outlaw? I was with you in the Temple every day and you did not arrest me.'

The Denial

They arrest Jesus and take him to the house of the High Priest. You follow at a distance, not wanting to be recognised as a disciple. You decide to wait and see if Jesus will be released so you sit down at the fire in the centre of the courtyard to warm yourself. You keep your head down, frightened that you'll be recognised.

But a servant girl notices you and says, 'You were with Jesus of Nazareth.' You are frightened for your life so you quickly reply, 'Oh no, I don't even know who you are talking about.'

You want to get up and leave the courtyard but that might draw too much attention to yourself, so you remain seated at the fire. You wonder to yourself how you ever got mixed up in all this. Nothing makes sense any more. And you ask yourself why you left your fishing nets – you would have been content with the simple life.

Shortly after, another man then recognises you and says loudly, 'This man was with Jesus.' The pressure is on now, you are adamant, 'I do not even know the man.'

About an hour later some other bystanders insist that you were with Jesus because they recognise that your accent is from the North, from Galilee. What else can you say, but deny that you have anything to do with him.

At once you hear a cock crowing in the distance and it is only then that you remember what Jesus said to you at supper ... 'Before the cock crows tonight you will deny me three times.'

You are ashamed of yourself and disappointed that you have failed Jesus. You leave the courtyard and weep bitterly.

Brought before Pilate

It takes you a long time to recover from denying Jesus the way you did. You hope now that Jesus will understand and forgive you. You are hearing rumours that Jesus has been brought before the Council – the elders, chief priests and teachers of the Law. You are surprised, for you are sure Jesus has committed no crime. You can see your friend Joseph of Arimathea coming out from a meeting of the Council. He looks worried.

You shout, 'Joseph, can you tell me what is happening? Is Jesus going to be set free? '

Joseph is glad to see you, for unlike the other members of the Council he does not agree with the decision made against Jesus. He tells you what happened during the meeting: 'Well, the Council asked Jesus, are you the Messiah? And he answered, "If I tell you, you will not believe me, and if I ask you a question you will not answer. But from now on the Son of Man will be seated on the right of Almighty God."' And Joseph goes on to

tell you that the Council was determined to accuse Jesus of something, so they tried to trap him by asking, 'Are you then the Son of God?' and Jesus replied, 'You say that I am.'

Well, you can imagine, that was all they needed to hear. They twisted his words but that didn't matter as long as they could accuse him of something.

So you ask Joseph, 'What's going to happen to him now?' 'I hear that in the morning he will be brought before Pilate, the Roman Governor,' Joseph answers. 'Well, keep me informed of what is happening, Joseph,' you insist.

Now you are frightened for Jesus and you ask yourself why doesn't he save himself? He is letting himself be led into a trap and you remember the words of the Prophet Isaiah :

Like a Lamb led to the Slaughter.

The next morning you hear from Joseph. He has been following the events of the morning closely. He tells you that Jesus was brought before Pilate and accused of corrupting the people by forbidding them to pay their taxes to Caesar and then claiming that he himself is a King! 'And what did Pilate say to all that?' you ask. 'He asked Jesus, "Are you the King of the Jews?" and Jesus replied, "So you say."'

'And what did Pilate do then?' you ask. 'He told us all that he could find no reason to condemn Jesus and so he sent him to Herod to see if he could find fault with him. But within the hour Jesus was sent back to Pilate,' Joseph replied.

Jesus is Sentenced to Death

You are standing among the crowd. People are jostling to get a better view. The atmosphere is tense. Among the crowd you can see Pharisees and elders of the Temple, it appears they are trying to stir up the people against Jesus. You can see Pilate coming out on the veranda. You can hear him telling the crowd that he finds no fault with Jesus and that he is letting him go. You feel relieved. But then the crowd begin shouting 'Crucify him! Crucify him!' You don't understand. Why are they shouting for Jesus to be crucified? Wasn't it only last week that these same people took branches of palm trees and went out of Jerusalem to meet him, shouting, 'God bless the King who comes in the name of the Lord!'

A hush falls over the crowd as Pilate raises his hands for silence. You can hear him making a compromise, 'Since it is the custom at Passover, I will set one prisoner free, you can choose between Barabbas or Jesus.'

You are certain that the people will shout for Jesus, since

Barabbas is a notorious rebel who had recently committed murder during a riot. However, 'Give us Barabbas. Set Barabbas free,' is the roar of the crowd. You try to stop them shouting, but you are helpless. You are frightened for Jesus. You get the impression that Pilate doesn't know what to do and you hear him asking the crowd, 'But what crime has he committed?'

Again the crowd are shouting, 'Crucify him! Crucify him!' You can hear Pilate passing sentence on Jesus. You are numb with disbelief. You can see Pilate going over to a basin and washing his hands of the whole nasty business and you hear him saying to his soldiers, 'Take him and whip him'.

You know now that there is nothing you can do to save Jesus. You bow your head.

The Scourging at the Pillar

It is about an hour later when you hear from a servant in the palace who was a supporter of Jesus.

He saw what happened to Jesus once the soldiers had taken him into the courtyard. He tells you that they stripped Jesus of his clothes, tied him to a pillar and flogged him with leather whips which had pieces of metal at the end.

You can imagine the pain that Jesus suffered. You can feel the crack of the whip against his back. You can imagine the strength drain out of him. And you know that he is suffering all alone because you and your friends have abandoned him.

The Crowning with Thorns

The servant from the palace continues to tell you that after the soldiers had flogged Jesus they made a crown for his head out of thorny branches. They then took a purple robe and put it on him and began to salute him by saying, 'Long live the King of the Jews!' And if that wasn't enough they hit him over the head with a stick and spat at him. He tells you that the soldiers fell on their knees and mocked him. When they had finished their game Jesus was led out to be crucified.

The Carrying of the Cross

It is hot and dusty in the narrow winding street. The people around you are noisy and excited. They hear there is to be a crucifixion. You can see Jesus approaching. He looks exhausted. You can see blood on his face and a deep cut on his forehead from the crown of thorns. He is staggering under the weight of the heavy timber crossbar. You can see he needs to rest but the soldiers are relentless with their whips.

Your heart is in your mouth when you see him collapse in the

'So Pilate, anxious to placate the crowd, released Barabbas for them, and having ordered Jesus to be scourged, handed him over to be crucified' *(Mark 15:15).*

Lord, grant that through your wounds we may be healed.

They put a purple robe on Jesus, made a crown out of thorny branches, and put it on his head *(Mark 15:17).*

dust. He has no strength to carry on. You want to help him carry his cross but you are frightened to come forward.

You can see tears come to his eyes in gratitude when Simon of Cyrene helps him to his feet and goes behind to take some of the weight of the cross.

In front of you some women are crying for Jesus and he turns to comfort them. Following behind are two common criminals who are to be crucified alongside Jesus. And you think of the injustice and humiliation Jesus is suffering as an innocent man.

You leave behind the dusty road leading to Calvary and hide yourself for fear the same fate will befall you.

Meanwhile, a small group of disciples and his mother, Mary, continue to watch as Jesus is nailed to the cross.

The Crucifixion

Beneath the cross his mother is standing; she is comforted by Mary Magdalene and John but they can find no words of comfort for him, as they watch helplessly.

She had watched as the nails had been driven into his wrists, hands and feet. And she could feel the pain in her own heart. It is about noon and an eerie darkness begins to settle, lasting into late afternoon.

He prays for his enemies, 'Forgive them Father! They don't know what they are doing'. He is finding it difficult to breathe. It hurts his mother to see the crowds mocking her son saying, 'Save yourself if you are the King of the Jews!'

Above the cross she can read the words, 'This is the King of the Jews'. She can even hear one of the criminals hanging beside Jesus hurling insults, 'If you are the Messiah save yourself and us!' She is surprised to hear the other criminal shouting at him, 'Don't you fear God? We are getting what we deserve, but this man is innocent, he has done nothing wrong'. And he turns to Jesus and asks Jesus to remember him. His mother hears Jesus saying,' I promise you that today you will be in paradise with me'.

She can see the agony in his face and she knows that he will die soon. She doesn't want to see him suffer any longer.

It was about three o'clock in the afternoon, when his strength left him. He had no strength left to struggle for his life and he cried out, 'My God, my God, why have you abandoned me?'

With his last breath, Mary could hear him whisper, 'It is finished. Father, into your hands I commit my spirit.'

And she wept for her son Jesus who had suffered great agony and who had been crucified between two criminals.

In Your Religion Journal

How did you feel as you watched Jesus suffer on the road to Calvary?
What were some of the things you heard?
Describe some of the things you saw.
In what way could you have helped Jesus as he suffered?
When you heard that Jesus forgave those who had tortured him what did you think?
What would you have said to comfort Mary as she stood at the foot of the cross?
When you heard that Jesus had died how did you feel?

Activity

Make a wall frieze by illustrating the five sorrowful mysteries.

In Your Religion Journal

Imagine yourself entering a room where Jesus is sitting quietly.
You take the seat opposite him.
Write out the conversation you would have with Jesus. Ask him questions about his own suffering and death.

When Jesus was crucified 2,000 years ago, crucifixions were very normal occurrences. Crucifixion had been used as a form of execution for almost 1000 years before the Romans adopted it as a form of slow torture. The Romans crucified slaves, foreigners and criminals, but at the time it was seen as too barbaric for Roman citizens. So Jesus' crucifixion of itself was a routine event and un-remarkable.

During the Roman period the most usual cross was T-shaped, so the top bar was nailed to the upright pole at the execution ground. The top crossbar would have weighed 75-125lbs, about as heavy as a bag of cement. Jesus was forced to carry part of the cross, to the place of execution. This was an added torture for Jesus for he had to carry it almost half a mile from Pilate's palace to Golgotha, through narrow winding streets. Jesus would already have been quite weak after being flogged at the pillar and crowned with thorns. He may not have eaten since the Last Supper with the apostles. Jesus would then have been offered a mixture of wine containing myrrh and gall. This was considered a pain reliever to deaden the pain as the nails were driven into the victim. Jesus refused it.

Nails would have been driven into Jesus' palms, wrists and feet. It is unlikely that his body-weight could have been support-ed if the nails had been driven through the palms of the hands alone since it is likely they would tear open. However, nails driven through the wrist bone would cause dislocation but the nails would still hold. A single nail would be driven through both feet and then into the upright cross. A notice with the name of the criminal and his crime was pinned to the cross.

Crucifixion did not cause the victim to lose a lot of blood but the pain was agonising. Nailed to the cross the body of the victim would have sagged downwards, causing agonising pain and severe cramp on the arms, shoulders and chest. He would then have found it difficult to breathe and in an attempt to buy some time, he would have pushed himself up by the nails in his feet and stretched his legs which would have enabled him to breathe, but at the same time caused unbearable pain. It was only a matter of time before the victim's heart would fail and his lungs would fill with fluid.

How painful is crucifixion?

Sometimes the executioners would nail a small ledge on the cross below the feet which allowed the victim to briefly lean and relieve the stress on the body. However, this only prolonged the agony and inevitable death. The executio-ner could shorten the ordeal by smashing the victim's legs, making it impossible for the dying man to push himself up to breathe and as a result death would come quickly from suffocation.

As we read in the gospel: *Then the Jewish authorities asked Pilate to allow them to break the legs of the men who had been crucified, and to take the bodies down from the crosses. They requested this because it was Friday and they did not want the bodies to stay on the crosses on the Sabbath, since the coming Sabbath was especially holy. So the soldiers went and broke the legs of the first man and then of the other man who had been crucified with Jesus. But when they came to Jesus they saw that he was already dead, so they did not break his legs. One of the soldiers, however, plunged his spear into Jesus' side and at once blood and water poured out (John 19:31-34).*

As a form of execution it was finally abolished in 337 AD. By then the Cross had become the traditional symbol of Christianity.

THE JERUSALEM HERALD

PASSOVER SABBATH
EST. 20 BC

Pilate grants permission to Joseph of Arimathea to bury a criminal!

Joseph of Arimathea, a leading member of the Jewish Council, was granted permission by the Governor, Pontius Pilate, to bury a man called Jesus, a criminal who was crucified yesterday. This is unusual as normally the bodies of executed criminals are thrown into a common grave. We have reason to believe that a reasonable sum of money was paid to Pilate to grant this request.

Our religious affairs correspondent caught up with Joseph as he was leaving his home in Gethsemane Road. At first he was reluctant to talk about the events surrounding the death and burial of Jesus as he felt it would not be safe for him to talk to the Press. Now that he is in hiding he agreed we could print his account of what happened.

'Well, as you know I am a member of the Jewish Council, but I did not agree with the decision and action they took against Jesus. They didn't understand him and so they were frightened of him. I always admired Jesus, but I was frightened to express this admiration publicly. You could say I was a secret disciple of Jesus.

I was there at Calvary when they nailed this innocent man to the cross. My heart went out to his mother who stood at the foot of the cross watching as her son suffered. I only saw a couple of his disciples there. Well, I can understand how they felt, they were probably frightened for their own lives and were in hiding.

Once Jesus died I knew that I had to act quickly, so I went to Pilate and asked him if I could take responsibility for Jesus' burial. He asked the Roman centurion, who had been on duty, if Jesus was already dead. Once he had been reassured, he gave the order that the body be handed over to me.

I was grateful to Pilate for giving me this opportunity to show my love and respect for this man I had admired. I knew that the women from Galilee and the disciples probably couldn't afford the burial spices and a tomb for Jesus and it was fortunate that I had just bought myself a tomb which could be used for his burial. I know Mary was relieved that her son would be given a proper burial. This was the least I could do for her.

My friend Nicodemus supplied the shroud that the body was to be wrapped in and the spices which were to be rubbed on the body. We had very little time because the sun was about to set, and as you know the Sabbath would begin, and we would have been forbidden even to bury the dead! We carried his body as far as the tomb and went down the steps that led from the outside to a narrow opening. Once inside the dimly lit tomb, myself, Nicodemus and the women used the first outer cave as a store for the spices, oil lamps and so on. It was there that we prepared his body and wrapped it in the shroud.

Just before sunset we went into the inner chamber of the tomb and laid his body out on one of the ledges cut in the wall. On leaving the tomb we rolled a huge granite rock across the opening. We leaned our heads against the stone for a while, because we all felt like the dream had ended. Roman soldiers stood guard outside the tomb for fear the disciples would steal the body.

We left the burial ground and began walking back to the city, just as everyone in the city was beginning to celebrate the Great Passover.

I just don't know what the future holds for all of us now. We'll have to wait and see!'

In Your Religion Journal

Imagine you are one of the disciples who is in hiding somewhere in Jerusalem. Write a letter to your family in Galilee telling them about the events surrounding Jesus' death and burial.

Copy and complete Holy Thursday and Good Friday on this calendar as a summary of the important events leading up to the death of Jesus.

Holy Week Calendar

Sun.	Mon.	Tues.	Wed.	Thurs.	Fri.
Jesus enters Jerusalem on a donkey. He is welcomed by people singing his praises and laying down palms for him to walk on. He returns to Bethany for the night.	Jesus visits the Temple and throws the traders out of the courtyard.	Jesus argues with the Pharisees and Sadducees in the Temple courtyard.	Religious authorities plot Jesus' death. A disciple of Jesus called Judas decides to betray him to the authorities.		

Discuss

Can you think of the different forms of slavery which exist within your own country and within the world today ? Gandhi, Martin Luther King, and Archbishop Romero wanted to free their people from different types of slavery. In each case can you say what form of slavery was oppressing their people and what sacrifice did each of these three people make on their behalf?

Why did Jesus have to die?

The freeing of a people from their slavery is never accomplished without great suffering and sacrifice.

Moses liberated the oppressed Israelite people from slavery to regain their dignity, freedom and independence.

However, this was accomplished only through hardship and suffering. Many lives were claimed as the Israelites travelled through the desert to the Promised Land.

Throughout his life Jesus was working to free all humanity from slavery: a slavery to sin and evil. But our liberation from sin was to cost a high price.

Jesus came among us as a human being, in order to be united with us and to bring us into unity with God. He wanted to share with us all that we have to endure, including suffering and death. Jesus' death was the way in which he could make an offering in love of his whole being to make up for all the lack of love that human beings are guilty of. He took upon himself all sins, including the sin of those who crucified him. God showed that he accepted the offering made by Jesus when he raised Jesus from the dead. In his crucifixion Jesus is saying to us, 'Do not be afraid that your sins are too great to be forgiven. Do not worry that you can never make up for the wrong you have done. I have already made up for it. Do your best and leave the rest to me.'

There was no profit for Jesus in suffering and dying. He did it for our sake. The crucifixion is the great proof of how much God loves us, even when we reject him and commit sin. St Paul tells us: 'What proves that God loves us is that Christ died for us while we were still sinners' (*2 Cor 5:21*). We don't need to earn God's love. It is there already .

In Your Religion Journal

Fit this jigsaw puzzle together using the words from the acclamation. When you have completed the jigsaw decorate the acclamation.

Lord and world the You are set have resur-rection Saviour you by your cross the free of us

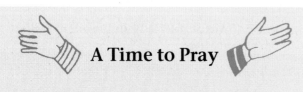

A Time to Pray

Let us reflect on the pain and suffering Jesus endured for us.

We despised him and rejected him;
he endured suffering and pain.
No one would even look at him —
we ignored him as if he were nothing.
But he endured the suffering that should have been ours,
the pain that we should have borne.
All the while we thought that his suffering
was punishment sent by God.
But because of our sins he was wounded,
beaten because of the evil we did.
We are healed by the punishment he suffered,
made whole by the blows he received.
All of us were like sheep that were lost,
each of us going his own way.
But the Lord made the punishment fall on him,
the punishment all of us deserved.

He was treated harshly, but endured it humbly;
he never said a word.
Like a lamb about to be slaughtered,
like a sheep about to be sheared,
he never said a word.
He was arrested and sentenced and led off to die,
and no one cared about his fate.
He was put to death for the sins of our people.
He was placed in a grave with evil men,
he was buried with the rich,
even though he had never committed a crime
or ever told a lie.

The Lord says:
'It was my will that he should suffer;
his death was a sacrifice to bring forgiveness.
After a life of suffering, he will again have joy;
he will know that he did not suffer in vain.
My devoted servant, with whom I am pleased,
will bear the punishment of many
and for his sake I will forgive them.
He took the place of many sinners
and prayed that they might be forgiven' *(Isaiah 53:3-13).*

The Resurrection

Jesus' friends regarded his death as a tragedy. They had pinned their hopes on him. They had left their homes and jobs to follow him. They expected great things of him. But he was put to death as a common criminal on a cross. His death left them disappointed and dispirited.
Jesus' death was the worst news they could have heard.

On a number of occasions during the three years that they were together Jesus had given them hints that he would be with them always. He told his disciples, 'The Son of Man will be delivered into the hands of men; they will put him to death; and three days after he has been put to death he will rise again' *(Mark 9:31/ Luke 9:44-45)*.

Then on Easter Sunday when it was discovered that Jesus had actually risen from the dead, they could not believe it was possible. Their friend Jesus whom they thought they wouldn't see again was risen from the dead and was with them. He appeared to them again and again, talked with them, walked with them and even ate with them.
The news was too amazing to understand or to believe at first. But soon the awe and amazement of Jesus' companions gave way to great joy and excitement. His rising from the dead was the best possible news his followers could have heard.

Read the account of the resurrection in Luke's gospel 24:1-12

Luke tells the Easter story in the final chapter of his gospel. He mentions four incidents:

The empty tomb (24:1-12);
The road to Emmaus (24:13-35);
The assembly in Jerusalem (24:36-49);
The ascension (24:50-53).

The Empty Tomb

Read and act out the following.

Good morning Jerusalem! This is Radio Zion FM, broadcasting our religious affairs programme 'Heart of the Matter'. My name is Joshua Hoffman and for the next hour I will be discussing the events of the past week in Jerusalem. You, the listeners, will have a chance to make your comments on the 'Phone In' during the programme. It's just gone 8.30 a.m. on a beautiful Sunday morning. I'll begin by summarising the events that made the headlines this week.

Preparations for the celebration of the Passover went smoothly...

Jerusalem comes to a standstill for the festive week...

A man from Galilee, along with two other criminals, was crucified at Golgotha on Friday...

I must interrupt this summary to bring you an unconfirmed report that a tomb on the outskirts of Jerusalem has been opened and a body is missing. For more details we go over at once to Daniel, our reporter at the scene.

Daniel: I am standing in the garden where the tomb of Jesus is located. He was crucified on Friday and was buried in the tomb of Joseph of Arimathea. When I was here yesterday the only sound to be heard was the singing of larks and the bleating of lambs on the hillside. Guards were on duty at the tomb as there was a rumour circulating in the city that the followers of Jesus would attempt to steal his body. Today, however, there is a buzz in the air, an atmosphere of apprehension and excitement. Followers of Jesus who recently arrived at the tomb found it empty. I spoke first to the women who discovered the empty tomb. Tell me, Mary, what were you doing visiting the tomb?

Mary: On Friday when we helped Joseph and Nicodemus to bury Jesus' body it was very rushed, because the sun was about to set. So Joanna and myself decided to come to the garden this morning with burial ointments to embalm the body of Jesus properly.

Joanna: Yes, that's right, we were minding our own business, and were busy discussing how we could get the huge stone rolled back from the entrance to the tomb.

Daniel: Well, what happened when you arrived at the tomb?

Mary: When we entered the garden we stopped, we could see the huge stone had already been rolled back. We raced to the open entrance of the tomb. I don't know about Joanna but I was really frightened, I didn't know what to expect.

Joanna: There was no body to be found anywhere. The burial shroud lay in the same place where we had left it on the ledge on Friday.

Daniel: Tell me what happened inside the tomb?

Mary: We were sitting in the tomb not knowing what to think. We were both in a state of shock. The tomb was suddenly filled with a blinding light. Against the wall we could see two figures who said to us, 'Why are you looking among the dead for one who is alive? He is not here, he has been raised from the dead.' And then they reminded us of something that Jesus himself had said when he was in Galilee, 'The Son of Man must be handed over to sinful men to be crucified and three days later rise to life.'

Daniel: Have you told anyone else this story?

Joanna: Oh yes, we were so overjoyed that our friend Jesus had risen from the dead we didn't waste a minute. We ran back to the city to tell the disciples. Mary was the first to arrive at the room where they had been hiding.

Mary: I was out of breath by the time I arrived at their hiding place. I hurried through the door and told them the amazing news that the tomb was empty and that we'd been told that Jesus is risen from the dead! Peter and John just looked at each other and told me that I was still in shock after what had happened on Friday. They thought I should go home and take a good rest.

Daniel: I'll interrupt you there, Mary, we have to go back to the studio for a commercial break....

In Your Religion Journal

What questions would you have asked the women on Easter Sunday if you had been interviewing them?

Daniel: With me here in the garden are the two guards who were on duty at the time the tomb was opened. I asked them what they saw.

Guard 1: Well, we had been on duty for about six hours. I think we were both getting tired and were looking forward to getting off for a few hours rest. The Pharisees had asked for guards to be posted outside the tomb to keep the body safe from thieves. There had been a rumour circulating that the disciples would try to steal the body. It was quite early in the morning, about 7.00 a.m., when we felt this earth-shattering trembling. It seemed as if it was coming from inside the tomb.

Guard 2: I can tell you I was terrified, I thought at first that an earthquake had hit Jerusalem. It all happened so quickly – a blinding light and the huge stone in front of the entrance to the tomb was being rolled back. The two of us could do nothing. We tried to move but we were stuck to the spot. It felt like being in a daze. It must have been only a couple of minutes at the most until we gathered our wits about us. We looked inside the tomb only to discover that the body was missing.

Daniel: What do you think happened to the body?

Guard 1:   I'm not sure. It seemed as if it just disappeared, vanished into thin air.
One minute it was there, the next it was gone.

Daniel: Did you tell your superiors what happened?

Guard 2:   Once we got our wits about us we thought we'd better get back to the city and report the bad news.

Daniel: And what did they say about the whole affair?

Guard 1:   We thought we'd be punished for being so careless, but that wasn't the case at all. They were quite understanding really.

Daniel: Is it true to say that the authorities gave you both a large sum of money to spread the story that Jesus' disciples had stolen the body?

Guards 1 & 2   We cannot comment on that statement. It is better if we finish the interview on that question!

Daniel: I have just caught up with Peter and John, the two disciples who visited the tomb after Mary Magdalen had told them her amazing news. I asked John what he found when he entered the tomb.

John: After Mary Magdalen left us, we thought about what she had told us. We were a little curious about her story, it just seemed such an impossible thing to have happened. Peter and I set out for the tomb. I'm a faster runner than Peter so I arrived outside the entrance to the tomb before him. I went inside to light the oil lamp, as it was still very dark in the inner chamber. By that time Peter had arrived so I let him go in first. I was a bit nervous of what we'd find.

Daniel: This is interesting. And what did you find, Peter?

Peter: We made our way into the back chamber of the tomb. We were astonished to find the shroud in exactly the same position as when Jesus was wrapped in it, but there was no sign of a body. I can tell you we were excited. It meant that Mary wasn't imagining the whole story after all. It confirmed what she'd said, that someone must have appeared to her and told her that Jesus is risen. We were thrilled at the thought of our friend Jesus coming back to life. He had said he would come back to life and this proved his claim that he was God's Son because power over death could come only from God.

Daniel: What can you say about the rumours that it was one of your own people who stole the body to make it look as if Jesus had risen from the dead?

John: Certainly not, we had nothing to gain by stealing the body.
In any case we would have had to get past the guard and roll away the sealed stone of the tomb.
Another thing which indicates that the body wasn't stolen is the fact that the shroud remained in exactly the same place even though the body was gone. Anyone wanting to steal the body would surely have carried the body off wrapped in its shroud or else simply thrown the linen bands in a corner.

Daniel: One last question, Peter. What do you and the other disciples intend doing now?

Peter: I think we will lie low for a while, it's still a bit soon after Jesus' death for us to come out and tell people the Good News that Jesus is risen. As witnesses of his life we have a lot to tell people about him. Maybe we'll be more courageous in a few weeks.

Daniel: Let's return to the studio for another commercial break....

Find Your Group

It's time now for the 'Phone In' to Radio Zion FM. The following people have made phone calls to the programme 'Heart of the Matter' concerning the events surrounding Easter Sunday. The presenter of the programme begins each call by saying 'Hello caller, can I have your name, please? What is your view of the events which we are discussing, please?'
In your group write and act out the phone calls from each particular point of view: the Jewish authorities; Mary Magdalen; the guards; Peter; John.

After the Resurrection

When the disciples met Jesus after his death, it was the same Jesus they had known before his crucifixion, yet now he was different, so different that they were slow, very slow to recognise him. He had conquered death. His risen glorified body would no longer be restrained by time and space.

Jesus was careful to show the disciples that he was really and truly risen from the dead. He was not a ghost. He encouraged them to touch him. He ate a piece of fish in front of them. He showed them the wounds made by his crucifixion. These things helped the disciples to understand that Jesus was definitely alive and real. He was the same person they had known before, yet his body was different. It was now his risen glorified body. One incident which shows how slow the followers of Jesus were to recognise him happened on the road to Emmaus.

The Road to Emmaus

Let's catch up with two friends of Jesus as they travel home to Emmaus, a small village about seven miles from Jerusalem. It's Sunday evening and they are returning to their village after the Passover weekend in Jerusalem.

Activity

Read Luke's account of the disciples on the road to Emmaus 24:13-35.

Cleopas: What a terrible disappointment! We had pinned all our hopes on Jesus. We were sure that he was the Messiah. Now he has ended up nailed to a cross like the worst of criminals.

Theo: Yes, Cleopas, it was a dreadful let-down. I don't know what the future holds for us.

Stranger: Good evening, friends. Can I travel with you for a while ?

Cleopas: Yes, certainly, come and join our company.

Stranger: You both look very downhearted. Has something happened?

Jordaens,
The Supper at Emmaus, *reproduced courtesy of the National Gallery of Ireland*

192

Cleopas:	You mean you haven't heard? Are you the only person staying in Jerusalem who hasn't heard about the man called Jesus? Everyone in Jerusalem is talking about him right now.
Theo:	Yes, Cleopas and myself were just discussing the events of the last few days. You see, we belong to a group of people which has followed Jesus as he journeyed throughout Israel. We had hoped he was the Messiah and our liberator. However, our chief priests handed him over to the Romans to be sentenced to death and he was crucified. It's now three days since he died and our hopes have died with him.
Cleopas:	There is just one faint hope. Some women whom we know went to the tomb where he was buried but they couldn't find his body. They even claim that angels told them that Jesus is alive.
Theo:	We went to the tomb ourselves to check out their story and right enough there was no sign of him.
Stranger:	I'm surprised at you two, you have little faith in all that the prophets have said. Haven't you read your Scriptures where the prophets have spoken of how the Messiah would suffer and die on his way to glory?
Theo:	That does sound familiar.
Stranger:	Let me refresh your memories. I'll explain these very texts of Scripture to you while we walk.
Cleopas:	Go on then, tell us more...
Theo:	Well, we've arrived at Emmaus already, the time has flown.
Cleopas:	It's a pity you have to travel on further. Look, it's getting late. Why don't you stay the night? You can continue your journey tomorrow.
Stranger:	Why not ? I'll stay the night. Let's go inside and have a meal.
Narrator:	During the meal the stranger took the bread, said the blessing and shared it....
	In this gesture of 'breaking the bread' they recognised him...but by then, Jesus was gone.
	Cleopas and his friend were so excited that they rushed all the way back to Jerusalem to tell the others what had happened to them.

In Luke's story the disciples at first failed to recognise the risen Jesus. For the early Christians, the realisation that Jesus is risen from the dead challenged them to put his teachings into practice in the way they saw themselves and others in the world around them. Also, for us today, when we realise that Jesus is risen from the dead and that the risen Jesus is present in our world, helping and guiding us, we are challenged to live out the gospel message in our own lives.

The Assembly in Jerusalem

The room was buzzing as Cleopas and Theo told the other disciples about their encounter with Jesus! 'Jesus is alive. He is risen and has appeared to us,' they shouted. Suddenly the room fell silent. Jesus himself was standing in the middle of them. 'Peace be with you,' he said.

The atmosphere was tense, the disciples were unsure of what way to react. But Jesus reassured them by saying, 'Why are you alarmed? Look at my hands and my feet, see the wound in my side from the nails and the spear'.

Jesus said to them, 'Come and eat'. By his eating with them the disciples were convinced that Jesus was not a ghost. They gave him a piece of cooked fish.

When they were all seated he began to talk to them and remind them of the things he had told them when he preached throughout Israel. He talked about the Law of Moses, the writings of the prophets and the Psalms. He helped them to understand more clearly the meaning of the Scriptures.

He reminded them that the Messiah must suffer and must rise from the dead three days later. Peter shouted out, 'Oh so that's what you meant, Jesus, when you said "The Temple of the Lord will be destroyed, yet within three days it will be rebuilt."'

As Jesus continued to talk with them, the disciples became clearer about all that had happened. Slowly they grew in courage and confidence. They became eager to go out and tell everyone the Good News. But Jesus told them to wait in Jerusalem until he had sent the Holy Spirit to help them.

Jesus' resurrection was the best news the apostles could ever have heard. His coming back to life made all the difference to his followers. It convinced them that Jesus was the Messiah, the Son of God, because they were certain that power over death could come only from God. It gave them Good News to tell everyone. They were eyewitnesses to the most amazing event and they wanted to tell people. Jesus had predicted his death, and that he would come back to life. If he was right about this, everything else he said should be true too.

Once the Holy Spirit had come and given them the strength and courage the apostles were ready to risk their lives to preach the Good News. His death and resurrection was at the heart of the Good News they preached everywhere they went.

Activity

Read Luke's account of the assembly in Jerusalem 24:36-49.

In Your Religion Journal

Imagine you were in the room when Jesus appeared to his disciples.
What did you see?
How did you feel?
What questions did you ask Jesus?

Find Your Group Discuss

Think of an incident in your life when you heard some good news. What was your first reaction?

In Your Religion Journal

You are interested in applying for a job with the Good News advertising agency. This job will require you to advertise and promote the Good News of Christianity. The agency has sent you an application form to be filled in. Answer the following questions.

the good news **n**g advertising agency

Name: _____

Address: _____

Date of Birth: _____

What is the Good News of Christianity ? _____

What qualifications have you for the job ? _____

_____

Give three reasons why you would be a good person for this job: _____

_____

What difference has the resurrection made to your life? _____

_____

What previous experience have you in promoting the Good News? _____

_____

There may be times when following Jesus becomes difficult. Are you prepared to accept these difficult times in your life? _____

Design an advertising slogan promoting the Good News in not more than five words. _____

Names of two referees: _____

_____

The Ascension

The gospels say that for forty days after he had risen from the dead, Jesus appeared to his disciples from time to time.

Gradually he began to explain to them that it would soon be time for him to leave them again and return to his Father.

He reminded them of the promise he made to them at the Last Supper, that the Holy Spirit would be there to help them. They were to wait in Jerusalem for the Holy Spirit to come.

Then Jesus took the disciples with him to the hillside at Bethany, where they had so often stayed. There he said goodbye. The last words of Luke's gospel say: '...he raised his hands and blessed them. As he was blessing them, he departed from them and was taken up into heaven'.

Activity

Read Luke's account of the ascension in 24:50-53.

Discuss

For what reason do you think the risen Jesus stayed with the disciples for forty days after he was risen from the dead? In what way is the risen Jesus present with us today ?

Class Activity

Design a banner/poster with the acclamation: Dying you destroyed our death; rising you restored our life; Lord Jesus come in glory.

Test Yourself.
Do the Looking Back exercises on page 228

Lesson Twenty-two

The Church

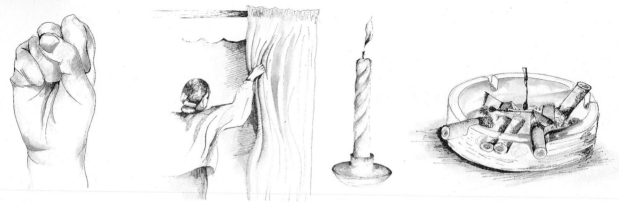

Discuss
What do the above signs indicate ?
Some signs are dead and lifeless. Some are full of life. Which of the above signs are dead and lifeless and which are not?

In Your Religion Journal

Draw pictures of other signs. Say what each one communicates. Which are living signs? Which are lifeless signs?

Draw the image of the vine and the branches in your religion journal.

There are many different kinds of signs.

The Church - A Living Sign

Before Jesus returned to heaven he said to his followers,'I will be with you always.' The Church is a sign that the risen Jesus is present in the world. The Church isn't a dead, lifeless sign. It is a living sign, made up of living people. We are the Church. Through us the risen Jesus is still alive and active in the world. The Church is like a living, growing plant and we are the branches of the plant.

The root of a plant or a tree is normally out of sight, but it is the vital part from which everything else grows. The visible parts may be damaged or destroyed, but provided the root remains alive, they can grow again and produce their fruit. It is the branches and flowers and fruit of the plant which tell us that the hidden root is still alive and active. That is the kind of sign the Church is – a living sign. We are alive. It is through the way in which we live and act that people come to know that Christ is still living and active in the world through us.

Jesus told his disciples, 'I am the vine, and you are the branches. Whoever remains in me, with me in him, bears fruit in plenty; for cut off from me you can do nothing' *(John 15:5)*.

The image of the vine and its branches is a good one to describe the Church.

The Sign of the Risen Jesus' continuing Presence with us.

Discuss

What kind of 'fruit' do you think Jesus wants the members of his Church to produce?

Discuss

Read through this passage from Matthew's gospel and discuss:
What are the three main things Jesus tells his disciples to do?
What do you think is meant by making someone a disciple ?
Who are the apostles sent to?

Jesus came to bring forgiveness and reconciliation, to show people how to live together in love, peace and justice and to gather everyone into union with God. He continues to do this through the Church. He entrusted the Church to the care of the apostles.

In Matthew's gospel Jesus says, 'Go, therefore, make disciples of all the nations; baptise them in the name of the Father and of the Son and of the Holy Spirit, and teach them to observe all the commands I gave you. And know that I am with you always; yes, to the end of time' (*Matthew 28:19-20*).

Today we are the people who make up the Church. We are challenged to carry out the command which Jesus first gave to the apostles. In our actions and in our relationships with one another we are challenged to show others how to live in today's world as followers of Jesus.

Read the following story. ## Jigsaw Pieces

Discuss

Like the little boy who had never seen the world and didn't know what it looked like, in today's world people have never seen Jesus.
How can the people who make up the Church show the world what Jesus is like?

There was a man one time baby-sitting with his own kids but he obviously didn't have enough practice at it. It was a wet Saturday. With time and motion studies and running a business he would be excellent but dealing with his own kids was another story. They were getting on his nerves.

Being inventive to some extent, he took down a magazine from a shelf opened it up and tore out a map of the world. He cut it up with scissors, jumbled it up to make a jigsaw, spread it out on the table and gave it to his seven-year-old lad to put together. He went on to give the second lad something to do. He was disgusted as well as amazed to look back very shortly afterwards and find that the first little lad was finished. He had all the pieces of the jigsaw put together for the map of the world. Amazed more than anything else, he said, 'How did you do it?' And the young lad said, 'Well, you said that this was the world but I had never seen one before and I didn't know where to start. But I turned over one of the pieces and there was a man on the other side, and when I put the man together the world was OK.'

A sign which makes Jesus known

Through the Church people get to know about Jesus, about what he taught, about what he has done and is still doing for us, about what he offers us and why he is important for us today.

Making Jesus known is a task for the whole Church. Everyone has a part to play. Do you remember that last year we studied the Church as 'The Body of Christ'? In one of his letters St Paul explained part of what this means. In our bodies, our eyes enable us to see, our ears to hear, our hands to do and make things. Usually all of these work together; when we play games, we use our eyes, hands and feet; when we study we use our eyes, ears, hands and so on.

Some members of the Church may have special functions and gifts, but we are all meant to work together to carry out the Church's task of making Christ's presence known. You might like to read the passage from St Paul again. It is 1 Corinthians 12:12-31.

Some members of the Church have special responsibilities in the task of keeping the Church united, in proclaiming the true faith, celebrating the sacraments and working harmoniously together to bring Christ's love to the whole world. These are the bishops, the successors of the apostles and the Pope, the successor of St Peter. The bishop maintains the unity of the Church in his diocese, the Pope has the responsibility to preserve the whole Church in unity under the guidance of the Holy Spirit.

However, every single member of the Church is important when it comes to making Christ known to the world. It is very important that we all play our part.

Discuss

Jesus called Peter 'the Rock' on which he would build his Church. Buildings need firm foundations or they will fall apart. The firmest foundation is solid rock.
In what ways do you think the Pope can act as a 'rock' for the Church?
In what ways can a bishop help to keep the Church in his diocese united?

Getting their act together

One day a group of second year students were given a project to do on the environment. There were eight students in the group.

Activity

Finish the above story in two different ways: the first showing what happened when the group co-operated and used good teamwork;
the second showing what happened when there was no co-operation among the group.
OR
Describe and act out dramas to show what happened.

Find Your Group

When Jesus was on earth he showed love and care and forgiveness to those who lived with him. He showed special care to the poor, the sick, the lonely. There are many people in the world today, in our parishes, in our country, in the wider world, who show in their lives some of the same qualities as Jesus showed in his.
List some people who are famous for the way in which they have cared for others.
Make a wall frieze entitled: *Signs of Jesus in the world today.*

In Your Religion Journal

Write about someone you know, someone at home or someone in your parish, who shows care and love for others, especially those in need.

Activity

Can you think of any stories which you have heard which show how important it is that all the members of a group co-operate with one another?

A Sign of Unity

Jesus came to bring everyone God's love and forgiveness. He wanted to unite everyone with God, so that they could become God's children, members of a united family, sharing God's life and love.

Baptism brings people into God's family, the Church, as God's children. That is why Jesus told his apostles to baptise. The Church is the living sign of the union between God and human beings. The Church shows us what it means to be united with God. The Church also makes it possible for us to be united with God. All this starts with Baptism, but it doesn't end there.

In Baptism we first become united with the risen Jesus as children of God, and united with each other as members of one family. We are called to live as children of God should.

In Confirmation we are specially commissioned to play our full part in the life of the Church. We are given the gifts of the Holy Spirit to help us do this.

In the Eucharist we join with Jesus in his great self-offering of love for us. We offer ourselves and our lives with him. Our union with the risen Jesus and with each other is strengthened when we receive him in Holy Communion.

The Church's Pilgrimage

We can think of the life of the Church and of each Christian, as a pilgrimage into God's Kingdom. Baptism and Confirmation make us part of the pilgrimage party and point us in the right direction. In the Eucharist we get strength and support for the journey. When we receive the Body of Christ we are assured that the risen Jesus is with us to give us all the help we need. Reconciliation brings us back to the pilgrimage, when we have wandered away.

Activity

Make a poster illustrating the Church's pilgrimage, showing the part that each of these sacraments plays.

A Sign Which Speaks Through Actions

To be a clear sign of Jesus' presence in the world, the Church needs to be a community which shows his love and compassion, a community which doesn't just believe in Jesus and talk about him, but which also acts like him.

You are like light for the whole world. A city built on a hill cannot be hidden. No one lights a lamp and puts it under a bowl; instead he puts it on the lampstand, where it gives light for everyone in the house. In the same way your light must shine before people so that they will see the good things you do and praise your Father in heaven (*Matthew 5:14-16*).

The light of Christ shines most clearly from the Church, when it is a community in which everyone cares for each other and is concerned for the needs of other people, just as Jesus was.
This is what the early Christian community did.

Discuss

How can you be a 'light for the world' at home, at school, with your friends ? Gandhi once said, 'I like your Christ but I don't like your Christians': what do you think he meant ?

Actions speak louder than words

Discuss

What do you think this proverb means? Can you think of times when people might use it?
How could this be true of the Church?

In Your Religion Journal

Make up a cartoon strip showing a situation where somebody uses the proverb:
Actions speak louder than words.

How the Friends of Jesus lived

The friends of Jesus made a great stir in the city. They lived day by day in God's Way as Jesus had shown them; Peter and James and John explained it to them.

They lived together like members of one family. When they had supper together, they 'broke the loaf', shared it as Jesus had done at the Last Supper on the night before he died, and remembered what Jesus had done for everybody everywhere.

They spent much time in prayer.

They lived together and shared everything with one another. They sold their property and possessions and shared the money out so that nobody went without anything he needed.

Every day they went to Temple worship and met at home to 'break the loaf' together. They shared their meals together with real happiness. All this was their way of thanking God for all he had done for them. The people in the city thought well of them. Day by day, with God's help, their numbers grew.

They were one in heart and mind, and none of them thought that their own things were just for their own use – they were for everybody to share. So the close Friends of Jesus, like Peter, made it very clear what 'Jesus being alive again' really meant.

They were a happy company. Everybody shared. The rich people among them sold their lands and houses, and brought the money they got to their leaders. It was then shared out as each had need.

Discuss

In what ways were the early Christians fulfilling the command of Jesus to be the light of the world?

Have you ever experienced a time when people acted like they did in the passage you've just read, in your family or in your neighbourhood ?

Here is one example. One of them, Joseph, was a rich man (Peter and his friends called him Barnabas). He was born in the island of Cyprus but he worked in the Temple, helping in the services there. He owned a field. He went and sold it and brought the money to the leaders.

More and more people, crowds of men and women, believed in Jesus and joined his company of Friends. Just as Jesus healed those who were ill, so did his Friends. People brought sick people on beds and mats out into the streets.

Of course, the Church is not perfect. Because we are all human it is made up of imperfect people but the light of Christ is within it. If we want to help that light to shine out more clearly, we have to imitate Jesus, and be true to our Baptism by trying to act as he told us to. In his instruction to the apostles, Jesus told them to teach people, 'to observe all the commands I gave you.'

Can you think of any of the commands that Jesus gave? Here are a few references to help you.

Matthew 5:43-45; 10:37-40. Luke 6:35-36; 22:19.

The Letter of St James

In the New Testament there is a letter by James, a cousin of Jesus, who was in charge of the Church at Jerusalem. He was concerned by the attitude of some members of the Church. Here is part of what he wrote.

As believers in our Lord Jesus Christ, the Lord of glory, you must never treat people in different ways according to their outward appearance. Suppose a rich person wearing a gold ring and fine clothes comes to your meeting and a poor man in ragged clothes also comes. If you show more respect to the well-dressed person and say to them, 'Have this best seat here,' but say to the poor person, 'Stand over there, or sit here on the floor by my feet,' then you are guilty of creating distinctions among yourselves and of making judgements based on evil motives (James 2:14-17).

Later in the same letter, James deals with people who thought it was enough just to believe in Jesus, without letting that affect the way they lived. This is what he wrote.

If one of the brothers or one of the sisters is in need of clothes and has not enough food to live on, and one of you says to them 'I wish you well. Keep yourself warm and eat plenty', without giving them the bare necessities of life, then what good is that? Faith is like that. If good works do not go with it, it is quite dead (James 2:14-17).

What James would call a 'living faith' is a faith which expresses itself in doing good. It is by showing that kind of faith that we help the Church to be a clear living sign of Christ's loving presence in the world.

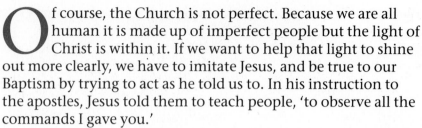

In Your Religion Journal

Check these references in your bible and then write a few sentences, saying in your own words, the kind of thing Jesus is telling us to do in each of these passages.

What would you have to do in your own life, if you wanted to fulfil these commands of Jesus?

Discuss

What do you think was wrong with the kind of attitude James was criticising?

Why do you think he said that a follower of Jesus shouldn't act like that?

In what ways are the poor discriminated against today?

How should Christians treat people who are very poor today ? Why?

Are there any other groups of people that might be discriminated against today?

What do you think James (or Jesus) would have said about this?

What kind of attitudes among Christians would help the Church to be a clearer sign of Jesus' love for everybody?

Discuss

What should a follower of Jesus do for those in need?

Can you think of any way in which you, as a class, can help people in need?

Research

1. Are there any church groups in your area which try to help those in need?

In what way does your parish provide help for the needs of people in the community?

2. Find out something about a religious order which tries to help the poor, sick or needy in your own country or throughout the world.

3. How does the whole Church in your country try to help those in need?

Margaret Bermingham

Margaret Bermingham was born in Co. Meath around the year 1515. At about the age of fifteen she married a wealthy Dublin merchant, Bartholomew Ball. It is said that Margaret had twenty children, though only five survived into adulthood, three boys and two girls. Both Margaret and her husband were devout Catholics and remained faithful to the Catholic religion through the years of the Reformation.

Her husband became Mayor of Dublin for the period 1553-54. He died in 1568. After his death, Margaret devoted herself even more exclusively to the cause of the Catholic Church in Ireland. The children of many merchants and landowners were sent to her home to be educated in the faith and her home was also a refuge for Catholic priests.

In the manner of the time Margaret's household included many servants. Margaret treated them as if they were her own children. They were well-trained in their duties, so that they were always in great demand in other

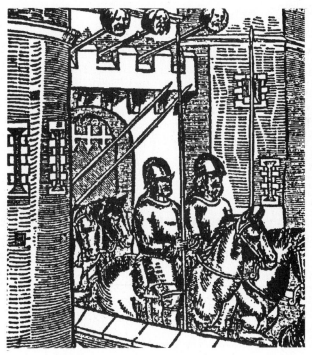

Dublin Castle

houses. And she also made sure that they were instructed in the faith.

Fr John Howlin, a Jesuit priest who had visited Margaret's house, said, 'They are like students graduating from the best of schools.'

Margaret was saddened by some of the things which were happening in the city at that time. The best loved relics of the Catholic Church, including St Patrick's crozier, were thrown on a bonfire and burnt in Christ Church Place. Mass could not be celebrated in any of the churches in Dublin. Her greatest sorrow was caused by the fact that her eldest son, Walter, became a convinced Protestant and a determined opponent of the Catholic religion.

The fact that Margaret offered hospitality to priests or bishops who were on the run, meant that almost every day Mass was celebrated in her house.

More than once in the late 1550s she was marched off to prison in the company of a priest caught in the act of saying Mass in her house. By using her influence Margaret was able to regain her freedom, which was not surprising for a lady of her position. Each time she went back to

204

doing exactly as she had before.

In the year 1580 her son Walter became Mayor of Dublin. He decided that drastic action was needed to save the city of Dublin from what he saw as the dangers of the Catholic religion. The obvious offender was his own mother. He ordered her to be arrested.

By this time Margaret was in her mid-sixties and was crippled with arthritis. Because she was no longer able to walk any distance she was put lying on a wooden hurdle and was drawn by a horse through the streets of Dublin. She was brought to Dublin Castle where she was to be imprisoned for the rest of her life. The cells in the castle were situated underground and were freezing in winter and stifling hot in the summer.

The ventilation was poor and there was no sanitation, so that the air was always bad. Some prisoners were lucky enough to get a candle to give a little light, otherwise they spent their time in darkness.

The prisoners got no exercise and there was no medical care. These conditions were particularly difficult for Margaret who had spent her life in comfort with an array of servants to look after her every need. The most difficult thing must have been that she could leave at any time, if only she would renounce her religion and take the Oath of Supremacy, accepting the Queen as head of the Church. Margaret would prefer to die!

After about three years in these conditions Margaret died around the year 1584.

Discuss

What are the most outstanding qualities which Margaret Bermingham had ?

What did she see as important ?

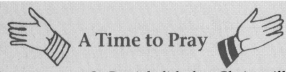

A Time to Pray

Let us pray, as St Patrick did, that Christ will be present in each one of us and through us present in the world today.

Christ be with me,
Christ be within me,
Christ behind me,
Christ before me,
Christ beside me,
Christ to win me
Christ to comfort and restore me,
Christ beneath me,
Christ in quiet,
Christ in danger,
Christ in mouth of friend, or stranger.

In Paul's letter to the Ephesians we read:

You are no longer outsiders and foreigners in God's world; you are fellow-citizens with all the friends of Jesus everywhere and members of God's family.
Let me make what I mean clear with an illustration.
Think of building a house. The builders lay the foundations, use the stones to build the walls and hold them together with a key-stone.
God's family is like a house. Inspired preachers among us and the first close friends of Jesus are foundations; Jesus is the keystone; you are the stones.
Jesus holds God's family together and helps it to grow; but he needs you, as the keystone needs the stones that make the walls
(*Ephesians 2:19-22*).

Let us pray that as members of the Church today we will learn how to work together so that through us the risen Jesus will be present in the world.

Baptism and Confirmation

How many of these are correct?

When someone has celebrated Baptism and Confirmation it means:

They are true Christians.

They are able to look after themselves.

They are followers of Jesus.

They have extra strength to do what is right.

They are really grown up.

They are responsible people.

They know lots of things about Jesus.

They have made a commitment to live in a certain way.

They will never sin again.

They have a responsibility to live as a member of the Church.

They are full members of the Church.

They should be treated as adults.

They are more holy than someone who has yet to celebrate these sacraments.

Sort out the Symbols.

Which symbols belong to Baptism and which symbols belong to Confirmation? Which symbols belong to both?

In Your Religion Journal

If you have already celebrated the sacraments of Baptism and Confirmation, write out five things that they mean for your life.

What will we do about Paul?

The young people from St Mary's Terrace at the southern end of the town had taken on a project. It had been decided that the town would enter a contest to find the tidiest town in the country.

A committee was set up and they had allocated the various tasks which needed to be done to different groups from around the town. St Mary's youth club had offered to set to work cleaning up a piece of wasteland which had always been an eyesore and gave those entering the town a bad impression from the beginning.

They had already put a lot of work into it, meeting in the evenings after school and at the weekends. They were pleased with the way the place was beginning to look and they were actually enjoying the work. There was just one problem, Paul!

Paul just didn't seem to want to pull his weight. Last week he had promised faithfully that he would paint the railings. Then when the time came he didn't turn up. Before that he had offered to approach all the shops in the town which had a gardening section and request some free flowers and shrubs to make the place look better. Of course, on the day, Paul found that he had a football practice and didn't turn up until all the shops had closed. Whenever he did turn up he seemed to be more interested in distracting the others than in trying to get the job done.

His companions were really fed up with him at this stage.

'I wish he'd either opt in or opt out,' said Gerard.

'That's right, if he wasn't here, we'd just sort out the tasks which need to be done in a different way. While he is here we are depending on him to play his part,' added Margaret.

'Yes' agreed Dermot, 'and Paul keeps letting us down.'

Belonging to a group

Whenever we join a group we take on certain commitments. Can you say what commitments are taken on by those who join the following groups ?

> A football team
> A drama group
> A parish council
> A branch of the St Vincent de Paul Society
> A residents' association.

The other side of the coin is that when we join a group we can look forward to certain advantages that we would not otherwise have. Can you say what would be gained by someone who joined each of the groups mentioned above?

Discuss

How do you think you would have felt if you had been one of the group?

Why did the rest of the group keep depending on Paul to do his bit?

Have you ever seen anyone behave as Paul did?

Why do you think Paul acted as he did?

What do you think the group could do about Paul?

Do you think Paul felt a sense of commitment or belonging to the group?

How is this shown in the story?

What groups do you feel a sense of commitment or belonging to?

How do you show this in your actions as part of these groups?

In Your Religion Journal

Finish off the story.
What did they do about Paul ?

The Eagle Learns to Fly

ONCE UPON A TIME, while walking through the forest, a farmer found an eagle tangled in a bush, too young to fly. He took the young eagle home with him and put him in the chickenyard – where the eagle soon learned to eat chickenfeed and to behave as chickens do.

A month or so later, a naturalist who was passing by spotted the eagle in the chicken-yard awkwardly pecking at kernels of corn. She enquired of the farmer why an eagle, the king of all birds, was living in a chickenyard with chickens.

'He has never learned to fly,' replied the farmer. 'He behaves as chickens behave. You might say that he is no longer an eagle.'

'Still, he has the heart of an eagle and can surely be taught to fly,' insisted the naturalist. After talking it over, the two agreed to find out whether this was possible. Gently the naturalist took the eagle in her arms and said, 'You belong to the sky and not the earth. Stretch forth your wings and fly.'

The eagle, however, was confused, not knowing who he was. Seeing his friends, the chickens, he jumped down to be with them again.

On the following day, the naturalist took the eagle up onto the roof of the barn and urged him again, saying, 'You are an eagle. Stretch forth your wings and fly.' But the eagle was afraid of his unknown self and jumped down once more to the chickenyard.

On the third day the naturalist rose early, took the eagle out of the chickenyard, and climbed with him to a high mountain. There she held the King of Birds high above her and encour-aged him again, saying, 'You are an eagle. You belong to the sky as well as to the earth. Stretch forth your wings now. Fly!'

The eagle looked around, back towards the chickenyard and up to the sky. Still he did not fly. Then the naturalist lifted him still higher straight towards the sun. And it happened that the eagle began to tremble. Slowly he stretched his wings. At last, with a triumphant cry, he soared away into the heavens.

It may be that the eagle still fondly remembers his friends, the chickens.

Yet, as far as anyone knows, he has never returned to the chickenyard.

Discuss

Explain why the bird, though he was an eagle, was unable to fly.

What needed to happen before he could fly?

In Your Religion Journal

Was there ever a time when you felt confused about whether or not you were really part of a group?
Write about how the experience affected you.

208

When we have celebrated the sacraments of Baptism and Confirmation we have taken our place as members of the Church.

The Church

When parents bring their child to the church to be baptised they want certain things from the Church for the child.

What do you think the Church has to offer to people?

The Church also makes demands on those who want to belong. They are the same demands as Jesus made on those who wanted to be his followers.

In Your Religion Journal

Write out ten things which you think the Church has to offer to you.

Find Your Group

The Church has decided to launch a campaign encouraging new members to join.

Your group is in charge of publicity.

Make a poster encouraging people to become members of the Church.

Make sure your poster sets out all the advantages.

Discuss

Can you remember any other gospel stories which refer to the action of washing someone's feet? How do you think you would have felt that night, had you been one of the disciples?

Can you think of any situations where you can be of service to others?

Has it ever happened that someone else has been of service to you?

At Supper

Twelve apostles and Jesus seated around the table.

James: The city is bursting at the seams. I've never seen such crowds in my life.

Andrew: We were very lucky to find this room to have our meal.

Philip: I hope there won't be trouble before the festival is over.

Matthew: The authorities are on the look-out. The soldiers are everywhere.

Jesus stands up. He takes off his outer garment, ties a towel around his waist and pours some water into a basin.

Thomas: What are you going to do now, Lord?

Jesus: I am going to wash your feet.

John: *Quietly to Peter.* Wash our feet! Surely he knows that washing feet is the work of the servant. He's no servant. He's our Lord and Master.

Peter: He'll not wash my feet. You'll see!

Jesus: You do not understand now what I am doing but you will understand later.

Matthew: You're right, Lord, we don't understand what you are doing. It doesn't make any sense at all.

Jesus approaches Peter.

Peter: Never, at any time, Lord, will you wash my feet. You are not my servant. You are my Lord and Master.

Jesus: Peter, if I do not wash your feet you will no longer be my disciple.

Peter: Then Lord, do not wash only my feet, wash my hands and my head too.

Jesus faces the group.

Jesus: Do you understand what I have just done to you? You call me Master and Lord and it is right that you do so, because that is what I am. I, your Lord and Master, have just washed your feet. You then should wash one another's feet. I have set an example for you so that you will do just what I have done for you.

Philip: What does he mean? Surely he can't seriously be telling us to go around washing one another's feet!

John: Can't you see? Servants wash people's feet. Jesus is telling us that we must be servants of one another. Washing feet is the sign of a servant.

Matthew: Yes, of course, as followers of Jesus we must be servants of others.

James: And Jesus has been showing us how to do that for the past three years.

Read the account of the washing of the feet from John 13:1-17.

Commissioning

One of the symbols used in the sacraments of Baptism and Confirmation is anointing. The anointing is a sign that the person is being commissioned or set apart for a particular function. What do you think the person is being commissioned for?

When we celebrate the sacrament of Baptism we become members of the Church, we are part of the community of the Church. We belong to the group of people who are the followers of Jesus in the world today. We promise to live as he asked his followers to do. Confirmation confirms this.

Activity

Make a list of the various kinds of service that are offered to people by church groups in your parish.
With the other students in your class from your parish, make a poster to illustrate these. You may have to contact one of the priests in the parish to find out the necessary information.

You may find suitable captions and pictures in the daily newspapers.
Can you think of different situations where someone is commissioned to do a particular job? Find out all you can about some commissioning ceremony which takes place regularly in your country.

History of Baptism and Confirmation

Stage 1

After Jesus had returned to his Father, the early Church consisted of a small group of believers who gathered together regularly to listen to the story of his life, death and resurrection and to take part in the breaking of the bread as Jesus had requested.

Many miracles and wonders were being done through the apostles, and everyone was filled with awe. All the believers continued together in close fellowship and shared their belongings with one another. They would sell their property and possessions, and distribute the money among all, according to what each one needed. Day after day they met as a group in the Temple, and they had their meals together in their homes, eating with glad and humble hearts, praising God, and enjoying the good will of all the people. And every day the Lord added to their group those who were being saved... (Acts 2:43-47).

As we read in Acts, they were noted by all who knew them for the way in which they lived together. Many people who saw the lifestyle of the believers and were impressed by it wanted to join the group. When they showed that they were interested they were invited to listen to the gospel being preached. They joined in the life style of those who belonged to the Church.

They were officially received into the Church in a simple ceremony which consisted of the pouring of water and the laying on of hands; a celebration of the forgiveness of sins and of the coming of the Holy Spirit. Baptism and Confirmation were part of the same rite and were not seen as separate sacraments.

Stage 2

By the third, fourth and fifth centuries those wishing to join the Christian community went through a long period of preparation, called the Catechumenate, and those taking part were called catechumens. They had instruction in the beliefs and way of life of the Christian community. They joined in prayer and worship with the Christian community on Sundays.

They were dismissed after the homily of the Mass since the act of sharing in the Eucharist in Holy Communion was only for those who were already baptised. At the Easter vigil the catechumens were initiated into the community. They were baptised, confirmed and for the first time took part in the Eucharist. The ceremony consisted of the following parts:

- The candidates for initiation went to the baptistry, often a separate building near the entrance to the church;

- They renounced Satan and committed themselves to Christ;

- Then they stripped completely, showing that they were leaving their old clothes and their old life behind;

- They were then anointed all over their bodies, like athletes being rubbed down before a fight. It symbolised their readiness to fight against evil;

- The font was blessed and the candidates would enter the water, perhaps going down three steps into the pool;

- They were immersed three times in the name of the Father, and of the Son and of the Holy Spirit.

- They came out of the water and were clothed in white garments;

- They returned to the full assembly where they were greeted with a kiss of peace by the bishop and were then anointed with chrism;

- They were then full members of the faithful and they joined in the celebration of the Eucharist.

The anointing, which was always performed by a bishop, though it was at this stage part of the larger ritual, is the basis of what we today know as the sacrament of Confirmation. At this stage most of those being initiated into the Church were adults, converts to the Christian community.

Infant baptism was to come later.

Stage 3

As long as dioceses were small and it was possible for bishops to preside at the Easter vigil this format for the sacraments of initiation held.

However, when the size of the Church increased so that it was no longer possible for the bishops always to be present at the Easter vigil, the question arose as to what ought to be done with the part of the ritual that was traditionally carried out by the bishop.

In the East, the decision was made that whoever presided at the Easter rites would do the anointing. In the West, Pope Innocent in 412 AD insisted that this anointing was reserved for the bishop. At first it was celebrated shortly after the Easter vigil but gradually it was pushed back further and further.

At this time also St Augustine's teaching on original sin prompted an increase in infant baptism. Parents began to fear that infants might die before being baptised and, because of original sin, would not go to heaven. And so what started out as one rite became separated, with baptism by water being celebrated by the priest as soon as possible after the birth of the baby, and the ceremony of anointing by the bishop taking place as long as fourteen years later.

Stage 4

With the years it was noted that the numbers of people presenting themselves for the anointing by the bishop decreased.

At times it had become so haphazard that if someone on a journey happened to meet a travelling bishop, they would request the anointing. The bishop would dismount and the ceremony would take place on the spot. It also happened though that many people never had the opportunity to take part in the ceremony of anointing.

In 1215, at the Fourth Lateran Council, the ceremony of anointing by a bishop was defined as a sacrament in its own right – the sacrament of Confirmation – and so we have for the first time, the list of seven sacraments. The general practice then became infant baptism, followed by confirmation, which took place not earlier than age seven and not later than age ten.

Stage 5

In 1972 the Rite of Christian Initiation Of Adults was issued. This restores the original order of the three sacraments of initiation for adults who are joining the Church. The candidate is baptised, symbolising a turning away from old ways and the taking on of the new commitment to Christ. This commitment is then confirmed in the sacrament of Confirmation. The newly initiated person is welcomed for the first time to the table of the Eucharist.

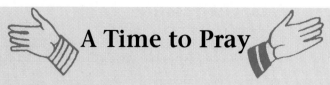

A Time to Pray

Read slowly and reflectively the following extract which tells us how we should live as followers of Jesus. In it Jesus is showing us in simple words what God's Way is really like and how we must try to live in God's Way.

God's Way Must be Our Way

THESE ARE OUR ORDERS.

Love your enemies,
do good to those who hate you,
bless those who curse you,
pray for those who treat you badly.

LIVING GOD'S WAY MAKES A DIFFERENCE.

If you love those who love you,
what is there special about that?
Everybody does that sort of thing.
If you favour those who favour you,
what is there special about that ?
Everybody does that sort of thing.
If you lend money to those you hope will help you,
what is there special about that ?
Everybody does that sort of thing.

WE MUST DO MORE THAN OTHERS.

Love your enemies;
do good and lend,
expecting nothing back.

IT CAN BE PUT QUITE SIMPLY.

Be merciful
as God your Father is merciful.

WE MUST SET THE PACE.

Don't judge and you won't be judged;
don't condemn and you won't be condemned;
forgive and you will be forgiven;
give and you will be given
good measure,
pressed down,
shaken together,
running over,
will be poured into your lap.

IT AMOUNTS TO THIS.

The measure you give
will be the measure you get.

The Eucharist

The image of a great banquet or meal is often used in scripture to help us to imagine the kingdom of God. In Isaiah chapter 25 we read: *'Here on Mount Zion the Lord Almighty will prepare a banquet for all the nations of the world – a banquet of the richest food and finest wine. Here he will suddenly remove the cloud of sorrow that has been hanging over all the nations. The Sovereign Lord will destroy death forever! He will wipe away the tears from everyone's eyes and take away the disgrace his people have suffered throughout the world.* In the gospels, Jesus also used the image of a great feast to help people understand the kingdom of God.

Read the following extracts.

The Parable of the Great Feast

Jesus said 'There was once a man who was giving a great feast to which he invited many people. When it was time for the feast, he sent his servant to tell his guests, "Come, everything is ready!" But they all began, one after another, to make excuses. The first one told the servant, "I have bought a field and must go and look at it; please accept my apologies." Another one said , "I have bought five pairs of oxen and am on my way to try them out; please accept my apologies." Another one said, "I have just got married, and for that reason I cannot come."

The servant went back and told all this to his master. The master was furious and said to his servant,"Hurry out to the streets and alleys of the town, and bring back the poor, the crippled, the blind and the lame." Soon the servant said, "Your order has been carried out, sir, but there is room for more." So the master said to the servant, "Go out to the country roads and lanes and make people come in, so that my house will be full. I tell you all that none of these men who were invited will taste my dinner!"' (*Luke 14:15-24*).

Discuss What do you think it is about sharing a feast or a meal that makes it a good image to use to help people imagine the kingdom of God? What is it about the feast described in the above passage that might help people to understand what the kingdom of heaven is like ?

Many of the meals that Jesus shared with others were with people who were unacceptable in the society of the time.

Jesus and Zacchaeus

Jesus went on into Jericho and was passing through. There was a chief tax collector there named Zacchaeus, who was rich. He was trying to see who Jesus was, but he was a little man and could not see Jesus because of the crowd. So he ran ahead of the crowd and climbed a sycamore tree to see Jesus, who was going to pass that way.

When Jesus came to that place, he looked up and said to Zacchaeus, 'Hurry down, Zacchaeus, because I must stay in your house today.'

Zacchaeus hurried down and welcomed him with great joy. All the people who saw it started grumbling, 'This man has gone as a guest to the home of a sinner!'

Zacchaeus stood up and said to the Lord, 'Listen, sir! I will give half my belongings to the poor, and if I have cheated anyone, I will pay him back four times as much.' Jesus said to him, 'Salvation has come to this house today, for this man also is a descendant of Abraham. The Son of Man came to seek and to save the lost' (*Luke 19:2-10*).

Discuss Why do you think the people grumbled when they saw what Jesus did? Why did Jesus go to eat with Zacchaeus? Why did Zacchaeus decide to change his ways?

Activity Act out the above story.

When Jesus shared food, there was always enough for everybody.

Read the following story.

After this, Jesus went across Lake Galilee. A large crowd followed him, because they had seen his miracles of healing those who were ill. Jesus went up a hill and sat down with his disciples.

The time for the Passover Festival was near. Jesus looked round and saw that a large crowd was coming to him, so he asked Philip, 'Where can we buy enough food to feed all these people?'

Philip answered, 'For everyone to have even a little, it would take more than two hundred silver coins to buy enough bread.' Another of his disciples, Andrew, who was Simon Peter's brother, said, 'There is a boy here who has five loaves of barley bread and two fish. But they will certainly not be enough for all these people.'

'Make the people sit down,' Jesus told them. So all the people sat down; there were about five thousand men. Jesus took the bread, gave thanks to God, and distributed it to the people who were sitting there.

He did the same with the fish, and they all had as much as they wanted.

When they were all full, he said to his disciples, 'Gather the pieces left over; let us not waste any.' So they gathered them all up and filled twelve baskets with the pieces left over from the five barley loaves which the people had eaten (*John 6:1-13*).

Discuss

How do you think you would have answered the question Jesus put to Philip?

Had you been the boy with the five loaves and two fishes, do you think you would have given them to the apostles?

The following words are all connected with sharing meals. Find them in the Wordsearch. Write a paragraph about meals using all or some of the words.

FRIENDSHIP, EATING, FOOD, HUNGER, TALKING, DEATH, MEAL, HEALTH, LIFE, TASTE, COOKING, DRINK, TABLE, SMELL, SHARING.

F	R	I	E	N	D	S	H	I	P	A	R	H
O	D	O	A	S	S	H	A	R	I	N	G	P
O	T	D	T	A	L	K	I	N	G	X	D	Y
D	N	Q	I	F	B	R	E	A	D	J	M	T
B	O	C	N	S	D	E	A	T	H	D	E	A
H	U	N	G	E	R	B	O	A	C	I	A	B
E	Y	M	G	D	I	H	N	S	M	E	L	L
A	X	T	F	S	N	P	R	T	W	S	K	E
L	I	F	E	C	K	U	K	E	L	K	B	R
T	A	W	U	L	E	J	P	V	G	E	Q	F
H	M	C	O	O	K	I	N	G	O	H	N	Z

Lanfranco, The Last Supper, *reproduced courtesy of the National Gallery of Ireland*

The meals which Jesus shared during his life on earth pointed in a symbolic way to the kingdom of God. There was always enough for everybody. Everybody was invited, nobody was excluded. People were challenged to see things in a new way and sometimes to make changes in their lives.

All this was possible because Jesus was present. The risen Jesus is also present at Mass. The risen Jesus is present at Mass in many ways. He is present in the celebrant, the priest. He is present in the word which is read from the scriptures. He is present in the consecrated bread and wine. The body of Christ which we share in Holy Communion is a sign of our communion with God and with one another. When we receive Holy Communion the risen Jesus is present uniting us more fully with God and with one another. St Paul says, 'Because there is one loaf of bread, all of us, though many, are one body, for we all share the same loaf' *(1 Cor 1:17)*.

Holy Communion

In Holy Communion we receive the body and blood of Christ so we are not only challenged to go out and do as Jesus asked but we know that the risen Jesus is with us giving us the strength and courage we need to do this.

Activities

Think of situations in the world today where it is not possible for people to sit and share a meal because of war or famine.

Find newspaper cut-outs and headlines about these situations.

Arrange these to make a collage.

Think of a suitable caption as a title for the collage.

OR

Think of situations of poverty and deprivation in your own country which make it difficult for people to find the money to buy food for their families.

Find newspaper headlines and cut-outs to illustrate these. Arrange them to make a collage.

Think of a suitable caption as a title for the collage.

Find the name of an organisation in your country which works to lessen world hunger.

Find out as much as you can about the organisation.

Why was it founded?

By whom was it founded?

How does it find funds for its work?

What projects has it been involved in?

You could ask for some literature about the organisation or perhaps you could arrange for a representative to come and visit the class.

Write a report on your findings.

When we go to Mass we take part in the Eucharistic meal. It is different from other meals because it is a ritual meal with a very special meaning and because the food we consume is different from other food. The bread that we share is no longer ordinary bread. It has truly become, in a manner only God can fully understand, Jesus Christ himself, the Bread of Life. We do not take part in this Eucharistic meal to satisfy physical hunger. The action of sharing and eating is a symbolic action. It is a sign that the one Christ, who has been offered up, is being given to all as their spiritual food – to strengthen their union with him and to nourish his life within them. It is a sign that, just as all share the same food, so all are bound together in the unity of the one Christ they have all received.

At Mass we share in the Eucharistic meal with all members of the Church. Because the Church is open to all who are willing to share its faith, no one is excluded on the grounds of colour, class, race, language, intelligence or anything like that. We stand beside people who are richer or poorer than ourselves, people who dress differently, speak differently, people whom we would never invite into our home to share a meal. Not one of them is excluded and there is always enough for everybody.

Hunger for food is not the only hunger which human beings experience. There are many different human hungers – the many things which people long for. For instance, we long for goodness, for happiness, for truth, for unity and so on. When we share in the Eucharistic meal we are assured that if we live up to the challenge of the Eucharist, all our deepest human longings will be fulfilled. When we enter the kingdom of God, there will be no more suffering, no more tears and no more pain.

When we take part in the Eucharistic meal it reminds us of the meals that Jesus shared with people during his life on earth and particularly of the Last Supper. It also reminds us of the passion, death and resurrection of Jesus. It signifies and makes present the sacrifice of Jesus on the cross. It points in a symbolic way to the conditions that Jesus urged his followers to work for in the world. He challenged us to make the world a place where people share all the resources available in such a way that there will be enough for everybody. When we share the Eucharistic bread we are challenged to become more aware of those in need and to search for ways in which we can work to improve their situation. It also points to the kingdom of God. We are all invited. There is a place for everybody.

 A Time to Pray

Let us spend some time reflecting on some of the sayings we find in John's gospel, which Jesus said to his disciples on the night before he died.

Whoever accepts my commandments and obeys them is the one who loves me. My Father will love whoever loves me; I, too will love him and reveal myself to him (John 14:21).

Think quietly of some of the commands which Jesus gave to his followers. Which do you find easiest to do? Which do you find most difficult?

Peace is what I leave with you. It is my own peace I give to you. Do not be worried and upset; do not be afraid (John 14:27).

Think of times you have felt upset, worried or afraid. Ask God to help you find the peace that Jesus spoke of.

I am the vine, and you are the branches, whoever remains in me and I in him will bear much fruit (John 15:5).

What fruit do you think followers of Jesus should bear in today's world?

My commandment is this: love one another, just as I love you (John 15:12).

In what way did Jesus love his disciples?

The Sacrament of Anointing of the Sick

Find Your Group Discuss

Have you ever been seriously ill? What was it like? How did you feel? What was most difficult? What helped? Do you know anyone who is seriously ill? What effect has it had on them and on their lives?

Martin has a bad septic throat. He feels weak. He gets hot all over and then, before he knows it, he's shivering with the cold.
His mother drove him to the doctor's surgery. The doctor gave him an injection and some tablets. He'll have to stay in bed for a few days.

Anne had an accident on her bicycle last week. The brakes went just as she was nearing the bottom of a steep hill. Anne remembers just one moment of terror and then everything went blank. The bicycle went bang into the high wall on the corner. Anne was very lucky. She could have been very badly injured. As it was she ended up with a lot of very sore ribs and a broken leg.

Dave Mullen lives on his own since his wife died ten years ago. He has always been a bit of a loner since then. The neighbours would like to help but they're never very sure as to what would be the best thing to do.
In the last few months Dave has had very bad rheumatism. He now finds it difficult and painful to move around the house. Getting something ready for himself to eat has become a major task.

There are many ways in which we can help and support those who are sick. We can show them love and care by visiting, by spending time trying to cheer up the person who is sick, by helping them to keep in touch with the things which are happening in their work place or among their friends.

When people are ill, they often cannot carry on with their normal lives. They may not be able to do many of the things they used to do before. They may not be able to get out and about. They may feel cut-off and lonely. They may feel use-less and a burden on others. They may be in pain. They may feel worried and frightened. They may be tempted to lose their faith and trust in God. If they are dying or in danger of dying, they may be afraid of death.

Discuss

Apart from the physical suffering caused by the illness, people may also be suffering from fear, loneliness, anxiety etc.
Can you think of other factors which might cause suffering?

Discuss

How do you think sickness might affect the people in the examples above, physically, emotionally, mentally?

How could the people around help them to cope?

Have you ever helped someone who was sick?

What did you do?

How do you think it helped the sick person?

Healing

When someone is sick they, above all, long for healing. There are many different types of healing. If someone has a broken arm, the doctor puts a plastercast on it. Eventually the bone knits together again and we can say that the broken arm is healed.

If you were in bed with flu, you wouldn't be able to eat. Your head would probably ache. You'd be too hot. You'd be physically sick. You'd also probably feel lonely and bored. You'd long for the companionship which you usually feel when you are with your friends. If your friend came to visit you and spent some time trying to cheer you up by telling you the news from school you'd feel much better afterwards.

You'd still have flu but a different kind of healing would have taken place. You'd no longer feel lonely, bored or depressed.

220

In high school, blonde good-looking Joni Eareckson was voted 'Outstanding girl athlete' by her classmates.

Now Joni's daily exercise consists of minute movements. She can move her arm with a biceps and shoulder motion. So by hooking a fork into a metal slot on her hand brace, she can feed herself. And by keeping her fingernails long, she can turn the pages of a book. Most of her day is taken up with the process of drawing — with meticulous subtle nods and slides of her head as she bites down on a pen with her teeth.

Joni's face is alive, her eyes bright and expressive. But her positive attitude was born out of tragedy.

'Summer had been especially hot and humid that year, 1967. July was stifling. I practised with the horses in the morning, working up such a sweat that only a dip in the bay could cool me. My sister and I rode to the Chesapeake Bay beach and dived into the murky water.

'I was never content to swim laps in a pool or splash around in the shallow part of the bay. I liked free swimming in the deep water. A raft floating fifty or sixty yards offshore was a perfect target, and my sister and I raced to it. We were both athletic, and sometimes reckless.

'When I reached the raft, I climbed on it and quickly dived off the side. It was a fast motion, done almost without thinking. I felt the pull of the water... and then a stunning jar – my head crashed into a rock on the bottom. I couldn't move. It was awful. With my mind I was telling my muscles to swim, but nothing was happening. I held my breath and waited, suspended face-down in the water.

'My sister, noticing I hadn't surfaced, searched underwater until she found me. She pulled me to the top. I gasped for air. I tried to hold on to her, but again my muscles would not respond. She draped me over her shoulder and began paddling towards the shore.'

Joni spent the next several months in a hospital bed. The pain was not great, and doctors hoped some of her nerves would repair themselves. At first her room was crowded with visitors and flowers and gifts.

It was easy for Joni to be happy. Showered with attention, she simply waited to get well. Only after several months of medical reports did it sink in that she would not get well. Her whole lifestyle would change. No more sports cars, horse shows, lacrosse matches. Maybe no more dates.

'I was devastated. My life had been so full. I had been involved in as many school activities as I could fit in. And suddenly I found myself all alone, just a bare body between two sheets.'

The inevitable questions that follow a tragedy crept in. Why did it happen to her? Why so cruel a blow at such a prime time in her life? Was God trying to punish her? She became despondent; she begged her best friend to bring pills so that she could commit suicide...

The turning to God was slow. The change from bitterness and confusion to trust in God dragged out over three years of tears and violent questionings.

'The first months, even years, I was consumed with the unanswered questions of what God was trying to teach me. I probably secretly hoped that by figuring out God's ideas I could learn my lesson and then God would heal me.

'Slowly my focus changed from demanding an explanation from God to humbly depending on God. Before the accident my questions had always been: how will God fit into this situation? How will God affect my dating life? My career plans? The things I most like to do? All those options were gone. It was me, just a helpless body and God.

'Okay, I am paralysed. It's terrible. I don't like it. But I thought, can God still use me, paralysed? Can I, paralysed, still worship God and love God? God has taught me that I can.

'Maybe God's gift to me is my dependence. I will never reach the place where I'm self-sufficient, where God is crowded out of my life. I'm aware of God's grace to me every moment. My need for God is obvious every day when I wake up, flat on my back, waiting for someone to come and dress me. I can't even comb my hair or blow my nose alone!

'Somehow – and it took me three years to admit – God proved to me that, I, too, can have fullness of life. I have friends who care. I have beauty of scenery surrounding my studio. Though I can't splash in the creek and ride the horses, I can sit outside and my senses are flooded with smells and textures and beautiful sights.'

Discuss

Joni has not been healed physically, but in what other ways has Joni been healed?

How did Joni change in the way she thought about God?

How do you think that Joni's new attitude to God has helped her?

The Healing Ministry of Jesus and the Church

We often read in the gospels of Jesus' compassion for the sick, and of occasions when he healed them.

Can you remember some times when Jesus healed people? Which one is your favourite?

Jesus sent out his apostles to preach and heal, and in Mark's gospel we learn that as part of their healing ministry they anointed people with oil (*Mark 6:13*).

The Church Today

The Church is the body of Christ in our world today. And so the Church has to continue to bring Jesus' healing touch into people's lives. It does this in many ways. Whenever we, as members of the Church, show care or compassion for someone who is sick, the Church is, through us, looking after the needs of the sick person.

One special way in which the Church brings healing to those who are sick is through the sacrament of the Anointing of the Sick. Here is a description of the sacrament which is found in the New Testament, in the Letter of St James.

Is there anyone who is ill? He should send for the church elders who will pray for him and rub olive oil on him in the name of the Lord. This prayer made in faith will heal the sick person; the Lord will restore him to health, and the sins he has committed will be forgiven (James 5:14-15).

Here the word 'elder' is a translation of the Greek word 'presbyter'. This is the official title of the people we nowadays usually call 'priests'.

There are two main parts to the celebration of the sacrament: prayer and anointing with oil.

The two symbols of the sacrament are anointing with oil and laying on of hands. We have already explored these symbols as they are used in the sacrament of Confirmation.

In Your Religion Journal

Write and illustrate your favourite story of an incident where Jesus healed someone.

Illustrate the two symbols. Write a paragraph on each saying why you think it is an appropriate symbol for the sacrament of Anointing of the Sick.

Celebrating the Sacrament

The Anointing of the Sick is not just for people who are dying. It is for any member of the Church who is seriously ill or weakened by old age and once they have at least begun to be in danger of death.

As is the case with all the sacraments, a community celebration is best. Sometimes groups of sick people are anointed during the celebration of Mass. Parishes occasionally have a special Mass for the Sick when the sacrament is celebrated for many sick people at once. This also happens in places of pilgrimage such as Knock and Lourdes.

When the sacrament of the sick is celebrated publicly in this way it allows all members of the Church to take part in Jesus' healing ministry and to pray publicly for those who are sick. It allows sick people to see and experience the loving support and prayers of the whole community of the Church.

Most often, of course, the sacrament is celebrated at home or in hospital. In this case, friends, relatives and those who care for the sick are encouraged to take part. However when someone is suddenly in danger of death, for instance, after an accident or when somebody has a heart attack, one of the things that happens is that the priest is sent for so that the person can celebrate the sacrament of the sick immediately. It is an opportunity for the person who is sick to be reconciled with God, and to be strengthened by receiving the Body of Christ in Holy Communion.

The Rite of the Sacrament

After giving a short introduction, the priest either leads everybody present in an act of repentance, similar to the Penitential Rite at Mass, or he may privately hear the sick person's confession and give absolution. Then a suitable passage of scripture is read.

PRAYERS

The priest leads all present in prayers for the sick person.
Here is one form of these prayers.

Look kindly on our sick brother/sister.
Give new strength to his/her body and mind.
Ease out our brother's/sister's sufferings.
Free him/her from sin and temptation.
Sustain all the sick with your power.
Assist all who care for the sick.
Give life and health to our brother/sister on whom we lay our hands in your name.

To each of these prayers everyone responds:
Lord hear our prayer.

Can you think of any prayers you would like to add to these?

IMPOSITION OF HANDS

The priest then lays his hands on the head of the sick person.

What do you think this is meant to show?

ANOINTING WITH OIL

Using olive oil, specially blessed by the bishop on Holy Thursday morning, the priest anoints the sick person on the forehead, saying:
Through this holy anointing may the Lord in his love and mercy help you with the grace of the Holy Spirit.

Then on the palms of the hands, saying:
May the Lord who frees you from sin, save you and raise you up.

Everyone responds:
Amen.

Can you remember which other sacraments have an anointing with oil as part of the rite? What do you think the significance of the anointing is in the sacrament of the sick?

CONCLUDING PRAYER

The priest says a concluding prayer. Here is one possible form.

Lord Jesus Christ, our Redeemer
by the power of the Holy Spirit
ease the suffering of our sick brother/sister
and make him/her well again in mind and body.
In your loving kindness forgive his/her sins
and grant him/her full health
so that he/she may be restored to your service.
You are Lord for ever and ever. Amen.

Then all present join in saying the Our Father.
Afterwards the priest will normally give Holy Communion.

Healing and Curing

Those who celebrate the sacrament of Anointing of the Sick are not promised freedom from suffering and illness, but they are promised that Jesus Christ will always be with them to strengthen them and support them through all their trials. The sacrament may bring about the curing of physical illness, if that is truly for our eternal welfare.

Whether the sacrament brings about a cure or not, it will always bring about healing, if it is received in faith. It can give the sick person peace and hope and confidence because they are reassured that Jesus Christ is with them always, even in death.

In the sacrament the risen Jesus comes to heal in the way in which he knows we most need healing.

He comes to strengthen our faith and trust, to give us the ability to bear trials with patience and to come closer to him through them.

Think for example of Lourdes. Only a comparatively few people are cured of their illnesses at Lourdes, but very many have a healing experience, which enables them to find peace and to face up to life with more confidence and trust in the love and care of God.

In Your Religion Journal

Draw a picture illustrating the Anointing of the Sick and its meaning.

Activity

Talk to someone who has been to Lourdes about their experience.

Test yourself. Do the Looking Back exercises on page 228

Looking Back

When you have completed lesson 4

Do you remember?

What is the name of one scientific theory about the origin of the planet earth?

What is the smallest unit of living matter called?

What words would you use to describe how the Hebrew people understood God?

The account of each of the seven days of creation is split into five different parts. Can you say what these parts are?

In which book of the Bible do we find the account of creation?

Can you name five different factors which cause damage to the environment?

What are the six basic elements necessary for life?

Who is the patron saint of ecologists?

What does it mean to say that we are created 'in God's image'?

What do you think?

If people from another planet were to visit the earth, what part of creation do you think they would be most impressed with?

What is the worst form of destruction of the environment taking place in the world today? Why?

In your own life

Think of a time when you were aware of the wonder of God as it is shown in the work of creation. Describe what it was like.

Name one positive thing you will do in the next week which will help to preserve and protect the environment.

Think about it !

When have you last thanked God for the gift of life in the world around you, in the people who are closest to you, in your own body?

Spend some time doing this in the near future.

When you have completed lesson 7

Do you remember?

List some of the changes which take place during adolescence in a boy's body, in a girl's body.

Name three things which young people find difficult to cope with during adolescence.

Name three things which parents find difficult to cope with during their children's adolescence.

List six characteristics of someone who is able to behave in an adult manner.

What is one of the images which Jesus used to describe life with God in heaven?

Describe an occasion when Jesus showed true friendship for someone.

List four characteristics of true friendship.

What do you think?

What stage of life are you most looking forward to? Why?

What is the best thing about belonging to your family?

In your own life

Decide on one thing you can do to show that you appreciate all the love and care that you experience in your family.

Decide on one thing you can do to show a friend that you appreciate him or her.

Think about it !

Compose a prayer of thanks to God for your family.

When you have completed lesson 10

Do you remember?

Unlike plants or animals, human beings have the ability to choose. However, our choices are limited. List some things which we cannot choose.

Who led the Israelites to freedom from Egypt?

Why did the Pharaoh eventually agree to allow the Israelites to go free?

Why did he change his mind?

List six different situations where someone might be enslaved.

What is a covenant?

What covenant did God make with the Israelites?

Name three times when the Israelites lost confidence in God during their journey through the desert.

What do you think?

What words would you use to describe slavery?

In what ways are the ten commandments helpful for us in our lives today?

In the past week:

which of the commandments have you found difficult to obey?

Which of the commandments have you found helpful?

In your own life

Think of one situation in your life where you have not been using your freedom to make the best possible choices.

How might you change this in the future?

Think about it !

Have you ever caused anyone to be enslaved?

When you have completed lesson 12

Do you remember?

Explain moral evil.

Explain physical evil.

What does our conscience do for us?

How do we develop our conscience?

How does reconciliation happen?

Give one example of a situation where Jesus showed us what God's forgiveness is like.

What words would you use to describe what God's forgiveness is like?

What do you think?

Which of the characters in the story 'The Prodigal Son,' do you think you are most like in your actions: the father; the younger son; the older son? Why?

In your own life

Think of a time when you followed your conscience even though it was difficult.
Think of a time when you failed to follow your conscience.

Think about it !

Is there someone with whom you need to be reconciled?
What could you do about this?

When you have completed
lesson 14

Do you remember?

When does the season of Advent begin?
How long does it last?
Who prepared the first crib?
Where is it located?
What are the five joyful mysteries of the rosary?
What happened at the Annunciation?
Name the feast celebrated on the 6th January.
Name the three Kings.

What do you think?

In what way can our Advent resolutions help us enter into the real spirit of Christmas?
How can you improve your preparation and celebration of Christmas?
What can we learn from the way Mary answered God?

In your own life

What practical things can you do for those in need in your community this Christmas?

Think about it !

How would you explain the meaning of Christmas to someone who has never heard of Christ?

When you have completed
lesson 16

Do you remember?

When did the first major split in Church history occur?
When did the second split take place and what is it known as?
When do the Churches celebrate Christian Unity week?
What is the chief representative of the Methodist Church known as?
People who have chosen to have their baptismal vows confirmed in the Methodist faith are known as? What is the name of a Presbyterian church?
At what age are candidates usually confirmed in the Church of Ireland?

At what age does a young Jewish boy become Bar Mitzvah?

What does Bar Mitzvah mean?

What is the text in Deuteronomy 6:4-9 known as?

How many Jewish feasts can you name?

The Day of Atonement is known as?

Which feast is celebrated five days after the Day of Atonement?

What does the feast of Purim celebrate?

When is the Festival of Lights celebrated?

What do you think?

What can we learn from other Christian denominations?

In what way can the first three commandments help people to put into practice what they are told in the Shema?

In what ways can the Jewish religion be considered a way of life?

In what ways can the Christian religion be considered a way of life?

In your own life

Think about ways in which you could get to know more about Christians from other denominations in your community.

Is it possible for your class to arrange a visit to a synagogue or to ask a rabbi into your school to tell you more about Judaism?

Think about it !

Compose a prayer for Christian unity.

When you have completed lesson 19

Do you remember?

What was Luke's background?

Luke's gospel falls into seven sections. What are these sections?

What characteristics of Jesus are shown in Luke's gospel?

Name the twelve apostles.

Name one story from Luke's gospel which shows:

the healing work of Jesus;

how Jesus related to women;

how Jesus helped people to understand the kingdom of God.

What impressed you most about Sally Trench?

Name four different types of prayer. Name two stories told by Jesus which encourage us not to give up praying.

Name five incidents from the gospels which speak about Jesus praying.

What do you think?

What do you think most impressed Luke about Jesus?

Which prayers do you find it easiest to say?

What opportunities do you have to serve God and others right now?

In your own life

How often do you pray?

Which prayers do you use?

Do you need to make any improvements in this area of your life?

Think about it !

Which story from Luke's gospel do you like best? Why?

When you have completed lesson 21

Do you remember?

What are the five sorrowful mysteries?

Where in Luke's gospel do we find the passion and death of Jesus?

What significance was there in Pilate washing his hands after he condemned Jesus to be crucified?

Who helped Jesus to carry the cross to Calvary?

What were Jesus' last words on the cross?

How could an executioner shorten the ordeal of a victim who was hanging on the cross?

What would the executioner offer the victim as a pain reliever, before crucifixion?

When was crucifixion finally abolished?

Which member of the Jewish Council offered his tomb as a burial place for Jesus?

What are the four incidents that Luke mentions in the final chapter of his gospel?

Who discovered that the tomb was empty on Easter Sunday?

On what road were two followers of Jesus travelling when Jesus accompanied them on their journey?

Can you name these two followers?

What happened forty days after Jesus had risen from the dead?

What do you think?

What did Jesus achieve for us by suffering and dying on the cross?

In your own life

In what way is the risen Jesus present in your life today?

Think about it !

How would you explain, to someone of another religion, the *Good News* of Christianity?

When you have completed lesson 25

Do you remember?

Jesus said to his followers, 'I am the vine, you are the branches'.
What does this mean?

How can you be a sign that the risen Jesus is present in the world today?

List two symbols used in Baptism.

List two symbols used in Confirmation.

How did Baptism and Confirmation become two separate sacraments?

Why is the image of a feast or a banquet a good one for the Eucharist?

What are the two symbols of the sacrament of Anointing of the Sick?

Explain them.

What do you think?

What is happening that tells you that the risen

Jesus is still present in the world today?

If you were asked to create a ceremony for young people of your own age who wanted to make a commitment that they would follow Jesus, what symbols would you use?

What actions would be part of the ceremony?

What readings?

Your friend says that he or she is bored at Mass. How would you respond?

How do you think the celebration of the sacrament of the sick might help the family of someone who is dying?

In your own life

How can you improve the way you celebrate Mass?

Think about it !

What part of your religion programme did you most enjoy this year? Why?